"This is an important new contribution, examining how a decade of austerity policy has impeded the governance and delivery of healthcare in English prisons. Drawing on detailed health statistics, interviews with key stakeholders, and official publications, the author unravels the complex relationships between economics, prison management, and the decline in health and safety in prisons since 2010."

Professor Alison Liebling,
University of Cambridge, United Kingdom

"How has it come to this? The prisons crisis is most acute in the prison healthcare system and this author uses that focus to argue that the crisis is a consequence of an ideologically constructed austerity programme. Based on interviews with 87 policy makers and ranging across sociological, legal, political and economic literature, Nasrul Ismail provides a sharp and distinctive analysis of the prisons crisis that should be on the reading list of everyone trying to understand the origins of the prisons crisis and the problems that beset prison healthcare."

Professor Nick Hardwick, Royal Holloway,
University of London, United Kingdom

"Drawing on an impressively wide range of sources and inter-disciplinary approaches, Nasrul Ismail has provided us with an analysis which is both urgently needed and deeply grounded. By demonstrating the pernicious effects and roots of austerity on the governance and delivery of healthcare in prisons, this book provides critical insights into the ways in which care is fundamentally undermined by the structures for its delivery and governance. This book is essential reading not only for those seeking to understand healthcare systems in prisons, but how prisons operate more generally."

Dr Mary Rogan, Associate Professor,
School of Law, Trinity College Dublin, Ireland

"Austerity was a choice. When the global financial crisis hit, governments could decide how to respond. The historical evidence, especially FDR's New Deal, argued strongly for a stimulus. Instead, in the UK, we saw a contraction of public spending. In this excellent forensic analysis, Nasrul Ismail reveals what this has meant for the prison system, whose occupants are so often the casualties of government failures."

Professor Martin McKee, Professor of European
Public Health, London School of Hygiene & Tropical Medicine

The English Prison Health System After a Decade of Austerity, 2010–2020

Austerity has reconfigured and scaled back the governance and delivery of public services and negatively affected society's most vulnerable groups. This book opens up the closed world of English prisons to examine its impact on prison health governance and healthcare delivery. It argues that austerity has been a decade-long, large-scale political experiment that has caused debt to balloon, eroded the prison health system and perpetuated a cycle of punishment resulting in sicker prisoners. In short, austerity has violated prisoners' human rights.

Drawing on interviews and data from existing longitudinal and economic analyses, the book demonstrates how austerity has resulted in high rates of recidivism, diminished what remains of the welfare state, and increased inequality and punitiveness. Despite a decade of failure, there is a marked political reluctance to dispense with austerity, and the governmental juggernaut continues to produce the same result. As the spectre of recession increases, caused in part by Brexit and COVID-19, these failures are ever more perilous.

This book blends the interdisciplinary perspectives of criminology, public health, sociology, law, social policy, politics, and economics to enable greater understanding of the impact of austerity on health governance, prison healthcare, the prison workforce, and prisoners' health and safety. It challenges current policy, practice and thinking, and is a must read for anyone who wants to reflect on how the political economic structure can affect the governance and delivery of healthcare services in marginalised settings, beyond prisons, and indeed beyond England.

Nasrul Ismail is Lecturer in Criminology at the University of Bristol. He has published widely on the impact of political economy on prison health and prisons.

Routledge Frontiers of Criminal Justice

The Virtual Reality of Imprisonment in Russia
"Preparing myself for Prison" in a Contested Human Rights Landscape
Laura Piacentini and Elena Katz

Life Without Parole
Worse than Death?
Ross Kleinstuber, Jeremiah Coldsmith, Margaret E. Leigey and Sandra Joy

Penal Responses to Serious Offending by Children
Principles, Practice and Global Perspectives
Nessa Lynch, Yannick van den Brink and Louise Forde

A Restorative Approach to Family Violence
Feminist Kin-Making
Joan Pennell

Interviewing of Suspects with Mental Health Conditions and Disorders in England and Wales
A Paradigm Shift
Laura Farrugia

Convictions Without Truth
The Incompatibility of Science and Law
Robert Schehr

The English Prison Health System After a Decade of Austerity, 2010–2020
The Failed Political Experiment
Nasrul Ismail

For more information about this series, please visit: www.routledge.com/Routledge-Frontiers-of-Criminal-Justice/book-series/RFCJ

The English Prison Health System After a Decade of Austerity, 2010–2020

The Failed Political Experiment

Nasrul Ismail

Routledge
Taylor & Francis Group
LONDON AND NEW YORK

First published 2023
by Routledge
4 Park Square, Milton Park, Abingdon, Oxon OX14 4RN

and by Routledge
605 Third Avenue, New York, NY 10158

Routledge is an imprint of the Taylor & Francis Group, an informa business

British Library Cataloguing-in-Publication Data
A catalogue record for this book is available from the British Library

Library of Congress Cataloging-in-Publication Data
A catalog record for this book has been requested

ISBN: 978-1-032-02195-9 (hbk)
ISBN: 978-1-032-02203-1 (pbk)
ISBN: 978-1-003-18233-7 (ebk)

DOI: 10.4324/9781003182337

Typeset in Bembo
by Apex CoVantage, LLC

Contents

Figures

Acknowledgements

"Why does your research focus on prisons? Not schools? Universities? Or care homes?"

When I tell people about my research interests, these are the common questions I get asked—by the ESRC panel who funded my study, fellow scholars at conferences, and immigration officers at airports. It piques people's curiosity, perhaps because of its peculiarity and dark aura. Generally, my answer is brief: prisons are a setting where the population health is overwhelmingly sick, we allow prisoners to exist in terrible living conditions which are not conducive to their needs, and then we release them into the same environment which makes them sick. My more detailed answer, however, goes far deeper.

I grew up in a small village in East Coast of Malaysia. Rampant poverty, drug dealing, drug-using, anti-social behaviour, and violent crime were prevalent. People lived in a vicious cycle from one generation to another, seemingly with no hope of escape. Those who broke the law were punished severely and given no structural support to help them reintegrate into the community.

One of these unfortunate people was my own brother who, after decades of substance misuse, found himself in a system that often prioritises punishment over rehabilitation.

This experience and early reflection were a turning point for me. I knew there was a world out there where I could reach my potential and attain social mobility. Motivated and driven by this notion, I worked as hard as possible to become the first person in my family to get A-levels, then an undergraduate degree, a Master's, and, finally, a PhD. Along the way, I was fortunate to be supported by various government scholarships since my family was unable to afford my education. I use my lived experience as my motivation because, one day, I want to return to this community with the skills and knowledge to engender genuine change.

A book is often portrayed as a solitary journey. However, the long list that follows suggests the opposite. This book has emerged out of my PhD thesis, which I successfully defended in June 2021. I am eternally grateful for the insight and support of my PhD supervisors, Dr Nick de Viggiani and

Professor Christina Pantazis. Nick inspired me to embark on prison health research since I did my MSc in Public Health between 2014 and 2017. My special thanks to Christina for her selfless time and care—from endless free lunches and coffees and thought-provoking questions ("*Do you ever believe that prisons can be rehabilitative?*") to helping me to secure a lectureship post at the School for Policy Studies, University of Bristol. When I received an email from Tom Sutton at Routledge asking whether he could meet me at a conference to discuss a book proposal, it was Christina who told me to "Go and meet with the editor, see what they have to say, and submit one". Fast forward, I managed to secure this book contract in the final year of my PhD. Without their guidance, my development as an early career academic would not have been achievable.

I am thankful to the School for Policy Studies, University of Bristol, where I had the opportunity to continue my research into the topic of prisons and the political economy. I am indebted to the School's vibrant research culture that enabled me to use my research for teaching, and allowed me to build vibrant networks with scholars who are part of the Centre for the Study of Poverty and Social Justice, the Centre for Research in Health and Social Care, and those beyond. I am grateful for my colleagues at the School for their continual support of my early career development.

I would also like to offer my sincere gratitude to the ESRC for their generous funding (ESRC Grant: ES/P000630/1). A particular thank you must go to the South West Doctoral Training Partnership (SWDTP) for their trust and belief in this study, and for their constant support as my journey continues. Their generosity has never failed to overwhelm me.

To the Routledge Editorial Team—particularly Tom Sutton and Jessica Phillips—thank you for your help since we first met at the Law Enforcement and Public Health Conference in Edinburgh in 2019. I am appreciative that you were able to envision how my PhD could be turned into this book. And thank you to the two anonymous reviewers who championed what I was trying to do whilst also providing constructive feedback, and also to those prominent scholars who have provided glowing endorsements for this book.

My deep appreciation also goes to all 87 research participants of this study. Each of you generously spent time with me talking about my research, in the snowy city of Vienna with hot chocolates and apple strudels, in the Victorian prisons of Northeast England, and many other locations besides. Thank you for teaching me so many new things about prisons and how they operate, and for welcoming me as part of your community. The level of perseverance and resilience that you demonstrate—behind closed doors, away from the public spotlight, in a system that continues to deteriorate—continues to amaze me. I hope I do justice in representing your voices in this book.

Last but not least, I thank my family and friends in both Malaysia and the UK. Grudgingly, they have had to learn to accept my academic journey, and provided me with support day after day. My gratitude for them can barely be expressed in words. Thank you for keeping me grounded.

I dedicate this thesis to my parents—in particular, my mother, who single-handedly raised our family after my father passed away. Thank you for the blessing for me to complete this doctorate and achieve the highest education level possible, despite not having the opportunity to go to university yourself. Even though you do not understand English—"I do not understand a word of your work"—you remain my biggest cheerleader every time I sent you a copy of my publications, constantly talking about my achievements to others.

I hope that, one day, this story will be an inspiration to someone in the small village where I come from. That they will come to know there is a world out there which can be explored, and that, through education, it *is* possible to work your way out of poverty and an environment where crime is rife. I will return to this community again, hopefully with opportunities to make a difference.

All these million-step journeys can begin with this book.

Acknowledgments

Chapter 1

Introduction

In 1848, Rudolf Carl Virchow, a pathologist who reported on the typhus epidemic in Silesia (now a region of Poland), observed how people oppressed by the aristocracy silently died of starvation. As the epidemic ravaged the poor and most vulnerable, the upper classes indulged in material luxuries and simultaneously increased the power of the courts and the army to protect their authority. Civil servants merely followed the government's directives. As the press continued to publish the details of the hunger-typhus epidemic, government ministries finally ordered an in-depth review, which was followed by public condemnations and calls for political and economic reforms that were critical to tackling the burgeoning outbreak (Virchow, 1848).

Something similar is happening in the United Kingdom today. Following a decade of austerity measures, inequality is rising: the rich are getting richer, the poor poorer. A fifth of the UK population—15 million people—lives in poverty, while the highest earners increased their wealth during the same period (Office for National Statistics, 2021; United Nations [UN] General Assembly, 2019). Austerity strips social protection—a key feature of the welfare state—further marginalising the poor. Some are eventually pushed into the criminal justice system (Wacquant, 2000). Prisons perpetuate the cycle of punishment, where individuals continue to suffer poor treatment (HM Inspectorate of Prisons [HMIP], 2021). Also, as populism and political support for penal justice have grown since the 1970s, so have both police powers within the community and the number of prisons (Hall, 1978, 2011; Newburn, 2007). Despite continual popular outcry against conditions in prisons and communities, politicians remain stubbornly idle.

Reconsidering austerity and its impact

This book examines how a decade of austerity policy has impeded the governance and delivery of healthcare in English prisons. It argues such policy uses imprisonment as a large-scale political experiment on prisoners that after a decade has catastrophically failed—not only for the system but also for prisoners' rehabilitation. These experiments point to discrepancies between the

DOI: 10.4324/9781003182337-1

intentions of austerity measures and their implementation. These experiments are wide-reaching, adaptive to various institutions and structures, and coercive in their implementation. Ultimately, their outcomes reinforce the dominant belief in imprisonment as a form of punishment—at the expense of rehabilitation.

Kevin Ward and Kim England (2007) identified four categories of neoliberalism: a hegemonic ideological project; a policy and programme; a state form (the 'rolling back' and 'rolling out' of state formations in the name of reform); and a governmentality (how relations among peoples and institutions are reimagined, reinterpreted, and reassembled to effect governing at a distance). I agree with Ward and England's analysis, and in this book I will critically explore the dynamics they uncovered. Following Pierre Dardot and Christian Laval (2013) and Jamie Peck (2015), it is best to consider neoliberal manifestations not as isolated phenomena but as elements of a complicated but coherent political nexus.

I seek to build upon a body of evidence that shows austerity has been implemented as a political ideology rather than as an evidence-based policy. In consequence, it has caused debt to balloon in the ensuing decade, eroded the prison health system, and perpetuated a cycle of punishment that has led to sicker prisoners, high rates of recidivism, and violations of prisoners' human rights (Committee for the Prevention of Torture and Inhuman or Degrading Treatment or Punishment [CPT], 2020; Ministry of Justice, 2020). Astonishingly, policymakers have largely glossed over and denied these failures.

The politics of austerity and health

Many perceive austerity as both a political ideology and a political outcome. Defined as a form of voluntary deflation via a reduction in government borrowing, austerity requires deep cuts in public expenditures to stimulate economic growth (Ortiz et al., 2011). Beyond falling budgets, its implementation hints at the chasm between the desire to uphold austerity—branded as 'economic efficiency'—and an ideological programme aimed at dismantling social structures, a programme built on economic fallacies (Krugman, 2012; Wren-Lewis, 2016). Indeed, austerity reflects an embrace of neoliberalism: a state policy that restructures processes according to the logic of supposed economic efficiency, minimal state intervention, and a preference for individual rather than collective rights (Harvey, 2010). Researchers suggest that the use of the term 'austerity' over 'neoliberalism' is strategic, as the former seems more authoritative and pragmatic than the latter, while also appearing ideologically neutral in response to the 'problem' of government debt (Farnsworth and Irving, 2018).

Experts tend to agree on the negative relationship between austerity and health, which is most visibly manifested in the approximately 130,000 preventable deaths in the United Kingdom resulting from austerity measures (Institute for Public Policy Research, 2019). Early research on austerity examined how high-risk groups, such as migrants and the homeless, are particularly vulnerable to financial cuts in services and benefits in silos (Suhrcke et al., 2011). Later, substantial evidence emerged suggesting that spending cuts to public services have worsened the many inequalities that cut across various minority groups, including women, Black and Minority Ethnic (BME), disabled, and lesbian, gay, bisexual and transgender (LGBT) communities (Cross, 2013; De Henau and Reed, 2016; Khan, 2015; Westwood, 2016). Yet few have articulated austerity's impact on the governance and delivery of public sector services. Existing studies focus on organisations, such as UK local authorities and the NHS, and how these services have undergone structural reconfigurations, scaled back their operations, and contracted out their services (Heald and Steel, 2018; McEldowney, 2016).

Such studies agree that austerity harms public health and the governance and delivery structure that seek to improve it (Heald and Steel, 2018; McEldowney, 2016). But investigations have stopped short of considering the governance of prison health and the delivery of prison healthcare services in England. How austerity affects different prison establishments is missing altogether. Without such efforts, we risk failing to understand adequately how austerity punishes prisoners beyond the loss of liberty.

Over the last decade, media and official publications have highlighted the crisis facing the English prison system (Committee for the Prevention of Torture and Inhuman or Degrading Treatment or Punishment [CPT], 2017; HMIP, 2021). To rectify the adverse situation, uncovering the role of the austerity programme in that crisis and, ultimately, describing its effects on prison health governance and the delivery of prison healthcare services within a broader construct of politically determined health- and location-based inequalities is critical. Politics and places matter for health, but health also matters for politics and places. This book therefore offers the first empirical evidence of austerity's uneven and detrimental impact on prisons and prison health and reveals its failure as a political experiment.

Research questions and methodology

The book asks seven questions: 1) How has austerity been mobilised as a vehicle to strengthen neoliberal constructs that impact prison health governance and the delivery of prison healthcare services in England? 2) How is austerity manifested in prison healthcare governance and healthcare delivery, as well as the supportive prison regime? 3) How has the top-down control of the prison service affected prison health governance and the delivery of healthcare across English prisons? 4) To what extent did longstanding issues of English prisons impact prison health governance and delivery of healthcare, as well as the broader prison regime, once austerity was established in 2010? 5) How has the government responded to the ongoing instability since 2010? 6) How do prison scrutiny mechanisms mediate austerity's impact? 7) What policy solutions should address the impact?

To answer these, I use data from 87 research participants from key organisations relevant to prison work at the international level (e.g., the UN, the World Health Organization [WHO], and the Council of Europe), the national level (e.g., HM Prison & Probation Service [HMPPS], NHS England, and Public Health England [PHE]), prison establishments (i.e., high, medium, open, resettlement and private prisons), and voluntary sector representatives at the national and regional levels. I supplement participants' views with insights from existing longitudinal and economic analyses to ensure a rounded view of the investigation. Grounded in public health and criminology domains, this book conducts its investigation through multiple disciplinary lenses: sociology, law, social policy, politics, and economics. Conducting interdisciplinary research, such as this topic, is inevitably complex. To deliver richer outcomes to untangle the impacts of austerity on prison healthcare, investigations need to go beyond the mono-disciplinary approach. Considering the scale of the investigation, a broad pool of participants were chosen to gather data in an in-depth and rigorous manner.

Given that I primarily interviewed policymakers, my work mostly focuses on the impact of the austerity measures on the prison health system, institutions, policies, financing, service delivery, and monitoring. Focusing on these structures, I believe, is key to unravel the impacts of austerity on the health outcomes of prisoners. The term 'prison' here refers to institutions that hold people aged 18 years and older who have been sentenced to a period of imprisonment by the courts for offences against the criminal law. My analysis excludes other locations that deprive people of their liberty, including police cells, youth offender institutions, military detention centres, immigration removal centres, and mental health institutions.

Likewise, the study excludes prisoners who have been released and monitored by the National Probation Service, as they are subjected to a different monitoring system and health setting. This research also explicitly focuses on prisons in England, as prisons situated in the devolved administrations of Wales, Scotland, and Northern Ireland are subject to different policy responses and enforcement and use a different health system (HMPPS, 2017).

Findings

Following the research questions, this book offers seven findings. First, it reveals that by using the construct of neoliberalism, austerity becomes a vehicle to justify scaling down public sector services (including prisons) as part of the deficit-reduction programme and privatisation of prisons and healthcare services. The book exposes as flawed the political claim that austerity is inevitable and necessary. Despite asserting that cuts were necessary to prevent economic extravagance, these experiments failed: debt has increased after a decade of austerity, however measured.

Second, the book shows the deterioration to the governance and delivery of healthcare services across English prisons, and to the supportive prison regime.

Austerity unevenly impacts different prison establishments, and the regression after its implementation was rapid, undermining its experimental successes.

Third, it examines how austerity and the broader neoliberal framework subvert prison rehabilitation to punishment. The peculiarity of prison health governance and delivery, working in a prevailing structure that prioritises top-down hierarchies and punishment over collaboration and rehabilitation, will expose the institutional gridlock of prisons and prison health. As austerity was implemented, prison leadership deteriorated. Such is revealed by the transient political leadership of prison service and the rampant growth of prison gangs and serious organised crime groups across English prisons. Overall, the book explains how these issues challenge English prisons' command-and-control governance and therefore impact the governance and delivery of adequate healthcare in prisons.

Fourth, contrasting the political claim that 'we are all in this together' (Cameron, 2010), this research demonstrates how the poor continue to bear the burden of austerity. It argues that the prevailing tough-on-crime rhetoric among politicians, the withdrawal of community services for vulnerable individuals, and deindustrialisation forced penal institutions to become first responders.

Fifth, it shows that the meagre political responses to the system's instability were inadequate. Building additional prisons, recruiting new prison officers, and blaming psychoactive substances only masks the root cause of system instability and hews to neoliberal politics. These responses have limitations and have had a compounding, circular effect: worsening the prison instability.

Sixth, the work assesses scrutiny mechanisms intended to reduce austerity's effects on the governance and delivery of health across prisons in England. It finds them still unable to hold the government accountable for the deterioration in each.

Finally, it explores potential solutions to the austerity programme. These upstream, structural recommendations range from improving public political literacy on austerity and prisons to tax adjustments for wealthy corporations and individuals. It also suggests attaching greater accountability for ministers.

Overall, the book is valuable because it demonstrates that austerity has failed to reduce the burgeoning national debt, failed to control governance and delivery of healthcare services effectively and efficiently, and failed to improve prisoner health in England. Yet, after over a decade of producing the same results, the government remains reluctant to scrap the agenda.

The layout of the book

The work is structured logically and best read chronologically. Chapter 2 reviews critical social sciences literature that demonstrates how the UK's Conservative politicians have conceptualised austerity since 2010. Here, I illustrate how politicians have created this crisis—tracing it back to the 1980s during the Thatcher era—and how they have resorted to neoliberal adjustments as solutions.

Chapter 3 introduces the drivers of prison health governance and delivery in England. Building on David Marsh's critical realist theory of how the central government maintains a firm grip on hierarchical coordination (Marsh, 2011), I highlight the peculiarity of prison healthcare and prison service in England—specifically in cases where the state dictates the minutiae of service delivery. I also explore how the government's structured, top-down, and command-and-control approach shapes the health system. Additionally, this chapter explores the role of health within a structure that prioritises punishment. I reflect on the vulnerability of a prison health governance system continually subjected to myriad political interference and increasing privatisation under a regime of efficiency, value for money and performance monitoring. This setting has impaired the potential for sustainable health gains. I subsequently examine literature that illustrates the effectiveness of the monitoring structure of both prison and prison healthcare services in addressing the systemic instability.

Chapter 4 explains how prisons fail to account for the needs of prisoners. In doing so, it draws on Loïc Wacquant's (2010) 'centaur state' (the deregulation of social and economic elites while disciplining marginalised groups to 'correct' their behaviour), Erving Goffman's (1961) theory of importation (how the subculture within prisons is originated and brought in from the outside world by those incarcerated), and Gresham Sykes' (1958) theory of deprivation (the deprivation of liberty, goods and services, heterosexual relationships, autonomy, and security). I argue that prisoners' poor health is the by-product of their experiences before incarceration and that inattention to their health needs during incarceration perpetuates their marginalisation. The chapter also argues that neoliberalism has limited political possibilities for reducing health inequalities among prisoners and the wider population, while violating human rights.

The subsequent five chapters present findings. They are based on the in-depth analysis of 87 interviews, which generated over 1,474 pages of transcripts and 689,664 narrative texts for analysis (see Chapter 12 for methodological appendix). Chapter 5 begins by outlining how the research participants interpreted, while either enacting or contesting, the meaning of austerity across various levels of governance. Based on the Benchmarking programme of the Ministry of Justice in 2012 that executed the government's reductions on prison spending (House of Commons Justice Committee, 2012), I report participants' perspectives on the government's justification for the imposition of austerity on prison health.

Chapter 6 discusses participants' accounts of deterioration in the governance and delivery of prison health—such as longer waits, insufficient consultation time, and frequent cancellation or postponement of appointments—that stems from austerity. Additionally, participants discussed the progressively harmful living conditions where prisoners spent more than 14 hours daily in unhygienic and overcrowded cells. This triggered boredom and restlessness and contributed to unprecedented (albeit underreported) spikes in self-harm, assault, and self-inflicted death (Ministry of Justice, 2019). As such, I describe how imprisonment goes beyond the deprivation of individual liberty and became a form of double punishment and double deprivation for prisoners. Rather than presenting a uniform trend, however, I illustrate participants' varying views of how different prison establishments suffered financial cuts disproportionately to others.

Chapter 7 illustrates how short terms and reactive policies of justice ministers since 2010 prevent consistent policymaking and implementation. It also shows staff difficulties in stemming the flow of psychoactive substances, which research links to increases in organised crime and prison gangs operating both within and beyond prison walls. I examine how these criminal groups not only impair prisoner health (for example, by intimidating vulnerable prisoners into buying drugs from them) but also create and administer their own forms of prison governance. This situation is linked to Jürgen Habermas's (1973) theory of the legitimation crisis of prisons: a decline in the confidence of administrative functions, institutions, or leadership. The chapter also details participants' observations on the challenges in commissioning and delivering healthcare services across English prisons, as well as the increasing privatisation of whole prisons and their services—including healthcare—as part of the ongoing neoliberal programme.

Chapter 8 considers background issues that have intensified governance and delivery of prison healthcare across English prisons. The diminishing social and welfare services in the deprived areas across England, and links between austerity and deindustrialisation, work as a disadvantage. Participants mentioned that this situation has ensured—despite being unequipped—that prisons have become first responders when community provisions are no longer available to numerous vulnerable individuals from these communities. This is happening against the backdrop of longstanding issues like a poor prison environment and harsher sentencing practices.

Additionally, this chapter examines participants' reactions to the government's policy responses to prison instability, particularly in regards to the nationwide recruitment campaign for new prison officers since 2016. This chapter concludes with reasons why nearly all participants were sceptical about the Treasury's announcements in 2019 that austerity was ending—especially given the backdrop of Brexit (at the time of interviews) and the global COVID-19 pandemic, which have been predicted to perpetuate the decline in the UK's economic growth.

Chapter 9 highlights participants' views on inherent failures in prison oversight mechanisms and how those failures helped create the space and conditions for the deep-seated crisis that austerity continually inflicts on prison structure. The chapter also explores participants' responses to third sector organisations that often fill advocacy gaps. To maintain their government funding, these organisations have absorbed neoliberal logic and failed to challenge austerity.

Chapter 10 considers measures to end austerity's effects on prison health. Following participants' remarks, these recommendations include improving the public's political literacy to expose a fiscal crisis that did not formerly exist, and nudging the political direction towards increased resources for prisons and the community via tax increases for profitable corporations and wealthy individuals. In parallel, the chapter suggests reducing the prison population, attaching augmented accountability for programmes to the relevant ministers, and encouraging prisoners to initiate civil and criminal litigations against the government. These would accelerate the reversal of austerity's impacts on prisoners and the prison health system.

Overall, Chapter 11 reiterates the central argument: the implementation of austerity on prison health is a failed political experiment. Such a failure is illustrated via these several concepts: austerity's supposed necessity; conceptualisation of prison health from the prism of punishment; stability of command-and-control governance of English prisons; political rhetoric of tough on crime and 'we are all in this together'; government responses to instil prison stability; and scrutiny organisations' continual monitoring. Using evidence, I reinforce the arguments that both austerity and imprisonment have failed in their respective objectives to reduce the mounting national debt and improve prisoner rehabilitation. Yet, after over a decade of failures, the government juggernaut of austerity and imprisonment continues to produce the same result—with marked political reluctance to dispense with these policies. With Brexit and COVID-19 possibly causing a creeping recession, these failures become ever more perilous.

References

Cameron, D. (2010) *Press Conference on The Coalition: Our Programme for Government: 20 May 2010*. London: HM Government.

Committee for the Prevention of Torture and Inhuman or Degrading Treatment or Punishment (2017) *Report to the Government of the United Kingdom on the Visit to the United Kingdom Carried Out by the European Committee for the Prevention of Torture and Inhuman or Degrading Treatment or Punishment from 30 March to 12 April 2016* [Online], available from: https://rm.coe.int/168070a773 (Accessed: 11th January 2018).

Committee for the Prevention of Torture and Inhuman or Degrading Treatment or Punishment (2020) *Report to the United Kingdom Government on the Visit to the United Kingdom Carried Out by the European Committee for the Prevention of Torture and Inhuman or Degrading Treatment or Punishment (CPT) from 13 to 23 May 2019* [Online], available from: https://rm.coe.int/16809e4404 (Accessed: 27th May 2020).

Cross, M. (2013) Demonised, Impoverished and Now Forced into Isolation: The Fate of Disabled People Under Austerity. *Disability & Society*. 28(5), pp. 719–723.

Dardot, P. and Laval, C. (2013) *The New Way of the World: On Neoliberal Society*. London: Verso.

De Henau, J. and Reed, H. (2016) 10 Years of Austerity: The Income on Low-income Households and Women. *Poverty*, pp. 6–9.

Farnsworth, K. and Irving, Z. (2018) Austerity: Neoliberal Dreams Come True? *Critical Social Policy*. 38(3), pp. 461–481.

Goffman, E. (1961) *Asylums*. New York: Doubleday/Anchor.

Habermas, J. (1973) *Legitimation Crisis*. London: Heinemann Educational Books.

Hall, S. (1978) *Policing the Crisis: Mugging, the State, and Law and Order*. London: Macmillan.

Hall, S. (2011) The Neo-liberal Revolution. *Cultural Studies*. 25(6), pp. 705–728.

Harvey, D. (2010) *The Enigma of Capital and the Crises of Capitalism*. London: Profile Books.

Heald, D. and Steel, D. (2018) The Governance of Public Bodies in Times of Austerity. *The British Accounting Review*. 50(2), pp. 149–160.

HM Inspectorate of Prisons (2021) *HM Chief Inspector of Prisons for England and Wales: Annual Report 2020–21* [Online], available from: www.justiceinspectorates.gov.uk/hmi-prisons/wp-content/uploads/sites/4/2021/07/6.7391_HMI-Prisons_Annual-Report-and-Accounts-2020_21_v6.1_WEB.pdf (Accessed: 1st February 2022).

HM Prison & Probation Service (2017) *Prison Finder A-Z Pages* [Online], available from: www.justice.gov.uk/contacts/prison-finder/prisonfinder-a-z (Accessed: 25th January 2021).

House of Commons Justice Committee (2012) *Oral Evidence Taken Before the Justice Committee: The Work of the Secretary of State, Wednesday 28 November 2012: Rt Hon Chris Grayling MP* [Online], available from: https://publications.parliament.uk/pa/cm201213/cmselect/cmjust/c741-i/c74101.htm (Accessed: 25th January 2021).

Institute for Public Policy Research (2019) *Ending the Blame Game: The Case for a New Approach to Public Health and Prevention* [Online], available from: www.ippr.org/files/2019-06/public-health-and-prevention-june19.pdf (Accessed: 25th January 2021).

Khan, O. (2015) *The 2015 Budget: Effects on Black and Minority Ethnic People*. London: The Runnymede Trust.

Krugman, P. (2012) *End This Depression Now*! New York: W.W. Norton & Company.

Marsh, D. (2011) The New Orthodoxy: The Differentiated Polity Model. *Public Administration*. 89(1), pp. 32–48.

McEldowney, J. (2016) Delivering Public Services in the United Kingdom in a Period of Austerity. In: Wollmann, H., Koprić, I. and Marcou, G., eds. *Public and Social Services in Europe: Governance and Public Management*. London: Palgrave Macmillan, pp. 41–54.

Ministry of Justice (2019) *HMPPS Annual Digest 2018/19* [Online], available from: https://assets.publishing.service.gov.uk/government/uploads/system/uploads/attachment_data/file/821148/HMPPS_Annual_Digest_bulletin_2018-2019.pdf (Accessed: 21st February 2020).

Ministry of Justice (2020) *Safety in Custody Summary Tables to March 2020* [Online], available from: https://assets.publishing.service.gov.uk/government/uploads/system/uploads/attachment_data/file/905014/Safety-in-custody-summary-q1-2020-final-tables.xlsm (Accessed: 25th January 2021).

Newburn, T. (2007) "Tough on Crime": Penal Policy in England and Wales. *Crime and Justice*. 36(1), pp. 425–470.

Office for National Statistics (2021) *Household Income Inequality, UK: Financial Year Ending 2020* [Online], available from: www.ons.gov.uk/peoplepopulationandcommunity/personalandhouseholdfinances/incomeandwealth/bulletins/householdincomeinequality-financial/financialyearending2020 (Accessed: 25th January 2021).

Ortiz, I., Chai, J. and Cummins, M. (2011) *Austerity Measures Threaten Children and Poor Households: Recent Evidence in Public Expenditures from 128 Developing Countries*. New York: UNICEF.

Peck, J. (2015) *Austerity Urbanism: The Neoliberal Crisis of American Cities*. New York: Rosa Luxemburg Stiftung.

Suhrcke, M., Stuckler, D., Suk, J. E., Desai, M., Senek, M., McKee, M., Tsolova, S., Basu, S., Abubakar, I., Hunter, P., Rechel, B. and Semenza, J. C. (2011) The Impact of Economic Crises on Communicable Disease Transmission and Control: A Systematic Review of the Evidence. *PLoS ONE*. 6(6), p. e20724. https://doi.org/10.1371/journal.pone.0020724.

Sykes, G. (1958) *The Society of Captives: A Study of a Maximum Security Prison*. Princeton, NJ: Princeton University Press.

United Nations General Assembly (2019) *Visit to the United Kingdom of Great Britain and Northern Ireland: Report of the Special Rapporteur on Extreme Poverty and Human Rights*

[Online], available from: https://undocs.org/A/HRC/41/39/Add.1 (Accessed: 25th January 2021).

Virchow, R. C. (1848) *Archiv für pathologische Anatomie und Physiologie und für klinische Medicin*. Berlin: Reimer.

Wacquant, L. (2000) The New "Peculiar Institution": On the Prison as Surrogate Ghetto. *Theoretical Criminology*. 4(3), pp. 377–389.

Wacquant, L. (2010) Crafting the Neoliberal State: Workfare, Prisonfare, and Social Insecurity. *Sociological Forum*. 25(2), pp. 197–220.

Ward, K. and England, K. (2007) Introduction: Reading Neoliberalization. In: England, K. and Ward, K., eds. *Neoliberalization*. Hoboken, NJ: Blackwell, pp. 1–22.

Westwood, S. (2016) LGBT Ageing in the UK: Spatial Inequalities in Older Age Housing/Care Provision. *Journal of Poverty and Social Justice*. 24(1), pp. 63–76.

Wren-Lewis, S. (2016) *A General Theory of Austerity*. BSG Working Paper Series 2016/014: May 2016. Oxford: University of Oxford.

Chapter 2

The spell of neoliberalism and austerity

Introduction

Evidence of austerity's effect on the general population's health is well publicised. Yet little exists on its impact on prison health governance and the delivery of healthcare services, which subsequently affect prisoner health and well-being in England. This chapter starts with a historical account of neoliberalism, investigating how its development provided a template for introducing and sustaining austerity as a UK government policy since 2010. I subsequently review how, in experimenting with austerity, policymakers framed it as a political rather than evidence-based choice. Then, I assess austerity's consequences for prisons and prison healthcare services. Beyond the immediate reduction of funding, this chapter infers a longer-term welfare state restructuring—a form of political experiment—in the context of increasing punitiveness and a tougher stance on crime. Altogether, these changes, although enacted in the name of austerity, are none other than the guiding norms of neoliberalism permeating the management of the English criminal justice system.

A history of neoliberalism

The UK's current neoliberal economics stem from Adam Smith's *The Wealth of Nations* (1776). Smith argued for the rights of free individuals to accumulate wealth and safeguard their property interests. He proposed that the government should play a minimal role in economic matters to allow trade to flourish. Britain adopted Smith's ideas, and the following century saw industrialisation and the rise of manufacturing, with the advent of waged labour, a factory system, free trade, and urbanisation dovetailing the revolution as the UK became 'the workshop of the world' (Hall, 2011, p. 709). For almost 200 years, its government internalised the liberal economic mindset through the rise of mass production, a large consumer market, and mass media (Hall, 2011).

However, post-World War II, societal movements based on collectivism, solidarity, and trust became fashionable (Taylor-Gooby and Leruth, 2018). And one English economist, John Maynard Keynes, usurped Smith as the dominant voice

DOI: 10.4324/9781003182337-2

of his age. His ideas would fundamentally change the theory and practice of macroeconomics and the government's economic policies. Keynes (1936) argued that the market had been left to its own devices for too long and that it showed no signs of correcting its negative externalities: protracted unemployment, poverty, and health disparities. He called for counter-cyclical fiscal and monetary policies to address them (Keynes, 1936). Britain embraced Keynesian economics, which saw over a third of the country's GDP redistributed to ensure acceptable standards in public services, promote greater social equality, provide benefits to those outside the labour market, and develop community infrastructure (Sen, 1977). It was a period dubbed 'the golden age', when the welfare state found consensus.

Despite Keynes' influence, in the background, neoliberal ideas were gaining traction among politicians, academics, policymakers, and influential journalists. They attacked the redistributive policies through the Walter Lippmann Colloquium, founded in 1938, and the Mont Pelerin Society, which began in 1947 (Dardot and Laval, 2013). When criticising the threat to freedom posed by the encroaching power of the state, these individuals assumed that no one has the perfect knowledge necessary to make economic planning work and to govern society (ibid.). Instead, they advocated for the genesis of a free society: the necessary conditions for the market to flourish, the need to prevent arbitrary rule and authoritarianism, and the need to restrict democratic involvement in decision-making processes (ibid.).

Nationwide inflation in the mid-1970s terminated the Keynesian reformation through the imposition of structural adjustment programmes by the International Monetary Fund (IMF) on Britain (Harvey, 2009). Austerity emerged as a crucial means of sustaining neoliberalism during this period. The New York financial crisis in the 1970s and the bankruptcy threat from Mexico in the 1980s led the IMF to bail out Mexico in a deal that would impose austerity on its citizens (Harvey, 2005). With the arrival of Margaret Thatcher, Ronald Reagan, and Helmut Kohl in 1979, 1981, and 1982, respectively, the UK, United States, and Germany underwent a reconstruction of the socio-economic landscape. These efforts accorded with the work of an Austrian-British economist, Friedrich von Hayek, and an American economist, Milton Friedman, which opposed Keynesian principles by espousing the self-regulating capacity of markets and scepticism of the state and collectivism (Martinez and Garcia, 1997).

Thatcher claimed that neo-Keynesianism had caused disastrous economic effects. She averred that "there is no alternative" policy to monetarism, creating a narrative about the benefits of thrift and hard work, with neoliberal policies to support them (Schmidt, 2002, p. 215). Right-wing commentators praised her approach; they reasoned that to institute more than a basic minimum of collective responsibility would constitute interference with free markets (Amable, 2011). Critics of Keynesian economics argued that such a policy had attempted "to provide for the poor and produced [poorer people] instead", and so the UK had "tried to remove the barriers to escape from poverty and inadvertently built a trap" (Murray, 1984, p. 9).

Following Thatcher, UK political parties have embraced varying styles of political economics. Yet neoliberalism remains in the background and has manifested into different governing forms. Also, toughness on crime has been steadfast until issues such as the global financial crisis and immigration superseded it (Hall, 2011). Unlike Thatcher's distinction of "the worthy poor" from "the feckless and the idle", Tony Blair's social-democratic legitimation underscored the need to create equal opportunities. However, he emphasised welfare would "not [be] a hammock but a trampoline", and not a "hand out but a hand up" (Schmidt, 2002, p. 269).

As growing neoliberalism bore down on the welfare state, criminal justice discourse increasingly dominated the political process. That the pair went hand in hand is unsurprising: Loïc Wacquant (2012, p. 242) describes them as the "two modalities of public policy towards the poor". And they only grew more coherent during this period. In 1993, a bipartisan consensus emerged called the 'second order', with both major political parties embracing an augmented position on crime (Reiner, 2011). One consequence was increased public attention to criminal justice operations. Moreover, criminal justice gained considerable exposure in popular media and political discourse, fuelled by images of dangerous offenders, vulnerable victims, and displaced elite and professional expertise (Garland, 2001).[1] Parallel with Robert Nozick's (1974) *Anarchy, State and Utopia*, the role of the state became to maintain law and order, while other interventions were viewed as either restricting individual liberty or interfering in market operations.

This neoliberal, minimal state mentality led governments to increase privatisation and labour market flexibility and reduce taxes and regulation (Hall, 2011; Harvey, 2010). Neoliberalism has also provided a template for competitive globalisation, imposing sweeping programmes of state restructuring and rescaling across a wide range of national and local contexts (Peck and Tickell, 2012). Ben Fine and Alfredo Saad-Filho (2017) argued—albeit in sharply dissimilar and logically incompatible ways—that differently endowed, property-owning individuals exchanging goods, services, and information in minimally regulated markets constitute the most desirable form of allocating resources and should prevail over an interventionist state and democratic processes. Borrowing Friedrich von Hayek's (quoted in Peck, 2010, p. 18) reference to it as the "flexible credo", the neoliberal project has been realised through a somewhat improvised, often experimental, and shape-shifting repertoire of pro-market programmes, projects, and power plays.

Prioritising short-term economic efficiency limits political possibilities for reducing health inequalities and causes human rights violations. Karl Polanyi (1944) warned that letting the market mechanism be the sole arbiter of the fate of human beings would lead to society's downfall, as governments would desensitise to the daily predicament of their members. The extreme austerity measures that the IMF and World Bank impose on countries receiving funds in a financial bailout lead debtors to deregulate capital markets, privatise economic activity, relax foreign investment, and reduce social spending (Hart-Landsberg, 2006). Both financial organisations depict human rights concerns as beyond the scope of the fiscal regime. Specifically, they conceive such issues as subject to cost-benefit analysis and the potential cost of trying to reconcile seemingly incommensurable values (Sarfaty, 2012). Discussions about marginalised and vulnerable populations, prisoners included, are therefore excluded from economic consideration. Nevertheless, the history of neoliberalism provided a template for introducing austerity in the UK since 2010, which will now be explored.

The 2007–2008 global financial crisis and austerity in the UK

In 2007, the UK bank Northern Rock announced insolvency—victim to a cascade of events in the credit market that ultimately caused the global financial crisis. The bank bailouts of 2008 followed, and the UK officially entered a recession along with most of the developed world (Basu, 2017). From this grew an annual gap in the state finance of £35bn, and the UK government were left scratching their heads (Farnsworth, 2018).

The Cameron-Clegg coalition embraced austerity shortly after coming to power in May 2010. The UK was not a member of the Eurozone. Yet, the then-Chancellor of the Exchequer, George Osborne, imposed severe fiscal reductions like those the European Commission, the European Central Bank, and the IMF ('the Troika') inflicted on other European countries such as Greece, Ireland, and Portugal as part of their bailout conditions (Gamble, 2014). In other words, though the UK government's objective was to reduce the budgetary deficit, they were not part of the Eurozone or bound by the Troika to do so. Deficits subsequently became the central political issue and austerity the rhetorical weapon of choice for politicians.

The early definition of 'austerity' developed around the concept of financial cuts. Defined as extreme retrenchment in public expenditure (Ortiz et al., 2011), austerity reflects a form of voluntary deflation via a reduction in government borrowing that requires deep cuts in public expenditures. It is based on a claim that such efforts will rebalance the economy and regain economic dynamism and competitiveness (Anderson and Minneman, 2014; Fontana and Sawyer, 2011; Schui, 2015). This definition of austerity is also based on the theory of expansionary fiscal contraction, which argues that a decrease in state spending will stimulate economic growth (Dellepiane-Avellaneda, 2015)—reasoning the UK government adopted.

The government justified reductions in public sector spending as part of its strategy to restore the economy to an equilibrium (Blyth, 2013). This strategy entailed lowering the deficit in the short term and maintaining confidence in the country's financial market in the long term (Gamble, 2014). The chancellor set a goal of achieving a ratio of public spending to GDP of 41% by 2015. And the Cameron-Clegg coalition exacted large spending cuts for public programmes to get there (ibid.). In this "rolling back [of] the state" (Taylor-Gooby and Stoker, 2011, p. 14), the government sought to appease financial markets by decreasing public sector spending to meet the burgeoning deficits created by the bailout of the banking sector without raising taxes; such efforts were designed to allow the government to continue borrowing at reasonable interest rates (Gamble, 2014; Midgley, 2014).

Some right-wing scholars have argued that austerity resembles a typical economic downturn pattern (Panitch and Konings, 2009; Thompson, 2013). Additionally, they have justified austerity as the due penance for financial mismanagement in preceding decades (ibid.). Austerity's great irony is that those who engineered or profited from asset bubbles avoid the brunt of the resulting austerity; workers and the poor suffer it instead (Callinicos, 2012). As Quinn Slobodian (2020, p. 6) underscored,

> if we place too much emphasis on the category of market fundamentalism, we will fail to notice that the real focus of neoliberal proposals is not on the market per se but on redesigning states, laws, and other institutions to protect the market.

Beyond financial cuts, economists and political scientists argue austerity is ideological because it will likely have a far-reaching impact on the population. Connecting austerity and neoliberalism, Simon Wren-Lewis (2016) argued that austerity measures have exceeded balancing the books; instead, they have become an ideological project that seeks to dismantle the welfare state via cuts on public services, built on the deceit that austerity is economically imperative. For Roger Clough (2018), austerity is a disingenuous word for promoting government rhetoric to the effect that there is no alternative—similar to Thatcher's slogan in the 1970s. Despite concerted attempts to reduce public spending, austerity increased government debt and deficit—the opposite of its intention (Blyth, 2013). "The austerity drive is not really about debt and deficits at all", Paul Krugman (2012, p. A27) asserted, "it is about using deficit panic as an excuse to dismantle social programs. . . . [E]conomic recovery was never the point; the drive for austerity [is] about using the crisis, not solving it". I adopt these critical definitions of austerity in this book and consider how austerity has been depicted as a political choice rather than an economic imperative.

Additionally, scholars have distinguished the existing implementation of austerity post-2008 financial crisis—termed 'neo-austerity'—from austerity in the previous decades (Farnsworth and Irving, 2018). While all phases of austerity characterise debt as a problem and claim state expenditure cuts are the solution, the 'socialised austerity' of 1945–1951 (Hill, 2015, p. 50) mainly focused on consumer restraint to support civic investment. And the 'permanent austerity' of the 1980s and 1990s—despite its legacy for welfare relations—did not prompt the political immobilisation required to reverse welfare expansion (Pierson, 1998).

Neo-austerity is unique for exploiting political opportunities in three ways (Farnsworth and Irving, 2018). First, its proponents used the post-crisis public debt narrative as a definitive and pragmatic economic truth to question the welfare state's affordability. Second, neo-austerity reconditioned social welfare expectations to the minimum, diminishing the solidarity that characterised post-war welfare state-building. Third, it enables social policy measures to support and promote private sector interests. This book will critically explore these three dynamics.

Austerity as a political choice

Since its inception, scholars have questioned the durability of austerity's macroeconomic policy (Blyth, 2013; Gamble, 2014). It depended on economists' misinterpretation of public debt and baseless claims the global recession overwhelmed the government. Nonetheless, such economic fallacies gave life to the policy and helped maintain it. That within ten years of its launch it had no credible economic support reveals austerity was clearly a political choice.

Misinterpretation of the impact of public debt

Comparatively, there are telling distinctions within the G7 economic bloc regarding their reaction towards the debt-to-GDP ratio. This is the ratio between a country's government debt and its gross domestic product, where a low debt-to-GDP ratio indicates an economy that can generate goods and services to pay back debts without incurring further debt. The UK was among very few major industrialised countries that increased public expenditures in the decade before the economic crisis (Shaoul, 2011; Streeck and Mertens, 2013). In 2010, Conservative politicians described the UK's 90% debt-to-GDP ratio as alarming. Yet other countries such as Japan had ratios as high as 240% (Konzelmann and Fovargue-Davies, 2019). The way in which the countries subsequently reacted showed a clear—and arbitrary—divide on what needs to be done when the debt-to-GDP ratio rises.

The UK's alarm at their debt-GDP ratio stemmed from several key misinterpretations of public debt, which Conservative politicians quickly leapt on to substantiate the call for austerity. First, economists claimed high debt could trigger economic sluggishness and unsustainable debt repayments (Reinhart and Rogoff, 2010). However, Mark Blyth (2013) debunked this myth, showing the forecast driving it was based on coding errors, selective exclusion of available data, and unconventional weighting of summary statistics. Second, European politicians began describing private household debt and public debt as analogous (ibid.). For example, Angela Merkel, the now former Chancellor of Germany, famously proclaimed that "the sustainable level of public debt was equivalent to that of private households" (Blyth, 2013). Economists discredited such false comparisons, which proposed that if the government desisted from excessive borrowing and concomitant spending, the economy would shrink from a lack of demand for goods and services (Blyth, 2013; Stiglitz, 2014; Weeks, 2019). These economists further warned that a liquidity-trap recession—when interest rates approach zero, and the economy remains in a recession—could occur (Blyth, 2013; Stiglitz, 2014).

The exposal of such theories as flawed did not stop right-wing economists pursuing austerity. They propounded that a fiscal contraction would improve business confidence and consumer expectations (Alesina and Ardagna, 2010). Opting to address shortfalls by imposing a tax increase would be deeply recessionary in the short and medium terms, such economists claimed, and would fail to address burgeoning debts (ibid.).

Because the UK fiscal cuts have deepened since 2010, the negative effects of austerity have become increasingly clear. The debt-to-GDP ratio rose from 74.7% in 2010 to 84.6% in 2020 (Office for National Statistics, 2021a). This parallels with research on European counterparts such as Romania, Estonia, Bulgaria, Latvia, and Lithuania, which shows that austerity measures coincided with increasing debt (Blyth, 2013).

Nevertheless, as Jason Hickel (2017, p. 156) argues, debt has been "a powerful mechanism for pushing neoliberalism around the world". The claim that austerity would reduce national debt justified a reduction in the size of many states, transferring the burden to the public sector and its workforce (Blyth, 2013; Grimshaw, 2013). With the same disregard for economic evidence, the coalition and subsequent Conservative governments have continued to blame the preceding Labour government for negligence with the public purse; they claimed to be serious about addressing the fiscal deficit while ignoring the more concrete theories on how to do it (Gamble, 2014; Hayton, 2014).

The claim that the global recession overwhelmed the government

In 2007, Naomi Klein (2007) predicted that neoliberal politicians opposed to 'big government' would use the coming global recession to pursue their political objectives in a way that would otherwise be impossible. Put simply, they could argue 'there is no alternative'. Klein's prediction was correct. As soon as it took office, the coalition government began asserting that the global recession had overwhelmed the state's power to stabilise the national economy (Prime Minister's Office, 2013).

Such claims were not new to politics. Far earlier, Linda Weiss (1987) had observed that governing institutions often overstate and overgeneralise state powerlessness and underplay their capacity for adaptability. Significant research (Nolan, 2015; Ortiz et al., 2011; Taylor-Gooby and Stoker, 2011) has suggested that the justification of austerity entailed such overstatements, further revealing austerity as a political choice, not an economic necessity.

In imposing cuts, the government ignored valuable commentary from the IMF and Organisation for Economic Co-operation and Development (OECD). The former warned that "a budget cut equal to 1 percent of GDP typically reduces domestic demand by about 1 percent and raises the unemployment rate by 0.3 percentage points" (IMF, 2010). The latter said of the UK's rapid financial consolidation that, by constraining monetary policy, it risked "adversely affecting the recovery" (OECD, 2011, p. 227). In contrast, countries that abandoned austerity and opted for fiscal stimulus—such as the United States and Iceland—witnessed a strong economic recovery, repaid their debts early, and improved their populations' health (Stuckler and Basu, 2013).

The UK government applied pre-emptive deflation as part of a domestic political manoeuvre. Considering austerity is economically unnecessary, implementing it constructed a misleading political narrative on the need to embrace it (Gamble, 2014). It also underplayed the political aspect of neoliberalism, containing it within financial responses (ibid.). Yet despite Conservatives painting such a dire situation, the economy has never returned to the lows of 2009 (OECD, 2018). That the economy never re-entered a recession is evidence politicians fabricated the crisis and resorted to neoliberal adjustments as solutions. The narrative on the economic recovery evolved from managing the risks of financial institutions to curbing the expansive welfare state (Clarke and Newman, 2012). This shift reflects the far-reaching impact of neoliberalism that uses the economy as a pretext to regulate public institutions.

Osborne promised to end austerity by the end of Parliament 2015. Yet six months before Parliament's dissolution, the Conservative-led coalition released details of its plans to cut public expenditure to around 35% of GDP by 2018 (Farnsworth and Irving, 2015; Vina et al., 2013). On narrowly winning the general election in 2017, the Conservative government delayed terminating the austerity programme until 2022, contingent upon the date of the next general election (The Conservative and Unionist Party, 2017). Former Chancellor of the Exchequer Philip Hammond announced in October 2018 that the era of austerity was ending; his successor, Sajid Javid, repeated the claim 11 months later (HM Treasury, 2019a, 2019b). These announcements were timed to secure the general election, which had no connection with their initial claim that the global recession overwhelmed the government. Thus, it demonstrates the experimentation nature of austerity given the ever-shifting end date while reinforcing that austerity is a political choice. Austerity's impacts on the public sector, including on prisons and prison healthcare services, were immediate and grave.

Impacts of austerity on the UK public sector services

The Treasury conducted a limited social impact analysis of reducing expenditures. Its justification was that assessing with any certainty how spending cuts might impact public services before imposing them would be impossible (HM

Treasury, 2018; O'Dea and Preston, 2010). A decade on, as Figures 2.1 and 2.2 show, the UK's spending on social protection is lower than the European average, and it spends slightly more than the European average on prisons (Eurostat, 2020). This trend typifies the punitiveness of neoliberalism: law and order are maintained as state welfare declines (Wacquant, 2000).

Austerity has had immediate social and health consequences. Spending cuts in the name of austerity have deprived the population of social protection and other social services, including health systems. The Poverty and Social Exclusion (PSE) UK study revealed that austerity has increased poverty and inequality: a third of the UK population is estimated to suffer financial problems, and about a quarter have an unacceptably low standard of living (Gordon et al., 2013). Austerity has severely impeded mental health provisions since 2010 (O'Hara, 2014) and increased suicides and depression (measured by prescription rates; Barr et al., 2015). More recently, the UN special rapporteur on extreme poverty and human rights, Philip Alston, systematically documented for the first time that, despite being the fifth-largest economy in the world, the UK has 14 million people in poverty—alongside record hunger, homelessness, and food bank dependency (UN General Assembly, 2019). These studies demonstrate the clash between efficiency, effectiveness, and equity, showing people unevenly share austerity's burden.

Measures on income inequality—such as the Gini coefficient,[2] Top 1% share,[3] S80/S20 ratio[4] and P90/P10[5] ratio—reveal income inequality increased between 2010 and 2020 (Office for National Statistics, 2021b) (Figure 2.3). The Palma Ratio,[6] on the other hand, remained stagnant (ibid.). Despite then-Prime Minister David Cameron's claim that "we are all in this together" (Cameron, 2010), selective austerity has protected high earners and major transnational corporations by reducing tax and enabling tax avoidance, but markedly disadvantaged those at the bottom of the income ladder (House of Commons Committee of Public Accounts, 2012).

The decline of public sector services following the implementation of austerity has impacted most of the population. Local authorities' spending (excluding education spending) per resident fell by almost a quarter in real terms between 2009–2010 and 2019–2020 (Institute for Fiscal Studies, 2021). Beyond organisational cost-saving initiatives, such as sharing back-office posts and efficiency savings, these public sector organisations have had to cut preventative and early intervention support to safeguard services in a significant manner. From the closure of 859 children's centres and family hubs (UNISON, 2019) to the 70% spending cuts in real terms for youth services in England and Wales spending (YMCA, 2020), local authorities shifted from universal to targeted services to meet the needs of the most vulnerable young people.

In parallel, around 4 million people in the UK live below the poverty line, with 1.5 million individuals unable to afford basic essentials (Social Metrics Commission, 2018). Rather than using the Universal Credit scheme to help with the cost of living for those who experienced job losses, housing insecurity

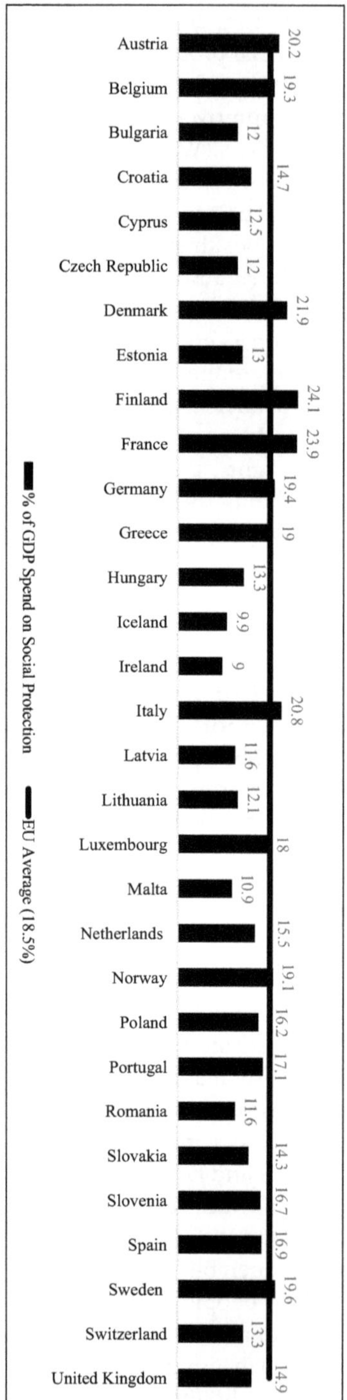

Figure 2.1 Percentage of GDP spend on social protection by European Countries 2018

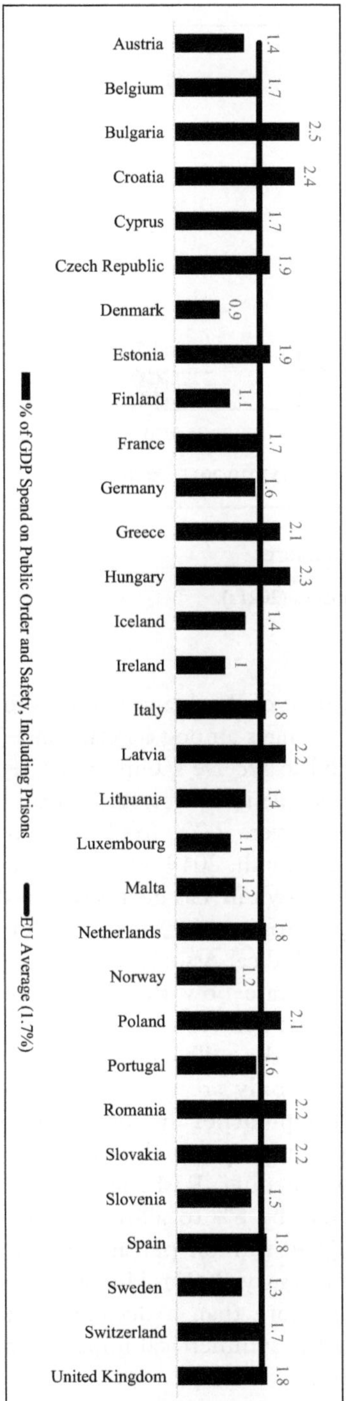

Figure 2.2 Percentage of GDP spend on prisons by European Countries 2018

Source: Eurostat (2020).

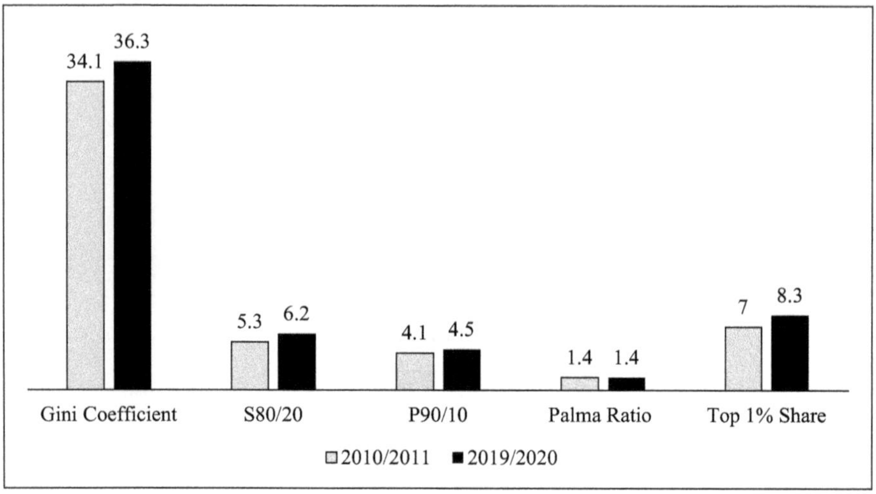

Figure 2.3 Income equality measures

Source: Office for National Statistics (2021a).

and illnesses, the Department of Work and Pensions focuses on economic savings and targets lifestyle changes among its claimants (UN General Assembly, 2019). The waiting period to receive a Universal Credit claim can take up to 12 weeks, which pushes people into debt, rent arrears, and hunger (Cheetham et al., 2020). In 2021, there were 2,200 food banks in the UK, up from 29 in 2010 (Citizen Network Research, 2019; House of Commons Library, 2021a). The notion of 'home as an asylum' has been severely deteriorated, with many individuals experiencing chronic stress, deterioration, or relapse of existing health conditions (British Medical Association, 2016).

These examples demonstrate how the decline of public sector services created a ripple effect on the individuals who depend on them. Altogether, they reinforce the notion of the rollback of the welfare state, which is a key trait of neoliberalism. Not only are the financial cuts unsustainable given preventative, long-term approaches are being compromised by the need to make short-term savings; they are also widening social inequality. The current Chancellor of Exchequer, Rishi Sunak, announced a reduction in Universal Credit taper rate by 8% to allow claimants to keep more of the payment and pledged £640 million per annum to address rough sleeping and homelessness (HM Treasury, 2021). However, this does not help reverse the damage inflicted by more than a decade of austerity. The next section, then, will illustrate the symmetrical impact of austerity on prisons and prison healthcare services.

Impacts of austerity cuts on prisons and prison healthcare services

Symmetrical to other public sector services, prisons experienced cuts to their budget. Daily spending on prisons totalled £3.48 billion in 2009/2010. By 2015/2016, it was 19% lower in real terms, at £2.3 billion (Institute for Government, 2019). This translated to a 30% decline in prison staff between 2009 and 2017 (CPT, 2017; National Audit Office [NAO], 2017). Despite some investment to reverse the spending fall in subsequent years, prison spending was still 14% lower in 2017/2018 compared with eight years earlier (Institute for Government, 2019). Despite these cuts to prisons and prison services, the prison population rose by 7% between 2010 and 2020 (Ministry of Justice, 2020a, 2020b). This raises the question of institutional safety as prisons were expected to house more individuals with a reduced budget.

A target was set for the HMPPS to deliver £900 million in savings by the end of 2015 without reducing the prison population (National Offender Management Service [NOMS], 2015). Consequently, HMPPS scrutinised and consolidated pay structures for management and operational staff, along with issuing early retirement offers, redundancies, fixed-term contracts for the existing workforce, and new pay levels in line with market rates—often lower than existing staff salaries. Meanwhile, it undertook structural measures, decreasing the number of headquarters and closing small and less cost-efficient prisons (House of Commons Justice Committee, 2015).

The total number of core prison operational staff in England and Wales consistently declined between 2012 and 2016 (Figure 2.4). This decline created a severe staffing deficiency, with 4.6 prisoners for every staff member in 2016/2017. This is more than double the average number of prisoners to staff in other European countries (European Public Service Union, 2016).

Following a 53% increase in the number of assaults (although it is likely to be an underestimate given inadequate reporting practice across prisons), the government launched a campaign between 2017 and 2019 to recruit more prison officers (CPT, 2020). But the effort has been insufficient to compensate for the contraction. The slight rise in staff numbers reflects greater reliance on inexperienced officers. A total of 2,640 frontline prison officers left the HMPPS in 2019, a 26% (n=552) increase in departures from 2018 and a reflection of an ongoing trajectory (CPT, 2017; HMPPS, 2019). Short terms of service are also growing: 38% of departing officers served under a year, compared with 31% the previous year (HMPPS, 2019). This rapid staff turnover exacerbates the problem of inexperienced officers in the prison system.

Additionally, overcrowding has persisted. The latest statistics show that 104% of adult prison places in England and Wales are in use (House of Commons Library, 2021b). Although remaining high, the rate of imprisonment has stabilised over the last decade. This is partly because the backlog of court cases (currently 45,500) has prevented a surge (Crest Advisory, 2020). However,

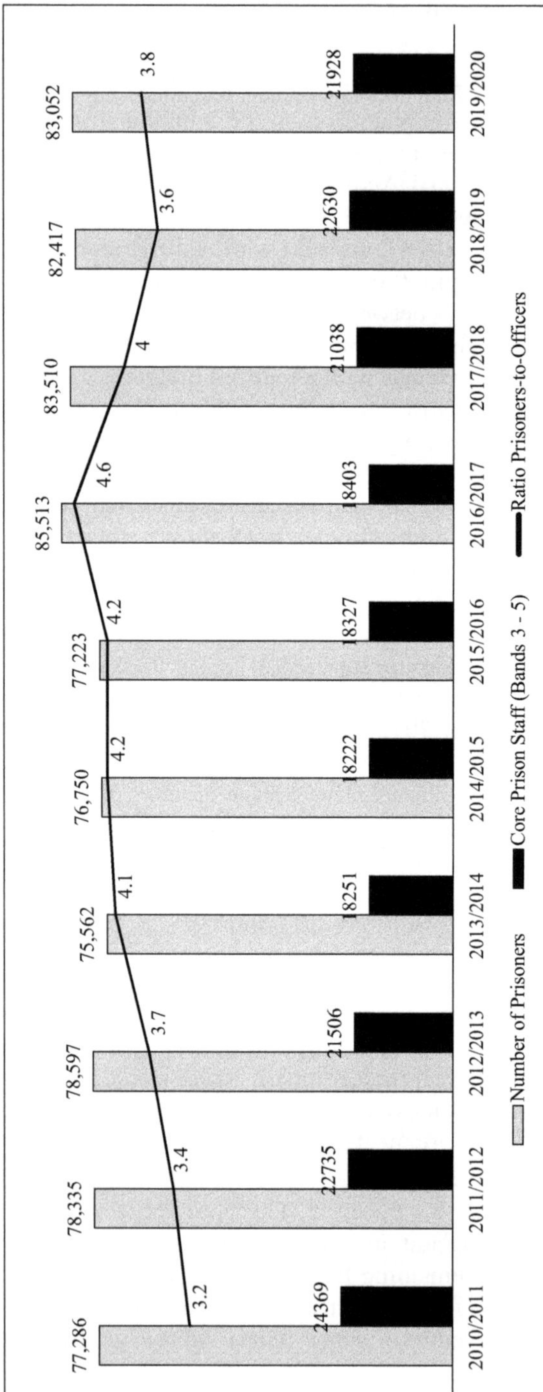

Figure 2.4 Number of core prison staff and prison population in England and Wales, 2010/2011 to 2019/2020

Source: Ministry of Justice (2020a, 2020b).

given the government has announced additional police resourcing, the extension of stop and search, and the review of sentencing for serious offenders, the prisoner-to-prison officer ratio is likely to worsen (House of Lords Library Briefing, 2019).

Under the coalition and the subsequent Conservative governments, expenditures on the NHS funding have been relatively protected (HM Treasury, 2010). However, growth has failed to keep pace with population growth. In 1979, NHS funding expanded 3.8%, but in 2010, it grew only 1.1% (Marmot, 2017), a rate that has remained steady between 2009/2010 and 2014/2015 owing to funding constraints (New Economics Foundation, 2018). As the New Economics Foundation (2018) noted, this represents the slowest growth since the 1950s. Thus, NHS funding has decreased in real terms over this period.

NHS funding for prison health was £400 million in 2016/2017. About £150 million of that went to mental health and substance misuse services (NAO, 2017). This plateaued funding was maintained throughout the austerity period (ibid.), despite an increased burden of disease in the prison population (see Chapter 4), and has strained the governance and delivery of prison healthcare in England. While spending cuts across the various public services vary, a basic point holds: prisons and prison healthcare have been disproportionately impacted, something scholars have yet to theorise. As Streeck and Mertens (2013) argue, austerity measures protect mandatory spending, which is often derived from statutory obligations. NHS England spending appears to follow this pattern. In contrast, prison spending appears to have fallen under discretionary funding, which is the most common target of austerity cuts in the consolidation of the state (ibid.). Less known, however, is the extent of the link between austerity and existing prison instability, a topic Chapter 4 explores further.

Punitiveness and tough on crime

With neoliberalism and inequality come punitiveness as a guiding social order. Both tend to neutralise social solidarity and lead to high levels of punitiveness (Cavadino and Dignan, 2006; Wilkinson and Pickett, 2009). The high incidence of punishment-use corresponds with neoliberalism's punitive nature (Rusche and Kirchheimer, 1939). Neoliberal societies are particularly prone to the culture of control (Garland, 2001); their dominant penal ideology has a pronounced tendency towards social exclusion, exclusionary modes of punishment, and strengthening of the coercive arm of the state (Cavadino and Dignan, 2006). Given the increasing economic inequality, higher levels of punishment are unsurprising (ibid.).

The rise of neoliberalism well sparks the return of the 'less-eligible' doctrine. It suggests that prisoners should receive lower-quality healthcare treatment than the poorest members of society (Sim, 1990), allowing the state to relinquish its moral obligations (Pantazis, 2016). But more crucially, we face the issue that when the welfare state's main function withers, the penal state flourishes in its place (Wacquant, 2000). In this context, the prison system becomes a major provider of state welfare, healthcare, and educational services.

Accompanying the growth of the penal system, politicians have engaged in an 'arms race' to convince voters that they are tough on crime (Lacey, 2008). Although a more populist and punitive penal environment can be traced to the mid-1970s, the decisive shift occurred in the early 1990s, when the main political parties vowed to be 'tough on crime' (Newburn, 2007). They used an emotional language of fear and anger, such as 'war on crime' and 'prison works', to portray individual deficits, such as violence and addiction, as requiring imprisonment (Sparks, 2007). Additionally, the state organises how politicians communicate and politicise risks (Sparks, 2000). Stuart Hall (1978) argued that the exaggerated outburst of public concern over the morality and behaviour of society represented politicians' attempts to persuade the working class that they are serious about tackling crime and the causes of crime. A comprehensive survey of media coverage revealed that networks spotlighted the lenient treatment of prisoners by prison officers while ignoring unacceptable living conditions and human rights violations in prisons (European Prison Observatory, 2013). A 2019 Ipsos MORI poll of the public revealed that only 17% of respondents considered crime and order to be important issues in the UK today, compared with the 25% who thought so in 2010—although there was a higher pre-2010 value (Ipsos MORI, 2015, 2019).

Proponents of being tough on crime often link falling rates of recorded crime to increased imprisonment. This assertion accords with former Conservative Home Secretary Michael Howard's classic argument that "prison works" (Parliament UK, 1993). Civitas, a UK right-wing think tank, also claims that crime is falling because of the incapacitating effects of prisons (Green et al., 2003). The latest figures show that the overall crime rate fell by 4% between July 2019 and June 2020 (Office for National Statistics, 2020), although violent and property crime have increased in line with the implementation of austerity since 2010. The reasons for this are complex and have been explored extensively elsewhere (Giulietti and McConnell, 2021; Walby et al., 2016).

However, only 32% of the public who responded to the nationwide Crime Survey for England and Wales believed that prison effectively punishes those guilty of crimes (Ministry of Justice, 2015). Indeed, such beliefs accord with the high reoffending rate of 45% for those released from custody and 61% of those serving a sentence of fewer than 12 months (Ministry of Justice, 2020c). These findings challenge the suggestion that "prison works"; its continuing orchestration through the tough-on-crime stance is thus seemingly a result of political choices. This is indeed a political orientation that seeks to perpetuate the status quo when responding to crime rather than addressing the root cause of criminality (Wacquant, 2010).

Summary

In this chapter, I have reviewed how the rise of neoliberalism offered a template for the government to implement austerity. We have seen how government austerity measures lead to fiscal consolidation and the consequent adverse impact on the population's health and well-being in the UK. In particular, the right-wing stance of being tough on crime and the privatising of services over the past few decades are evidence that the guiding norms of neoliberalism direct the current social order.

Although the government initially claimed austerity would reduce deficits, evidence of misinterpretations of public debts and fallacies about the global recession reveals that austerity's implementation was ideological, not requisite. Beyond spending reductions on public sector services—including prison spending—the broader notion of neoliberalism decimated state welfare and increased punitiveness. Cumulatively, these undercurrents have deepened inequality, insecurity, and disparity in society. The impacts on prison healthcare governance and delivery, however, remain to be theorised.

Notes

1 Chapter 3 analyses this more when describing the prison and prison healthcare governance.
2 The Gini coefficient ranges between 0% and 100%. 0% indicates that income is shared equally among all households, and 100% indicates the extreme situation where one household accounts for all income. Therefore, the lower the value of the Gini coefficient, the more equally household income is distributed.
3 Top 1% have incomes substantially higher than the rest of those in the top 10%. For the entire world, the top 1% earn 20% of the total income.
4 The S80/S20 ratio refers to the ratio of the total income received by the richest 80% to the poorest 20% of people.
5 The P90/P10 ratio is calculated as the ratio of incomes of the person at the 90th percentile to the person at the 10th percentile.
6 The Palma Ratio is the ratio of the income share of the richest 10% of individuals to that of the poorest 40% of individuals.

References

Alesina, A. and Ardagna, S. (2010) Large Changes in Fiscal Policy: Taxes Versus Spending. *Tax Policy and the Economy*. 24, pp. 35–68.

Amable, B. (2011) Morals and Politics in the Ideology of Neo-liberalism. *Socio-Economic Review*. 9, pp. 3–30.

Anderson, B. and Minneman, E. (2014) The Abuse and Misuse of the Term "Austerity" Implications for OECD Countries. *OECD Journal on Budgeting*. 14(1), pp. 109–122.

Barr, B., Kinderman, P. and Whitehead, M. (2015) Trends in Mental Health inequalities in England During a Period of Recession, Austerity and Welfare Reform 2004 to 2013. *Social Science and Medicine*. 147, pp. 324–331.

Basu, L. (2017) Living Within Our Means: The UK News Construction of the Austerity Frame Over Time. *Journalism*, pp. 1–8.

Blyth, M. (2013) Austerity as Ideology: A Reply to My Critics. *Comparative European Politics*. 11(6), pp. 737–751.
British Medical Association (2016) *Health in All Policies: Health, Austerity and Welfare Reform: A Briefing from the Board of Science* [Online], available from: www.bma.org.uk/media/2086/bos-health-in-all-policies-austerity-briefing-2016.pdf (Accessed: 25th January 2021).
Callinicos, A. (2012) Contradictions of Austerity. *Cambridge Journal of Regions Economy and Society*. 36(1), pp. 65–77.
Cameron, D. (2010) *Press Conference on The Coalition: Our Programme for Government: 20 May 2010*. London: HM Government.
Cavadino, M. and Dignan, J. (2006) Penal Policy and Political Economy. *Criminology & Criminal Justice*. 6(4), pp. 435–456.
Cheetham, M., Moffatt, S. and Wickham, S. (2020) *Universal Credit: The Wait for a First Payment* [Online], available from: https://committees.parliament.uk/writtenevidence/1481/pdf/ (Accessed: 25th January 2021).
Citizen Network Research (2019) *UK Food Banks in 2019* [Online], available from: https://citizen-network.org/library/uk-food-banks-in-2019.html (Accessed: 25th January 2021).
Clarke, J. and Newman, J. (2012) The Alchemy of Austerity. *Critical Social Policy*. 32(3), pp. 299–319.
Clough, R. (2018) *Rage Against the Cruelty of So-called Austerity* [Online], available from: www.theguardian.com/society/2018/nov/15/rage-against-the-cruelty-of-so-called-austerity (accessed: 25th January 2021).
Committee for the Prevention of Torture and Inhuman or Degrading Treatment or Punishment (2017) *Report to the Government of the United Kingdom on the Visit to the United Kingdom Carried Out by the European Committee for the Prevention of Torture and Inhuman or Degrading Treatment or Punishment from 30 March to 12 April 2016* [Online], available from: https://rm.coe.int/168070a773 (Accessed: 11th January 2018).
Committee for the Prevention of Torture and Inhuman or Degrading Treatment or Punishment (2020) *Report to the United Kingdom Government on the Visit to the United Kingdom Carried Out by the European Committee for the Prevention of Torture and Inhuman or Degrading Treatment or Punishment (CPT) from 13 to 23 May 2019* [Online], available from: https://rm.coe.int/16809e4404 (Accessed: 27th May 2020).
The Conservative and Unionist Party (2017) *Forward, Together: Our Plan for a Stronger Britain and a Prosperous Future* [Online], available from: www.conservatives.com/manifesto (Accessed: 25th January 2021).
Crest Advisory (2020) *Impact and Legacy of Covid-19 on the CJS: Modelling Overview* [Online], available from: https://b9cf6cd4-6aad-4419-a368-724e7d1352b9.usrfiles.com/ugd/b9cf6c_e16b3e351b12430bb79cd6a2830f88f3.pdf (Accessed: 25th January 2021).
Dardot, P. and Laval, C. (2013) *The New Way of the World: On Neoliberal Society*. London: Verso.
Dellepiane-Avellaneda, S. (2015) The Political Power of Economic Ideas: The Case of "Expansionary Fiscal Contractions". *The British Journal of Politics and International Relations*. 17(3), pp. 391–418.
European Prison Observatory (2013) *Prison in Europe: Overview and Trends*. Rome: European Prison Observatory.
European Public Service Union (2016) *Prison Staff Perspectives: An EPSU Survey of the Impact of the Economic Crisis on Prisons* [Online], available from: www.epsu.org/sites/default/files/article/files/Prison%20staff%20perspectives%20EPSU%20survey%20June%202016%20EN.pdf (Accessed: 19th September 2019).

Eurostat (2020) *General Government Expenditure by Function* [Online], available from: https://ec.europa.eu/eurostat/databrowser/view/gov_10a_exp/default/table?lang=en (Accessed: 25th January 2021).

Farnsworth, K. (2018) *The British Corporate Welfare State: Public Provision for Private Businesses.* SPERI Paper No. 24 [Online], available from: http://speri.dept.shef.ac.uk/wp-content/uploads/2018/11/SPERI-Paper-24-The-British-Corporate-Welfare-State.pdf (accessed: 25th January 2021).

Farnsworth, K. and Irving, Z. (2015) Austerity: More Than the Sum of Its Parts. In: Farnsworth, K. and Irving, Z., eds. *Social Policy in Times of Austerity: Global Economic Crisis and the New Politics of Welfare.* Bristol: Policy Press, pp. 9–42.

Farnsworth, K. and Irving, Z. (2018) Austerity: Neoliberal Dreams Come True? *Critical Social Policy.* 38(3), pp. 461–481.

Fine, B. and Saad-Filho, A. (2017) Thirteen Things You Need to Know About Neoliberalism. *Critical Sociology.* 43(4–5), pp. 685–706.

Fontana, G. and Sawyer, M. (2011) Fiscal Austerity. *Challenge.* 54(2), pp. 42–60.

Gamble, A. (2014) Austerity as Statecraft. *Parliamentary Affairs.* 68, pp. 42–57.

Garland, D. (2001) *The Culture of Control: Crime and Social Order in Contemporary Society.* Oxford: Oxford University Press.

Giulietti, C. and McConnell, B. (2021) *Kicking You When You're Already Down: The Multipronged Impact of Austerity on Crime.* Esen: Global Labor Organization.

Gordon, D., Mack, J., Lansley, S., Main, G., Nandy, S., Patsios, D., Pomati, M. and the PSE Team (2013) *The Impoverishment of the UK* [Online], available from: www.poverty.ac.uk/sites/default/files/attachments/The_Impoverishment_of_the_UK_PSE_UK_first_results_summary_report_March_28.pdf (Accessed: 25th January 2021).

Green, D. G., Grove, E. and Martin, N. A. (2003) *Civitas: The Institute for the Study of Civil Society Final Report for the Rethinking Crime and Punishment Project How Can the Criminal Justice System Reduce the Criminal Activities of Known Offenders?* [Online], available from: www.civitas.org.uk/pdf/CivitasRCP_Report.pdf (Accessed: 25th January 2021).

Grimshaw, D. (2013) Austerity, Privatization and Levelling Down: Public Sector Reform in the United Kingdom In: Vaughan-Whitehead, D., ed. *The Public Sector in Shock.* Cheltenham: Edward Elgar, pp. 1–27.

Hall, S. (1978) *Policing the Crisis: Mugging, the State, and Law and Order.* London: Macmillan.

Hall, S. (2011) The Neo-liberal Revolution. *Cultural Studies.* 25(6), pp. 705–728.

Hart-Landsberg, M. (2006) Neoliberalism: Myths and Reality. *Monthly Review.* 57(11), pp. 1–9.

Harvey, D. (2005) *A Brief History of Neoliberalism.* Oxford: Oxford University Press.

Harvey, D. (2009) *Cosmopolitanism and the Geographies of Freedom.* New York: Columbia University Press.

Harvey, D. (2010) *The Enigma of Capital and the Crises of Capitalism.* London: Profile Books.

Hayton, R. (2014) Conservative Party Statecraft and the Politics of Coalition. *Parliamentary Affairs.* 67, pp. 6–24.

Hickel, J. (2017) *The Divide: A Brief Guide to Global Inequality and Its Solutions.* London: Heinemann.

Hill, M. (2015) Conventional Wisdom on Government Austerity: UK Politics Since the 1920s. In: Farnsworth, K. and Irving, Z., eds. *Social Policy in Times of Austerity: Global Economic Crisis and the New Politics of Welfare.* Bristol: Policy Press, pp. 43–66.

HM Prison & Probation Service (2019) *Workforce Quarterly: March 2019* [Online], available from: https://assets.publishing.service.gov.uk/government/uploads/system/uploads/

attachment_data/file/801838/hr-publication-tables-march-2019.xlsx (Accessed: 21st February 2020).

HM Treasury (2010) *Budget 2010*. London: The Stationery Office, HC61.

HM Treasury (2018) *The Green Book: Central Government Guidance on Appraisal and Evaluation* [Online], available from: https://assets.publishing.service.gov.uk/government/uploads/system/uploads/attachment_data/file/938046/The_Green_Book_2020.pdf (Accessed: 25th January 2021).

HM Treasury (2019a) *Spring Statement 2019: Philip Hammond's Speech* [Online], available from: www.gov.uk/government/speeches/spring-statement-2019-philip-hammonds-speech (Accessed: 25th January 2021).

HM Treasury (2019b) *Spending Round 2019: Chancellor Sajid Javid's Speech* [Online], available from: www.gov.uk/government/speeches/spending-round-2019-sajid-javids-speech (Accessed: 25th January 2021).

HM Treasury (2021) *Oral Statement to Parliament: Autumn Budget and Spending. Review 2021 Speech* [Online], available from: www.gov.uk/government/speeches/autumn-budget-and-spending-review-2021-speech (Accessed: 25th January 2021).

House of Commons Committee of Public Accounts (2012) *Public Accounts Committee—Nineteenth Report—HM Revenue and Customs: Annual Report and Accounts* [Online], available from: https://publications.parliament.uk/pa/cm201213/cmselect/cmpubacc/716/71602.htm#evidence (Accessed: 11th January 2018).

House of Commons Justice Committee (2015) *Prisons: Planning and Policies. Ninth Report of Session 2014–15* [Online], available from: https://publications.parliament.uk/pa/cm201415/cmselect/cmjust/309/309.pdf (Accessed: 3rd July 2018).

House of Commons Library (2021a) *Food Banks in the UK* [Online], available from: https://researchbriefings.files.parliament.uk/documents/CBP-8585/CBP-8585.pdf (Accessed: 25th January 2021).

House of Commons Library (2021b) *The Prison Estate* [Online], available from: https://researchbriefings.files.parliament.uk/documents/SN05646/SN05646.pdf (Accessed: 25th January 2021).

House of Lords Library Briefing (2019) *Debate on the Queen's Speech: Day 4 Home Affairs, Justice, Local Government, Devolved Affairs and Constitutional Affairs: 21 October 2019* [Online], available from: http://researchbriefings.files.parliament.uk/documents/LLN-2019-0128/LLN-2019-0128.pdf (Accessed: 25th January 2021).

Institute for Fiscal Studies (2021) *What's Happened and What's Next For Councils?* [Online], available from: https://ifs.org.uk/uploads/7-What%E2%80%99s-happened-and-what%E2%80%99s-next-for-councils-.pdf (Accessed: 25th January 2021).

Institute for Government (2019) *Prisons* [Online], available from: www.instituteforgovernment.org.uk/publication/performance-tracker-2019/prisons#:~:text=In%20March%20 2019%2C%2050%25%20of,high%20of%2066%25%20in%202014 (Accessed: 21st February 2020).

International Monetary Fund (2010) *Will It Hurt? Macroeconomic Effects of Fiscal Consolidation* [Online], available from: www.imf.org/external/pubs/ft/weo/2010/02/pdf/c3.pdf (Accessed: 25th January 2021).

Ipsos MORI (2015) *Economist/Ipsos MORI March 2015 Issues Index* [Online], available from: www.ipsos.com/ipsos-mori/en-uk/economistipsos-mori-march-2015-issues-index (Accessed: 11th January 2018).

Ipsos MORI (2019) *Worry about Brexit and EU Has Fallen However Remains Britain's Number One Worry* [Online], available from: www.ipsos.com/ipsos-mori/en-uk/ipsos-mori-issues-index-january-2019-worry-about-brexit-and-eu-has-fallen-however-remains-britains (Accessed: 19th September 2019).

Keynes, J. M. (1936) *The General Theory of Interest, Employment and Money*. London: MacMillan.

Klein, N. (2007) *The Shock Doctrine: The Rise of Disaster Capitalism*. Toronto: Random House of Canada.

Konzelmann, S. and Fovargue-Davies, M. (2019) Interlude: "Mirror, Mirror on the Wall—Who Has the Highest Debt of All". In: Konzelmann, S., Himmelweit, S., Smith, J. and Weeks, J., eds. *Rethinking Britain: Policy Ideas for the Many*. Bristol: Policy Press, pp. 7–8.

Krugman, P. (2012) *End This Depression Now*! New York: W.W. Norton & Company.

Lacey, N. (2008) *The Prisoners' Dilemma: Political Economy and Punishment in Contemporary Democracies*. Cambridge: Cambridge University Press.

Marmot, M. (2017) The UK's Current Health Problems Should Be Treated with Urgency. *British Medical Journal* [Online], available from: https://blogs.bmj.com/bmj/2017/09/13/michael-marmot-the-uks-current-health-problems-should-be-treated-with-urgency/ (Accessed: 21st February 2020).

Martinez, E. and Garcia, A. (1997) *What is Neoliberalism? A Brief Definition for Activists*. Oakland, CA: National Network for Immigrant and Refugee Rights.

Midgley, J. (2014) Austerity Versus Stimulus: Theoretical Perspectives and Policy Implications. *Journal of Sociology and Social Welfare*. 41(2), pp. 11–32.

Ministry of Justice (2015) *Public Confidence in the Criminal Justice System—Findings from the Crime Survey for England and Wales (2013/14)* [Online], available from: https://assets.publishing.service.gov.uk/government/uploads/system/uploads/attachment_data/file/449444/public-confidence.pdf (Accessed: 25th January 2021).

Ministry of Justice (2020a) *Her Majesty's Prison and Probation Service Workforce Quarterly: March 2020* [Online], available from: www.gov.uk/government/statistics/her-majestys-prison-and-probation-service-workforce-quarterly-march-2020 (Accessed: 25th January 2021).

Ministry of Justice (2020b) *HMPPS Workforce Statistics Bulletin: 31 March 2020 Tables* [Online], available from: https://assets.publishing.service.gov.uk/government/uploads/system/uploads/attachment_data/file/891138/HR-tables-31-March-2020.xlsx (Accessed: 11th January 2018).

Ministry of Justice (2020c) *Proven Reoffending Statistics Quarterly Bulletin, October 2018 to December 2018* [Online], available from: https://assets.publishing.service.gov.uk/government/uploads/system/uploads/attachment_data/file/930446/Proven_reoffending_stats_bulletin_OctDec18.pdf (Accessed: 25th January 2021).

Murray, C. (1984) *Losing Ground: American Social Policy 1950–1980*. New York: Basic Books.

National Audit Office (2017) *Mental Health in Prisons* [Online], available from: www.nao.org.uk/wp-content/uploads/2017/06/Mental-health-in-prisons.pdf (Accessed: 11th January 2018).

National Offender Management Service (NOMS) (2015) *National Offender Management Service: Annual Report and Accounts 2014–2015* [Online], available from: https://assets.publishing.service.gov.uk/government/uploads/system/uploads/attachment_data/file/434548/NOMS_AR14_15_report_accounts_Final_WEB.pdf (Accessed: 11th January 2018).

Newburn, T. (2007) "Tough on Crime": Penal Policy in England and Wales. *Crime and Justice*. 36(1), pp. 425–470.

New Economics Foundation (2018) *Austerity by Stealth? Options for the Chancellor at the Coming Spending Review* [Online], available from: https://neweconomics.org/uploads/files/AUSTERITY-BY-STEALTH-Sep18.pdf (Accessed: 21st February 2020).

Nolan, A. (2015) Not Fit for Purpose: Human Rights in Times of Financial and Economic Crisis. *European Rights Law Review*. 4, pp. 358–369.

Nozick, R. (1974) *Anarchy, State, and Utopia*. New York: Basic Books.

O'Dea, C. and Preston, I. (2010) *The Distributional Impact of Public Spending in the UK: IFS Working Paper W12/06* [Online], available from: www.ifs.org.uk/wps/wp1206.pdf (Accessed: 25th January 2021).

O'Hara, M. (2014) *Austerity Bites: A Journey to the Sharp End of Cuts in the UK*. Bristol: Policy Press.

Office for National Statistics (2020) *Crime in England and Wales: Year Ending June 2020* [Online], available from: www.ons.gov.uk/peoplepopulationandcommunity/crimeandjustice/bulletins/crimeinenglandandwales/yearendingjune2020#:~:text=The%20police%20recorded%205.8%20million,April%20to%20June%202020%20period (Accessed: 25th January 2021).

Office for National Statistics (2021a) *UK Government Debt and Deficit: September 2020* [Online], available from: www.ons.gov.uk/economy/governmentpublicsectorandtaxes/publicspending/bulletins/ukgovernmentdebtanddeficitforeurostatmaast/september2020 (Accessed: 25th January 2021).

Office for National Statistics (2021b) *Household Income Inequality, UK: Financial Year Ending 2020* [Online], available from: www.ons.gov.uk/peoplepopulationandcommunity/personalandhouseholdfinances/incomeandwealth/bulletins/householdincomeinequalityfinancial/financialyearending2020 (Accessed: 25th January 2021).

Organisation for Economic Co-operation and Development (2011) *OECD Economic Outlook. Volume 2011/1*. Paris: Organisation for Economic Co-operation and Development.

Organisation for Economic Co-operation and Development (2018) *Quarterly GDP* [Online], available from: https://data.oecd.org/gdp/quarterly-gdp.htm (Accessed: 25th January 2021).

Ortiz, I., Chai, J. and Cummins, M. (2011) *Austerity Measures Threaten Children and Poor Households: Recent Evidence in Public Expenditures from 128 Developing Countries*. New York: UNICEF.

Panitch, L. and Konings, M. (2009) *American Empire and the Political Economy of Global Finance*. New York: Palgrave.

Pantazis, C. (2016) Policies and Discourses of Poverty During a Time of Recession and Austerity. *Critical Social Policy*. 36(1), pp. 3–20.

Parliament UK (1993) *Home Affairs and Education* [Online], available from: https://publications.parliament.uk/pa/cm199394/cmhansrd/1993-11-23/Debate-2.html (Accessed: 25th January 2021).

Peck, J. (2010) *Constructions of Neoliberal Reason*. Oxford: Oxford University Press.

Peck, J. and Tickell, A. (2012) Apparitions of Neoliberalism: Revisiting "Jungle law Breaks Out". *Area*. 44(2), pp. 245–249.

Pierson, P. (1998) Irresistible Forces, Immovable Objects: Post-industrial Welfare States Confront Permanent Austerity. *Journal of European Public Policy*. 5(4), pp. 539–560.

Polanyi, K. (1944) *The Great Transformation: The Political and Economic Origins of Our Time*. Boston, MA: Beacon Press.

Prime Minister's Office (2013) *Economy Speech Delivered by David Cameron* [Online], available from: www.gov.uk/government/speeches/economy-speech-delivered-by-david-cameron (Accessed: 25th January 2021).

Reiner, R. (2011) *Policing, Popular Culture and Political Economy: Towards a Social Democratic Criminology*. London: Routledge.

Reinhart, C. M. and Rogoff, K. S. (2010) Growth in a Time of Debt. *American Economic Review*. 100, pp. 573–578.

Rusche, G. and Kirchheimer, O. (1939) *Punishment and Social Structure*. New York: Columbia University Press.

Sarfaty, G. (2012) *Values in Translation: Human Rights and the Culture of the World Bank*. Stanford: Stanford University Press.

Schmidt, V. A. (2002) *The Futures of European Capitalism*. Oxford: Oxford University Press.

Schui, F. (2015) *Austerity: The Great Failure*. New Haven, CT: Yale University Press.

Sen, A. (1977) Rational Fools: A Critique of the Behavioural Foundations of Economics Theory. *Philosophy and Public Affairs*. 6(4), pp. 317–344.

Shaoul, J. (2011) The Economic and Financial Context: Paying for the Banks. In: Corby, S. and Symon, G., eds. *Working for the State: Employment Relations in the Public Services*. Basingstoke: Palgrave Macmillan, pp. 43–66.

Sim, J. (1990) *Medical Power in Prisons: The Prison Medical Service in England 1774–1989*. Milton Keynes: Open University Press.

Slobodian, Q. (2020) *Globalists: The End of Empire and the Birth of Neoliberalism*. Cambridge, MA: Harvard University Press.

Smith, A. (1776) *An Inquiry into the Nature and Causes of the Wealth of Nations*. London: W. Strahan and T. Cadell.

Social Metrics Commission (2018) *Social Metrics Commission Launches a New Measure of UK Poverty* [Online], available from: https://socialmetricscommission.org.uk/a-new-poverty-metric/ (Accessed: 25th January 2021).

Sparks, R. (2000) Risk and Blame in Criminal Justice Controversies: British Press Coverage and Official Discourse on Prison Security (1993–6). In: Brown, M. and Pratt, J., eds. *Dangerous Offenders: Punishment and Social Order*. London: Routledge, pp. 127–143.

Sparks, R. (2007) The Politics of Imprisonment. In: Jewkes, Y., ed. *Handbook on Prisons*. Devon: Willan Publishing, pp. 73–94.

Stiglitz, J. E. (2014) Inequality is Holding Back the Recovery. In: Johnston, D. C., ed. *Divided: The Perils of Our Growing Inequality*. New York: The New Press, pp. 44–49.

Streeck, W. and Mertens, D. (2013) Public Finance and the Decline of State Capacity. In: Schafer, A. and Streeck, W., eds. *Politics in the Age of Austerity*. Cambridge: Polity Press, pp. 25–58.

Stuckler, D. and Basu, S. (2013) *The Body Economic: Why Austerity Kills*. London: Allan Lane.

Taylor-Gooby, P. and Leruth, B. (2018) *Attitudes, Aspirations and Welfare: Social Policy Directions in Uncertain Times*. London: Palgrave Macmillan.

Taylor-Gooby, P. and Stoker, G. (2011) The Coalition Programme: A New Vision for Britain or Politics as Usual? *The Political Quarterly*. 82(1), pp. 4–15.

Thompson, H. (2013) UK Debt in Comparative Perspective: The Pernicious Legacy of Financial Sector Debt. *British Journal of Politics & International Relations*. 15(3), pp. 476–492.

UNISON (2019) *Shocking Picture of Austerity Cuts to Local Services is Revealed by UNISON* [Online], available from: www.unison.org.uk/news/article/2019/12/shocking-picture-austerity-cuts-local-services-revealed-unison/ (Accessed: 25th January 2021).

United Nations General Assembly (2019) *Visit to the United Kingdom of Great Britain and Northern Ireland: Report of the Special Rapporteur on Extreme Poverty and Human Rights* [Online], available from: https://undocs.org/A/HRC/41/39/Add.1 (Accessed: 25th January 2021).

Vina, G., Hutton, R. and Penny, T. (2013) *Osborne Pledges Five More Years of UK Austerity* [Online], available from: www.bloomberg.com/news/2013-03-20/osborne-pledges-five-more-years-of-u-k-austerity.html (Accessed: 25th January 2021).

Wacquant, L. (2000) The New "Peculiar Institution": On the Prison as Surrogate Ghetto. *Theoretical Criminology*. 4(3), pp. 377–389.

Wacquant, L. (2010) Crafting the Neoliberal State: Workfare, Prisonfare, and Social Insecurity. *Sociological Forum*. 25(2), pp. 197–220.

Wacquant, L. (2012) The Punitive Regulation of Poverty in the Neoliberal Age. *Criminal Justice Matters*. 89(1), pp. 38–40.

Walby, S., Towers, J. and Francis, B. (2016) Is Violent Crime Increasing or Decreasing? A New Methodology to Measure Repeat Attacks Making Visible the Significance of Gender and Domestic Relations. *British Journal of Criminology*. 56(6), pp. 1203–1234.

Weeks, J. F. (2019) *The Debt Delusion: Living Within Our Means and Other Fallacies*. Oxford: Polity Press.

Weiss, L. (1987) Globalisation and the Myth of the Powerless State. *New Left Review*. 225, pp. 3–27.

Wilkinson, R. G. and Pickett, K. (2009) *The Spirit Level: Why Equality Is Better for Everyone*. London: Penguin.

Wren-Lewis, S. (2016) *A General Theory of Austerity*. BSG Working Paper Series 2016/014: May 2016. Oxford: University of Oxford.

YMCA (2020) *Out of Service: A Report Examining Local Authority Expenditure on Youth Services in England & Wales* [Online], available from: www.ymca.org.uk/wp-content/uploads/2020/01/YMCA-Out-of-Service-report.pdf (Accessed: 25th January 2021).

Chapter 3

The governance and delivery of prisons and prison healthcare services in England

Introduction

"Accusing the politicians of ignorance and illiteracy is unfair. They are not fools. They have been around. They receive expert advice [from] the officials of the [Ministry of Justice] who are educated and intelligent". A Conservative politician emailed me this after reading my previous publications on this topic, where I argued that austerity and imprisonment policies in England are political choices that lack evidence to support their implementation. It was a relatively predictable disagreement, yet it enables me to make a broader point: the politicians knew what they did when they opted for austerity measures, and they ignored their impact on social policies, prisons included.

Before examining austerity's impact on prisoners, we must unpack the governance structure of prisons and prison healthcare in England. This structure experiences austerity before transferring it to the prisoners. And though a robust structure for governing and delivering prisons and prison healthcare is in place, incoherent policies concerning imprisonment, a fragile institutional base at all levels of governance, and persistent political intrusion weaken the potential for sustainable health gains.

In unpacking the governance structure, I first outline the theoretical definitions and understanding of the modes of governance before analysing the structure, process, and actors of HMPPS and NHS England. I seek to untangle a web of issues afflicting the governance structure, which stem from impending political ideologies closely resembling neoliberalism. Such ideologies include punishment over rehabilitation and increased privatisation of prisons and prison healthcare services. I then analyse the monitoring structure of both prison and prison healthcare services at the UK governmental level, the inadequacy of which has enabled these ideologies to flourish.

To understand how austerity impacts prison health governance and healthcare delivery across English prisons, we must assess how these structures function within a prevailing neoliberal framework. Existing literature tends to examine prison governance and prison healthcare governance discretely. Yet, these two governance structures influence one another and should be

DOI: 10.4324/9781003182337-3

considered together. Indeed, their interrelation is key to the mobilisation of prison healthcare delivery within a neoliberal framework. In this chapter, I interrogate these dynamics systematically for the first time.

Definition and modes of governance

Existing literature suggests 'governance' is a complex and multidimensional concept. Jan Kooiman (2003) defined it as a set of arrangements in which public and private actors aim to solve societal problems and phrase principles by which these activities are undertaken. To various public administration scholars, governance comprises structure and process (Davies, 2005; Marinetto, 2003). Often, structure relates to institutions and actor constellations highly subject to the actors' power (ibid.).

Academic literature on governance has evolved chiefly around top-down and dispersed governance modes. For top-down governance, David Marsh (2011) used the critical realist theory of governance to argue the government maintains a firm grip on hierarchical coordination. This descends from the Westminster model of British government, involving a unitary state, parliamentary sovereignty, strong cabinet government, ministerial accountability, majority party control of the executive, and institutionalised opposition (ibid.). The top-down nature is typically built on three assumptions: 1) chronological action in which policy intentions precede action; 2) a linear view of policy underpinned by a causal link between policy intentions, policy actions, and results; and 3) a hierarchy in which policy formation is more important than policy implementation (Hill and Hupe, 2015). Although hierarchical coordination is relatively rare, we find it in the criminal justice system, especially prisons, with unilateral and closed decision-making processes (Scharpf, 1997; Williams and Matheny, 1995).

In contrast, a dispersed governance model has grown markedly in government. From a public policy perspective, Roderick Rhodes (1996) suggested that "governance without government" denotes the hollowing out of a state, favouring self-organisation, inter-organisational cooperation, and resource exchange that the actors involved cannot impose externally. Rather, it results from these actors' interaction (Kooiman and van Vliet, 1993) and significant autonomy from the state: processes relating to an effort to organise and exercise political power in response to challenges and opportunities (Fidler, 2007).

Multilateral cooperation among actors involved in the agenda-setting process underpins a dispersed governance structure. It is designed to hold each actor accountable and encourage transparent dealings (Bexell et al., 2010; Scholte, 2011). The application of structure-actors-processes as a theoretical framework has led scholars such as Richard Dodgson and colleagues (2002), and Sarah Payne (2008) to establish a concept of health governance that I believe resonates with the nature of prison health governance: the actions and mechanisms that actors adopt to organise the promotion, organisation, and protection of the population's health. Ilona Kickbusch (2006) described the unique characteristics of health governance that differentiate it from other fields: the fluidity of knowledge transfer between sectors to address population health issues and the relevance of initiatives in other sectors that can affect population health. However, researchers often suggest dispersed, collaborative governance commonly suffers power imbalances (Ansell and Gash, 2007). For prison healthcare, the overall governance and delivery of the services are subjected to the control of the prison authorities. Such a structure is internally conflicting: the healthcare system focuses on well-being, while the prison system focuses on punishment and security—with the prison authorities acting as the final arbiter when the two systems collide. The health system is often complex, and thus its focus is not always aligned and requires negotiation across different agencies (Marks et al., 2010). This chapter will further explore the dynamics of power and alignment between prison and prison healthcare.

The HM Prison & Probation Service (HMPPS)

The delivery of prison healthcare services in England relies on the HMPPS (known as the NOMS until 2017). The HMPPS is the Ministry of Justice's executive agency, responsible for commissioning and providing offender services in the community and custody. England and Wales currently have 100 public-sector prisons and 14 prisons contracted to private organisations, such as Serco, Sodexo, and G4S (HMPPS, 2017). The security categories range from Category A (high security) to Category D (resettlement prisons), with most being closed prisons to prevent escapes.

Imprisonment has no specific aims derivable from legislation or policy documents. Legally, Rule 3 of the Prison Rules 1999 provides the Prison Service mission statement: to encourage and assist prisoners in leading a good and useful life. However, legal academics criticise this provision as too general. For instance, Stephen Livingstone et al. (2008, p. 7) says legislation comprises "a series of enabling and deeming provisions designed to give the Secretary of State maximum discretion in the organisation of the prison system". Alternatively, HMPPS (2021a) states that imprisonment's purpose is to carry out court sentences, prevent further victimisation, and reduce reoffending via rehabilitation programmes, such as education and employment. Although it is implicit within 'rehabilitation', this definition does not explicitly recognise the role of health. Legal scholar Keith Syrett (2011) argues the law functions as a control mechanism and sets parameters for the actions and decisions that institutions can take, so the lack of clarity on the aims of imprisonment is problematic. Too much depends on the discretion of the minister and bureaucrats to interpret the government mandate for prisons.

When funding prisons, the state has adopted managerialism, subjecting prison institutions to a regime of efficiency, value for money, and performance monitoring (Loader and Sparks, 2002). A study by prison criminologists Alison

Liebling and Ben Crewe (2012) revealed how senior prison managers discussed a "Tesco prison model", (p. 295) referring to the government's desire to standardise cheaper, larger scale, and austere punishment provisions to legitimise their prison management to taxpayers. However, as Malcolm Feeley and Jonathan Simon (1992) averred, this management style, which uses the language of probability, risk, control, and management of prisoners through numbers, dehumanises prisoners.

Besides cost-saving and efficiency measures, prison management is characterised by indicators and risk assessments such as Prison Service Instructions and Prison Service Orders (PSOs). These operational policies, with which prison governors must comply, address issues ranging from the use of force to health promotion in prison (Ministry of Justice, 2020). The management resembles a top-down framework that seeks to enforce compliance. Max Weber (1930) compared such bureaucracies to an iron cage that removes staff freedom and autonomy, especially in shaping the operation of their establishments. As Richard Sparks and Anthony Bottoms (1996) correctly noted, people legitimately view officials' behaviour as reflecting the system as a whole, despite it possibly differing from their leadership ethos because they cannot exercise discretion.

Overall, the law too vaguely defines the aims of imprisonment, with 'health' having no explicit role within the HMPPS's stated purpose of imprisonment. This lack of clarity is further reinforced by a top-down governance structure that pervades and employs an ethos of managerialism to prioritise efficiency, value, and performance.

Prison governors

Despite policy scholars' debate around prison governance, they have paid little attention to prison governors—those dictating the provisions across English prisons, including healthcare. Lionel Fox (1952, p. 9) argued prison governors are "the keystone of the arch. Within his own prison, he [sic] is supreme". Their responsibility is to ensure prisons function in an orderly manner by using their leadership to create a structured, stable, predictable, and acceptable environment (Liebling and Arnold, 2004).

Section 11 of the Prison Act 1952 states governors are responsible for all activities happening in the establishments they manage. They have the power to steer and motivate their workforces, which increasingly involve voluntary, community, and private sector organisations, to deliver prison services (Ministry of Justice, 2010). Shane Bryans (2007) theorised four types of prison governor: general managers operating their establishments according to performance indicators, chief officers adopting a people-centred approach, liberal idealists subscribing to the idea of prisoner reformation, and conforming mavericks repeatedly challenging the *status quo*. Although a single governor may shift between these categories, the 'conforming maverick' seems to be disappearing today given increasing regulations, instructions, and rules curtailing governors' ability to shape prison regimes, which witness a shift towards top-down governance (ibid.).

Prison officers

Criminologists have long recognised relationships between prison officers and prisoners are at the prison system's core. Characterised as low visibility yet highly skilled (Liebling and Price, 2001), prison officers have often been depicted as engaging in complex and varied work, not least because maintaining penal order relies significantly on personal authority and discretionary practices (Cheliotis, 2008; Crawley, 2013).

The government expects prison officers to act as mentors, counsellors, and social workers for prisoners (HMPPS, 2021b) despite lacking training to do so, unlike in other European countries (Eide and Westrheim, 2020). However, a micromanagement culture also pervades alongside a focus on punishment and control rather than care and empathy (Arnold, 2016). These two factors undermine the legitimate expectation that prison officers should fulfil roles that more resemble social work.

Today, over 30,000 prison officers in England, Wales, Scotland, and Northern Ireland are members of the Prison Officers' Association (POA, 2021). Historically labelled as resistant to change and militant (Liebling and Price, 2001), the POA has embraced cooperation over resistance more recently. In 2004, it was a signatory to the Joint Industrial Relations Procedural Agreement in which the POA agreed not to induce its members to strike. It thereby promoted enhanced constructive collaboration between managers and unions—such as being informed by threats of commercial competition from outside and adopting target-driven performance management from the inside (Bennett and Wahidin, 2008). A disinterest in national issues (e.g., political leadership on prisons) and greater concern for the prison in which the members work and their immediate environment reflect this change (ibid.). A combination of a lack of clear aims for imprisonment, the disappearance of the 'conforming maverick' governor, and the reliance on inadequately trained staff leaves this system of governance vulnerable to top-down, political interference.

Political interference

Tom Gash et al. (2010) identified three reasons public bodies support the governance structure and delivery of public services. First is to depoliticise decision making, second to increase managerial freedoms, and third to allow the government to access external skills and expertise. Despite the first reason, research finds politics interferes with public bodies. Larry Terry (1995) and Arjen Boin (2001) explain that the autonomy of civil servants highly depends on the current government's political values. Contemporary governance structures seek to align civil servants with their superiors' objectives (Hood, 2000). This aligns with Antonio Gramsci's (1971) classical theory of the ideological incorporation of hegemony through state apparatuses—which includes prisons—while protecting ministers from blame in a crisis.

How much agency civil servants can exercise in the daily operation of public services is unclear. Anthony Giddens' agency and structure theory (1984) explains how structures can be both enabling and constraining and how actors can create and adapt to those structures. Using this theory, Michael Pusey (1991) argued ministers can frame constraints as economic rationality while using technical efficiency to give a false impression of abundant choice. Ministers thereby contribute to structural inequality, which critical realists Colin Hay (2002), David Marsh (2003), and Stuart McAnulla (2005) propose significantly influences the British political system, concentrating power towards central government.

The government continues to direct the criminal justice system, particularly prisons, from the top down. That is despite such efforts losing traction in other public sector systems in favour of a dispersed governance structure. The Learmont Report in 1995 recognised prisons are a politically sensitive area, so ministerial involvement will typically be relatively high (Hansard, 1995). Reaffirming active top-down management of the criminal justice system, Richard Chapman (1984) argued prison leadership should be reserved for ministers, as civil servants are merely expected to execute ministerial visions. This idea accords with Max Weber (1978), who conceptualised bureaucracy as a form of rational-legal authority whereby politicians direct public officials who do not dominate the government. A recent quote by the current Justice Secretary, Robert Buckland, signifies this position: "I am not here to run every prison operationally, but I am here, I hope, to set a clear steer to the civil servants about what I expect to be done" (House of Commons Justice Committee, 2019a).

One potential implication of this minister-civil servant relationship is that civil servants cannot be held accountable for a system failure. But practically the situation is different. Prison governors must manage conflicting expectations—of care and of punishment—and potential misalignment of their statutory obligations with the ministers' political preferences. These conflicts can undermine prison health governance and delivery in favour of appeasing the vertical ministerial power (Cäker and Nyland, 2017). Since ministers are typically transient, regularly moved for strategic political reasons, this makes coordination challenging (Flinders, 2002). The difficulty is exemplified in a series of reforms that came with turnover of eight justice ministers since 2010, whose policies on sentencing, running prisons, and increasing the size of prison estates were based on their fickleness.

From Prison Medical Service to NHS England

From the 19th century, the Prison Service adopted a biomedical paradigm that has supported prison healthcare work (Smart, 1985). Its statement of purpose "is to look after [prisoners] with humanity and help them lead law-abiding and useful lives in custody and after release" (Home Office, 1991, p. 3), and originally, the Prison Medical Service was responsible for the physical and mental health of prisoners (Home Office, 1968). However, a single-minded prioritisation of security and discipline undercuts the perception of prisoners as patients (HMIP, 1996). Prison Services provided healthcare while being responsible for the correctional mission, forcing on staff two objectives that might sometimes conflict (ibid.). Healthcare could be compatible with rehabilitation; however, staff were focused on security, punishment, discipline, and deterrence, resulting in a serious compromise of prisoners' health and well-being (Hudson, 1993). The presumption that "if [prisoners] are not [known to be] ill, *de facto* they are healthy" became expedient as staff sought to resolve their multiple roles (Morris et al., 1963, p. 193).

Policy changes in the last three decades suggest a growing understanding of prison healthcare problems, if not how to address them. In 1990, the Strangeways Prison Riot prompted *The Woolf Report* which, among other criticisms, described the failure of the prison service to uphold the National Health Service's standards of treatment and the ensuing widespread prisoner anxiety and unrest (Sim, 2002). The 1992 replacement of the Prison Medical Service with the Health Care Service for Prisons began a shift towards integrating the healthcare responsibilities of the Prison Service into the National Health Service (ibid.). This integration primarily sought to extricate Prison Services from the conflicting objectives of healthcare and punishment.

In 2000, the government published "The Future Organisation of Prison Health Care", a policy document outlining a partnership between the Prison Service and the NHS to improve prisoners' health services over five years (ibid.). The Prison Service ceased controlling the prison healthcare service in 2006, and it became part of the NHS's commissioning and delivery, formally establishing the NHS as a conduit between the community and prison health systems (Hayton and Boyington, 2006). This turning point saw the prison healthcare services embrace the notion of equivalence, which proponents claim ensures prisoners can access the same healthcare as members of society at large (Leaman et al., 2017).

There is a consensus that England leads the world generally and Europe specifically in standards for prison healthcare (Leaman et al., 2017; Gatherer and Fraser, 2009). This is because England's prison health framework acknowledges the relationship between prisons and the wider community and because England's multisector partnership can provide resources and ideas, reduce duplication of effort, and share operational risks to promote efficiency without compromising health (Leaman et al., 2017).

The stability of prison rehabilitation is challenged when the increasing number of prisoners is not met by adequate funding of the prison healthcare services. In England and Wales, 174 of every 100,000 people are incarcerated—notably higher than the global average of 132 (House of Commons Library, 2019). These statistics question the sustainability of the prison healthcare services in England, especially when more individuals are being incarcerated and not rehabilitated adequately into society.

Prison healthcare workforce

Joe Sim (1990, p. 5) questioned the dual loyalty of healthcare professionals in prisons because prison authorities could force them into "controlling the behaviour of the ill-disciplined and recalcitrant" through treatment and medication. The quality of treatment and care that treatment agencies and healthcare staff could give depended on the command prison authorities, with their priorities of security and control, had over them (De Viggiani, 2007). However, public health academics and practitioners favour a more contemporary explanation. They argue that the professionalisation of prison healthcare workers, transparency, the use of evidence-based guidance, and the responsiveness of services have increased the quality of care since the NHS assumed prison healthcare in 2006 (Leaman et al., 2017). Situations have vastly improved since 2006, although expanded resources and guided focus on prevention would provide further improvements.

But issues regarding recruitment and retention, workload, and working environment have increasingly gained policy traction. Even as prison staff have decreased, staff retention in the health sector has been poor (The Health Foundation, 2019). In 2019, England faced a shortfall of 39,520 nurses and 9,000 doctors across the NHS (NHS Improvement, 2019). Although official statistics did not disaggregate these rates among prison providers, nearly half of prison nurses (45%) say staff shortages compromise care provision (House of Commons Select Committee, 2018). Furthermore, the most recent CPT inspections of English prisons documented numerous unfilled GP and healthcare staff posts (CPT, 2020). These observations point to serious inadequacies in prison healthcare staffing—a trend likely to worsen given the lack of a coherent government approach to recruitment and the migration policies and uncertainties of Brexit (The Health Foundation, 2019).

Studies increasingly portray how increasing workloads have led prison healthcare staff to feel unsupported, experience low morale, and terminate employment (Forrester et al., 2013; Ginn, 2012). Tension from reorganisation, operational efficiency imperatives, and management of local needs have reinforced the sense of helplessness among this workforce (Exworthy, 2010). And this has come with increased violence among prisoners that subsequently subject staff to the violence, which compromises staff well-being and safety (Plugge et al., 2017; Watson et al., 2004). How employees deal with these pressures remains unclear, with scholars calling for more research (Plugge et al., 2017). Compared with the clear progression of political infiltration into the governance of the prison system, the prison healthcare system is more insulated.

Punishment

Punishment is a key trait of neoliberalism. Georg Rusche and Otto Kirchheimer (1939) argued that the mode and degree of state punitiveness in a society is largely determined not by crime trends but by economic and fiscal forces.

Through the adoption of exclusionary measures to police, control and incarcerate the poor, punishment has been, and continues to be, acute in countries that have embraced neoliberalism, the UK included (Cavadino and Dignan, 2006). This structure then dictates how the governance of the prison system and the prison healthcare system operate within a prevailing neoliberal framework.

Prisons are the main mode of punishment in neoliberal states. As Michel Foucault noted, prisons represent "the darkest region in the apparatus of justice" (Foucault, 1979, p. 256). And they continue to occupy a central position in the criminal justice system in England. Despite their failure as a tool of punishment, prisons still exist and produce the same results of failing to rehabilitate and maintaining high reoffending rates, despite political reluctance to get rid of them (ibid.). Punishment is one way, albeit not the best, of getting people to understand that they have caused harm; however, this contradicts the broader goal of rehabilitation.

Since the latter part of the 20th century, politicians have attacked the rehabilitation ideal as soft on crime and ineffective at reducing reoffending (Cullen and Gendreau, 2001). Such attacks result in practices that stress incarceration and deterrence—both punitive in nature (Pratt, 2007). They also have health implications. Joe Sim (1990) proposed prisoners suffer from "less eligibility", deemed undeserving of anything more than what the lowest social class in a free society experiences. The extent the state chooses to exercise power over health governance and align it with the prevailing political ideology influences its structure (Peck and Tickell, 1994).

As observed (section 3.2.1), the central government imposes vague and conflicting regulations and instructions on prison governors, and cost-cutting often takes precedence (Bryans, 2007). As such, governors are required to interpret these mandates between structures and agencies (Bennett, 2016). Therefore, prisons have become a by-product of Weberian bureaucracy, whereby staff freedom and autonomy in shaping the operation of their establishments have been removed by the central government. As such, prison governors are ill-equipped to translate vague and often conflicting goals, such as punishment and rehabilitation, into integrated action (Boin, 2001). The Weberian bureaucracy has resulted in governors having no autonomy and simply being forced to enact punishment as a trait of neoliberalism to preserve security and public safety.

Public Health academics Linda Marks (2014) have argued that command-and-control management techniques are unsuited to complex systems like healthcare, where flexibility, innovation, and local problem solving are needed. However, Marks failed to propose how healthcare systems, especially prisons, could thrive within a top-down system. This explanation is necessary given NHS England cannot control political interference, but must operate under it nonetheless. The prison healthcare services must often negotiate carefully between rehabilitation and punishment in a prevailing neoliberal system.

Apart from punishment, we can see other traits of neoliberalism influencing the prison health services. These are deregulation through commissioning and the privatisation of services, as well as the impotence of the monitoring structure of prison healthcare and overall prison operations. Subsequent sections will explore these issues.

Privatisation

A state is neoliberal when the market governs distribution of social goods and services according to the principles of market efficiency and effectiveness (Foucault, 1979). England's move towards privatising prisons, including their healthcare, education, and welfare services embodies that process and enables the state to govern public services from a distance. In the process of privatisation, we also observe two contemporary characteristics in prison and prison health governance that are the result of neoliberalism: deregulation—which is enmeshed with the contradiction of centralisation—and preference for economic efficiency over collective rights.

Deregulation involves dismantling laws so that the government relinquishes its oversight power to the private sector (McGregor, 2001). The coalition government in 2010 instituted such deregulation through 'Localism' and the 'Big Society' (Cameron, 2010). These efforts sought to give local actors autonomy in shaping local economies while shrinking the state, thereby decentralising state power (ibid.). Advocates argued that decentralisation would lead to faster and more thorough responses to citizens' needs, with greater sensitivity to their contexts and conditions (Brodie, 2000). Critics, however, are quick to highlight the lack of results (Grimshaw et al., 2017; Halsall et al., 2015).

Centralisation of criminal justice policy and practice illustrates the trend towards localisation (Newburn, 2007). Despite the guise of localisation towards private sector organisations, centralisation of central government power remains vicariously intact for prisons. Given central government's firm control of how prisons are run, the policy has thus become more punitive, more politicised, and more populist (ibid.), which highlights neoliberalism in action.

From the 1980s, cost reduction and efficiency were central to the argument for contracting and competitive tendering for public services (Walsh, 1991). Commissioning became understood as a process where needs are assessed, resources planned and prioritised, and delivery purchased and monitored to attain the best outcomes (Allen et al., 2020). Successive British governments since the 1980s have used procurement variously to support the evolution and development of private business and particularly the procurement sector (Crouch, 2011; Whitfield, 2001).

There is an understanding that the government should be "steering and not rowing" prison healthcare (Osborne and Gaebler, 1992, p. 25). This has led increasingly more politicians to believe a shared arrangement between public, voluntary, and private-sector organisations can deliver prison services. The arrangement allows the state to uphold the legal principle of subsidiarity, whereby decisions regarding prison health governance are deliberated and enforced at the lowest level possible, rather than dictated at the central government level (Morgan, 2011). Devolved risk—based on leaving governance responsibilities with regional and local actors who have a better capacity to respond—appeals to the government because of the perception it improves the capacity to tailor services to the needs of a particular community (ibid.). Commitment towards a shared public-market ownership of health from both Conservative and New Labour governments demonstrated acceptance of neoliberal ideas to govern public services at a distance (Newman, 2012).

Regulation 9(4) of the Public Contracts Regulations 2006 supports commissioning. In particular, the supply of products or the provision of services with a value generally of at least €134,000 (or ~£117,552) requires public-sector organisations to use a prescribed procurement procedure to provide "equal access to economic operators" and that must not have "the effect of creating unjustified obstacles to the opening up of public procurement to competition". Such regulations open opportunities for profit and not-for-profit sectors to help run prison services. With the primary aim of improving quality, flexibility, and efficiency of prison operations, the Health and Social Care Act 2012 increased the competition for health services by welcoming "any qualified provider" to issue a proposal to manage public services (Krachler and Greer, 2015). As such, non-profit social enterprises (e.g., community interest companies) and private-sector players (e.g., Care UK and Virgin Care) deliver prison healthcare alongside NHS Trusts. Such privatisation has only intensified over the last ten years (HMPPS, 2019; Ministry of Justice, 2009).

Intensifying privatisation of prisons

The move toward further privatisation began with the introduction of the Prison Unit Cost Programme—also known as the Benchmarking Programme—in 2012 (House of Commons Justice Committee, 2012). It required that public prisons reduce their operating costs at the same level as the private sector (ibid.). The programme's objective was explicitly to provide an alternative to wholesale competition for prison space from private companies as a means of delivering cost savings across prisons (ibid.). Such efforts further embedded the neoliberal principles of market forces and competition.

England has the most privatised prison system in Europe (Prison Reform Trust, 2019). Competition to run prison services is the crux of the programme. This is proposed as a "means to secure new services to improve existing service delivery, encourage innovation and drive value for money" (Ministry of Justice, 2011, p. 4). The policy rests on a perception that creating a competitive and mixed market, where successful contractors from voluntary and private organisations, local communities, and the public sector are paid to reduce recidivism, makes penal institutions more efficient (ibid.). Custodial contracts represented 16% of HMPPS's overall expenditures in 2018/2019, for a total of £6.8 billion (HMPPS, 2019)—a dramatic increase from £0.2 billion in 2009 (Ministry of

Justice, 2009). Seemingly, austerity has played a role in this explosion of private contractor involvement in the penal system, as privatisation is claimed to decrease costs by not running the service in-house.

Privatisation heightens doubt, fear, and insecurity about the quality of public services (O'Hara, 2014). In turn, these feelings rationalise further privatisation based on the belief that "government is inept, the market works, and that anything and everything that can be done to deliver the services of the state through the mechanisms of the market is of benefit" (Murphy, 2011, p. 29). This belief results in what Richard Murphy (2011, p. 5) called the cowardly state, saying it "sees responsibility and runs away from it". Paul Krugman (2012) argued that the government hoped that a "confidence fairy" (p. 3) would magically rescue the economy after fiscal reductions through privatisation. He argued that savings have been enormously unattainable (ibid.).

Privatisation also defies the logic of neoliberalism and in particular deregulation. Private contractors must still be managed and policed considering markets are not self-correcting and prisoners cannot provide appropriate quality control (Fitzgibbon and Lea, 2018). Inevitably, privatisation in England and Wales is placing additional strains on an already inadequate regulatory system. Due to how these institutions escape regulation, neoliberalism in the current economic condition has led to a consolidation and centralisation of power into the hands of a few institutions that escape public control (Harvey, 2010).

Scholars are coming to recognise misconceptions around the efficiency and quality of the services provided by prison privatisation. Admittedly, Sanjiv Sachdev (2004) claimed prison contractors in Britain projected efficiency by reducing labour costs, and Christoph Hermann and Jörg Flecker (2012) asserted that privatisation, liberalisation, and marketisation of public services led to lower costs and superior quality. Nonetheless, these claims were fallacies when private contractors have been shown to provide services that compromised the quality of the services (Hacker, 2004). Tom Sasse and colleagues (2019) illustrated that the political claim that outsourcing delivers between 20% and 30% savings lacked evidence. Additionally, the government does not always establish a sufficient understanding about the services that were outsourced, and its fixation on the lowest price usually accompanies unreasonable expectations on service efficiency and effectiveness (ibid.).

The efficacy of private prisons for rehabilitation remains underexplored. In Australia, Jane Andrew and Damien Cahill (2007) and Daniel Baldino et al. (2010) argue a lack of accountability, oversight framework, and quality control of private security operators undermines the penal sector's image. If we generalise these experiences to English prisons, relations between prisoners and those governing them may well be based on the penal commercialisation. Considering the lack of accountability structure to scrutinise how prisoners are treated in private prisons, opportunities to pursue the prison rehabilitation agenda could be limited. Furthermore, removing healthcare services from some of the private prison contracts is difficult (House of Commons Justice Committee,

2019b). Therefore, for those prisons HMPPS directly commissions, some governors have raised concerns about worsening standards of healthcare, as they were not subjected to the NHS England delivery framework (ibid.). Without such a framework, commercial interests may subordinate the role of rehabilitation and social justice in prisons.

Recent data highlight the failure of privatisation and the poor inability of private contractors to deliver their promises of cost efficiency and high quality. HMP Birmingham's transfer from G4S to the Ministry of Justice following continual high levels of violence and poor standards in 2019 was evidence private sector organisations ran state facilities ineptly (Ministry of Justice, 2019a). Moreover, the bankruptcy of Carillion—a facilities management company with a footprint across prisons in the South of England—cost taxpayers an estimated £72 million (Sasse et al., 2019). So not only did Carillion fail to deliver on its mandates, but it also required the state to subsidise its failure.

Corporate welfare is direct or indirect government subsidy, support, or rescue packages to business (Dawkins, 2002). The reality of corporate welfare, as per Kevin Farnsworth (2013), disputes the claim that private sector organisations are independent. Despite the neoliberal idea to reduce state intervention in the market, private businesses still depend extensively on public services and state benefits. Uniquely, the political right and left both oppose corporate welfare's existence. For the right, public expenditure distorts markets to the detriment of all (Moore and Stansel, 1996). For the left, corporate welfare operates as a tool of political corruption designed to reward elite interests at the expense of those in genuine need (Dawkins, 2002). Yet, despite its poor track record across the English criminal justice system, corporate welfare persists. Indeed, the Ministry of Justice continues to use private providers to manage newly built prisons and even announced in 2018 a competition to operate two new prisons (House of Commons Library, 2018; Ministry of Justice, 2019b).

Overall, the claim that private sector services provide better efficiency and quality for prison services has been discredited, as has the existence of corporate welfare that diametrically opposes state interference with the market. Altogether, these errors prove the misconception of the neoliberal agenda, even though the government increasingly relies on privatisation to deliver penal services.

Monitoring structure of English prisons

Considering the closed nature of prisons, checks and balances on power within the prison and prison healthcare governance structure are paramount. They are especially critical given well-documented power abuse (Liebling and Crewe, 2012). This section will analyse the monitoring structure of English prisons and prison healthcare—from governmental to non-governmental—and its effectiveness in addressing the governance structures' potential democratic deficits across English prisons to date.

In line with the rollback of the state function of neoliberalism, Noam Chomsky (1999) contended that the retrenchment of government from various areas of economic and political life creates a democratic deficit. Such a deficit engenders monitoring and accountability problems. These problems leave the monitoring structure of prison healthcare and the overall prison operations impotent and might compound the existing austerity measures in place and help neoliberal ideals infiltrate prison and prison healthcare governance.

European region monitoring

Legal scholars observe that protecting prisoners' rights features strongly in the European approach to punishment (Snacken and Dumortier, 2012; van Zyl Smit et al., 2014). Structural elements of this approach include the European CPT and the European Court of Human Rights (ECHR), which enforces the European Convention on Human Rights—key to prisoner protection in England.

The European Convention for the Prevention of Torture and Inhuman or Degrading Treatment or Punishment set up the CPT in February 1989 to prevent torture through non-judicial means. Meanwhile, the European Court of Human Rights interprets the European Convention on Human Rights, which is an international treaty drawn up within the Council of Europe in 1949 during the first post-war attempt to unify Europe. All 47 member states of the Council of Europe have ratified these two conventions, which become binding on these 47 states, the UK included.

The CPT consists of independent experts elected for a four-year term by the Committee of Ministers of the Council of Europe and is responsible for scheduled and unscheduled inspections of individual prisons and thematic reports on issues—such as healthcare—which cut across the whole system. The CPT has repeatedly criticised prison conditions detrimental to health, such as overcrowding, poor ventilation, lighting and heating, and poor hygiene and sanitary conditions, which are increasingly widespread in English prisons (CPT, 2017, 2020). Chapter 4 will discuss these criticisms in detail.

The legally binding provisions of the ECHR across all member states often strengthen the findings of the CPT. In its landmark judgement of *Kudla v Poland* [2000] ECHR 512, the state must ensure imprisonment does not subject prisoners to distress or hardship exceeding the unavoidable level of suffering inherent in imprisonment. Imprisonment was low on the ECHR agenda until 1975. That year it handed down its first major decision on prisoners' rights involving the UK government in the case of *Golder v United Kingdom* [1975] 1 EHRR 524, which led to an improvement in healthcare standards in European prisons. ECHR jurisprudence on prisons has since evolved, focusing on prisoners' health, social and welfare rights, and their participation in democracy.

ECHR often refers to the recommendations the CPT sets that strengthen prisoners' rights via international case law. That law subsequently has led to improved conditions in prison systems across Europe. These judgements have a real-time application that continually benefits prisoners beyond the reactivity of prisoners taking legal actions against individual governments, including the UK (Karamalidou, 2017; van Zyl Smit and Snacken, 2009). Research has demonstrated that a human rights approach is the most effective and safest way of managing prisons (Coyle, 2009).

Critics, however, have noted that the ECHR contains no explicit benchmark for the right to health, that some provisions aim too low, and that the convention occupies soft law status (Betteridge, 2004). Yet, it remains the most successful form of governance, whereby case law regarding Articles 2 and 3 of the convention has created minimum legal requirements for both the right to health and the ban on inhumane treatment—especially on deficient material conditions and unacceptable prison practices—that signatory states must meet, although with varying implementation success (Lines, 2008). This jurisprudence has clarified the obligations in Articles 2 and 3 and most likely made them irreversible—particularly given their ubiquity across Europe (van Zyl Smit and Snacken, 2009). Outside of the legal jurisprudence, the political weight of the treaty itself is their strongest asset.

Beyond these immediate benefits and drawbacks, the CPT and the ECHR can, to some extent, prevent neoliberalism from infiltrating the prison and prison healthcare governance systems. The CPT, for instance, freely enters settings regarded by the state as their *sancta sanctorum*, which outsiders are usually prevented from accessing (Daems, 2013). The European Court of Human Rights judgements have also opened the closed prison system to independent monitoring bodies, such as ombudsman (O'Connell et al., 2021). However, Brexit threatens much of this stability. While the UK government has stated that it "is committed to membership of the European Convention on Human Rights" (Department for Exiting the European Union, 2018), the potential repeal of the Human Rights Act 1998 (ECHR) might render ECHR decisions less effective, and the UK will not be bound by changes to EU law. Additionally, relying on European mechanisms to prevent torture and preserve prisoners' health alone is insufficient; one must turn to the monitoring of prisons by the national authorities.

Cross-government departmental monitoring

The governance and delivery of prison healthcare in England involve multisector cooperation across governmental departments. Formed in 2012, the National Partnership Agreement for Prison Healthcare in England 2018–2021 (Ministry of Justice, 2018) governs the commissioning, delivery, and monitoring of prison healthcare. HMPPS, the Ministry of Justice, the Department of Health and Social Care, NHS England, and PHE formally oversee the delivery of this agreement. It aims to promote collaboration on improving prisoner health outcomes, reducing health inequalities among prisoners, addressing health-related drivers of prisoners' offending behaviour, and improving continuity of care across criminal justice pathways (ibid.).

Reports, though, have criticised the deficiency of the partnership. In a NAO review on mental health in prisons (NAO, 2017), government agencies collected insufficient data about services, treatment, and outcomes in prison. For instance, 31,328 prisoners reported mental health issues in the HMIP surveys, but NHS England recorded mental health treatment for only 7,917 prisoners, suggesting at least 75% went untreated (NAO, 2017). The House of Commons Health and Social Care Committee (2018) provides a possible explanation for this failure. It criticised prison health contracts for failing to reflect population health needs, with gaps in key services including dentistry, mental health services, and speech and language therapy. Regardless, without robust data, assessing the prevalence of ill-health in prisons and directing resources appropriately to address deficiencies is nigh impossible. The prevailing structure of neoliberalism makes it difficult for prison healthcare to function effectively, especially when punishment tends to be prioritised over health.

Over the last 40 years, the House of Commons Select Committees have been responsible for scrutinising each Whitehall department executive decision. The committees are generally well-regarded, and their establishment in 1979 is routinely cited as a key event in British parliamentary history (Kelso, 2009). They rely heavily on external witnesses to provide evidence as part of the scrutiny and recommendation processes (Helboe et al., 2015). The House of Commons Justice Committee is the main committee examining the policies of prisons and prison healthcare. However, joint committees—such as the Joint Committee on Human Rights and the Public Account Committee—often examine prison and prison healthcare issues from human rights and finance management perspectives, respectively.

These parliamentary committees are viewed as critical to monitoring and influencing government policy. Meghan Benton and Meg Russell (2013) found that the government accepted and implemented approximately four in ten recommendations from these committees. Public embarrassment and media attention towards their review activities have influenced policy reforms (ibid.). While parliamentary inquiries have consistently kept the issues of prisons on the political agenda, the reality is that government compliance persists (Brazier and Fox, 2011; Rogers and Walters, 2006). Prison scholars have yet to examine these parliamentary committees' effectiveness in developing and implementing paradigm shifts for prison and prison healthcare. However, the lack of implementation of the parliamentary committee recommendations by the government signals the weakening of this monitoring structure and provides opportunity for neoliberal politics to infiltrate.

Independent prison inspections

Compared with other aspects of England's prisons, the effectiveness of prison inspections and monitoring has attracted little scholarly attention. The HMIP monitors service delivery, reporting the findings of its inspections directly to the Secretary of State for Justice concerning the treatment and conditions of prisoners—as outlined in section 5A of the Prison Act of 1952 (as amended). In line with its reputation for "conspicuous independence" (Morgan, 2002, p. 146), the HMIP works through announced and unannounced inspections. The Care Quality Commission (CQC) usually accompanies the HMIP inspections, verifying places of detention comply with the CQC Code of Practice to prevent and control infections and other related health guidelines. Both HMIP and CQC form the UK NPM and are answerable to the UN Optional Protocol to the Convention against Torture and Other Cruel, Inhuman or Degrading Treatment or Punishment (OPCAT) (National Preventive Mechanism [NPM], 2021).

Both announced and unannounced prison inspections draw on five datasets: 1) a confidential survey of a representative proportion of the prisoner population; 2) prisoner focus groups; 3) individual interviews with staff and prisoners; 4) documentation analysis; and 5) inspector observations during the inspection (HMIP, 2020). The inspections are based on a set of expectations from the HMIP that derive from various international and regional standards relating to the quality of service in prisons. These include the promotion of health and well-being among prisoners (ibid.).

Robust prison health governance and monitoring have not prevented a reduction of standards, something the HM Chief Inspector of Prisons' Annual Reports continually demonstrate. The HM Chief Inspector of Prisons has been calling for urgent notifications for HMPs Nottingham, Exeter, Birmingham, Bedford and Bristol, and the Feltham Young Offender Institute since January 2018 (HMIP, 2019). It has cited surges in deaths, drugs, degrading living conditions, and overall failure in maintaining institutional safety (ibid.). Also, it detailed stark implementation gaps where almost half of the HMIP recommendations for improvement have not been achieved in 2019/2020 (HMIP, 2020). This suggests that inspections of prisons and their healthcare services have failed to ensure prisoners' health and well-being.

The Prisons & Probation Ombudsman (PPO) is another effort that has not prevented failures in prisoner health. The PPO was established in 1994 (PPO, 2021) following recommendations from *The Woolf Report* on the need for an independent complaint adjudicator for prisoners. It investigates complaints submitted by individual prisoners who have failed to obtain satisfaction from the HMPPS. Most complaints concern mismanagement of prisoner property, staff's excessive use of force, and fatal incidents involving prisoners, the latter of which increased by 6% to 334 in 2019 (PPO, 2019). While PPO investigations have been useful in revealing the causes of the prisoner deaths, the organisation does not address the broader political questions on power, values, and interests in punishment (Aitken, 2021; Tomczak, 2018). Their abstention from addressing political questions gives a way for neoliberal principles to infiltrate the monitoring system, which should have preserved prisoner health.

A third mechanism that has insufficiently protected prisoner health is the independent monitoring boards (IMBs). Established in 1898, their function is to be watchdogs for the daily life and regime in an individual prison; they are empowered to investigate complaints from prisoners regarding their prison conditions (Livingstone et al., 2008). These boards consist of over 1,300 volunteers from local communities who visit prisons 50,000 times a year and report their findings to the Secretary of State on the conditions and treatment of prisoners (ibid.).

However, IMBs have recently assumed a more managerial agenda: they are increasingly becoming a purely monitoring body as opposed to an advocate for prisoners given their independent status (Behan and Kirkham, 2016; Bennett, 2016; Padfield, 2018). Their localised nature, too, does not provide a coherent and collective picture of issues experienced by prisoners, sits rather uncomfortably with the centralised nature of English prisons, and provides a space for neoliberalism to penetrate the governance structure. Additionally, findings from studies on the awareness of human rights among prisoners are inconsistent, creating scepticism about the boards' efficacy. For instance, one investigation by Susie Hulley and colleagues revealed that "some prisoners are well-informed about their rights" (2011, p. 20). However, a more recent study by Anastasia Karamalidou (2017) identified an almost total lack of awareness of human rights among prisoners in English prisons.

Despite occupying a prison monitoring remit, HMIP, PPOs, and IMBs lack uniform foci and efforts, which could be detrimental to monitoring prison health. These organisations have expressed serious concerns about prison staff's failure to implement improvements following their reports (House of Commons Justice Committee, 2019b). HMIP has undermined the message by stating that the English prison service is not entirely in crisis, although only a minority of prisons are relatively safe, calm, professional, and have caring staff (HMIP, 2019). However, the PPO, in its annual report, described the prison system as in crisis (PPO, 2017). Additionally, these monitoring organisations lack formal powers. And while they have developed relatively informal mechanisms for implementing some improvements (Hood et al., 1999), they cannot constitute an effective remedy for rectifying human rights breaches of prisoners.

Advocacy by voluntary organisations

Voluntary organisations, particularly those with an advocacy remit, can demand transparency and accountability from the government for its treatment of prisoners. Many of these organisations provide services and campaign for the improvement of services for prisoners, although there are some influential advocacy organisations—such as the Howard League for Penal Reform and the Prison Reform Trust—that solely focus on challenging the government through the policy and legal routes.

Research suggests a reorientation of these organisations towards a neoliberal structure has undermined this function to hold the government to account. Social movements and human rights activists have witnessed equality and justice being morphed to fit within a consumerist logic (Clarke, 2008; Hall, 2011; Massey, 2011). Stuart Hall (2011) referred to "disaffected consent", whereby the authorities use tactics, such as resource allocation, to disseminate their neoliberal logic via charitable organisations' aims and objectives. According to Milton Harris and Artur Raviv (1979), being a beneficiary of state financial assistance reinforces the principal-agent relationship and eventually erodes the autonomy of organisations. Increased dependence on state funding has raised concern that independence and autonomy of the voluntary sector would be undermined, especially when there are strains between service providing and advocacy roles (Baggott, 2013; Carmel and Harlock, 2008; Martikke and Moxham, 2010). As Janet Newman (2012) proposed, these efforts question how far the local democracy championed by these actors can challenge the hegemonic processes.

Little research exists on how voluntary organisations, particularly those detached from the state, respond when expected to incorporate neoliberal mutations into their work. Indeed, the preceding ideas are largely theoretical; empirical research has yet to emerge that investigates precisely how the state's extensive resources and political power could force voluntary organisations to conform to a top-down agenda.

Furthermore, recent developments have shown these non-state actors can be readily silenced—in the form of gag clauses within their contracts—from challenging the government's prevailing political ideologies. The Lobbying Act of 2014 imposed restrictions on openly criticising government policies. The Citizens Advice Bureau was among the first major organisations to acquiesce to the clause, taking £51 million in contracts to provide advice to Universal Credit claimants in exchange for promising not to criticise publicly the Department for Work and Pension (Disability News Service, 2019). The then-chair of the National Association for Voluntary and Community Action, John Tizard, criticised the law, arguing the government was distorting England's pluralistic democracy and devaluing charities (The Guardian, 2019). How the gag clause will affect prison health organisations remains to be seen. It could tamper with their independence in challenging adverse treatment of prisoners.

Summary

This chapter has outlined the structure of governance and delivery for prisons and prison healthcare in England. I argue that the absence of a clear aim of imprisonment blurs the role of health and rehabilitation, especially when government prioritises punishment, cost-saving, and efficiency over rehabilitation.

Prisons have always struggled with prioritising the health of their prisoners even before neoliberal forces began infiltrating its governance structure. However, that neoliberalism prioritises punishment and incarceration over health only compounds the issue. Increasing privatisation continues this prioritisation, with research revealing misconceptions around moral legitimacy, service efficiency, and quality. Although various monitoring organisations exist, they lack sufficient power and independence to instigate reforms, with independent organisations—such as voluntary ones—being subjected to a gag clause in return for funding. The effects of this pervasive structure of neoliberalism will be seen in the next chapter, in which I will analyse the current state of prisoner health in England.

References

Aitken, D. (2021) Investigating Prison Suicides: The Politics of Independent Oversight. *Punishment & Society*. 24(3), pp. 477–497. https://doi.org/10.1177/1462474521993002.

Allen, P., Checkland, K., Moran, V. and Peckham, S. (2020) *Commissioning Healthcare in England: Evidence, Policy and Practice*. Bristol: Policy Press.

Andrew, J. and Cahill, D. (2007) *Value for Money? Neoliberalism and New South Wales Prisons*. New South Wales: University of Wollongong.

Ansell, C. and Gash, A. (2007) Collaborative Governance in Theory and Practice. *Journal of Public Administration Research and Theory*. 18, pp. 543–571.

Arnold, H. (2016) The Prison Officer. In: Jewkes, Y., Crewe, B. and Bennett, J., eds. *Handbook on Prisons*. Oxford: Routledge, pp. 265–283.

Baggott, R. (2013) *Partnerships for Public Health and Well-being: Policy and Practice*. London: Palgrave Macmillan.

Baldino, D., Drum, M. and Wyatt, B. (2010) The Privatisation of Prisoner Transfer Services in Western Australia: What Can We Learn from the Ward Case? *The Australian Journal of Public Administration*. 69(4), pp. 418–430.

Behan, C. and Kirkham, R. (2016) Monitoring, Inspection and Complaints Adjudication in Prison: The Limits of Prison Accountability Frameworks. *The Howard Journal of Crime and Justice*. 55(4), pp. 432–454.

Bennett, J. (2016) *The Working Lives of Prison Managers: Global Change, Local Culture and Individual Agency in the Late Modern Prison*. London: Palgrave Macmillan.

Bennett, J. and Wahidin, A. (2008) Industrial Relations in Prisons. In: Bennett, J., Crewe, B. and Wahidin, A., eds. *Understanding Prison Staff*. Cullompton: Willan Publishing, pp. 117–131.

Benton, M. and Russell, M. (2013) Assessing the Impact of Parliamentary Oversight Committees: The Select Committees in the British House of Commons. *Parliamentary Affairs*. 66(4), pp. 772–797.

Betteridge, G. (2004) Bangkok 2004. Prisoners' Health and Human Rights in the HIV/AIDS Epidemic. *HIV AIDS Policy Law Review*. 9(3), pp. 96–99.

Bexell, M., Talberg, J. and Uhlin, A. (2010) Democracy in Global Governance: The Promises and Pitfalls of Transnational Actors. *Global Governance*. 16(1), pp. 81–101.

Boin, A. (2001) *Public Institutions: Leadership in Two Prison Systems*. Boulder: Lynne Rienner Publishers.

Brazier, A. and Fox, R. (2011) Reviewing Select Committee Tasks and Modes of Operation. *Parliamentary Affairs*. 64(2), pp. 354–369.

Brodie, J. (2000) Imagining Urban Democratic Citizenship. In: Isin, E. F., ed. *Democracy, Citizenship and the Global City*. Oxon: Routledge, pp. 110–128.

Bryans, S. (2007) *Prison Governors: Managing Prisons in a Time of Change*. Devon: Willan.

Cäker, M. and Nyland, K. (2017) Inter-Organizational Cooperation Challenging Hierarchical Accountability: The Dominated Actors in a Municipal Joint Venture. *Financial Accountability & Management*. 33(1), pp. 102–120.

Cameron, D. (2010) *Big Society Speech* [Online], available from: www.gov.uk/government/speeches/big-society-speech (Accessed: 11th January 2018).

Carmel, E. and Harlock, J. (2008) Instituting the "Third Sector" as a Governable Terrain: Partnership, Procurement and Performance in the UK. *Policy & Politics*. 36(2), pp. 155–171.

Cavadino, M. and Dignan, J. (2006) Penal Policy and Political Economy. *Criminology & Criminal Justice*. 6(4), pp. 435–456.

Chapman, R. A. (1984) *Leadership in the British Civil Service*. London and Sydney: Croom Helm.

Cheliotis, L. (2008) Resisting the Scourge of Managerialism: On the Uses of Discretion in Late-Modern Prisons. In: Bennett, J., Crewe, B. and Wahidin, A., eds. *Understanding Prison Staff*. Cullompton: Willan, pp. 247–261.

Chomsky, N. (1999) *Profit Over People: Neoliberalism and Global Order*. New York: Seven Stories Press.

Clarke, J. (2008) Living With/in and Without Neoliberalism. *Focaal: European Journal of Anthropology*. 51, pp. 135–147.

Committee for the Prevention of Torture and Inhuman or Degrading Treatment or Punishment (2017) *Report to the Government of the United Kingdom on the Visit to the United Kingdom Carried Out by the European Committee for the Prevention of Torture and Inhuman or Degrading Treatment or Punishment from 30 March to 12 April 2016* [Online], available from: https://rm.coe.int/168070a773 (Accessed: 11th January 2018).

Committee for the Prevention of Torture and Inhuman or Degrading Treatment or Punishment (2020) *Report to the United Kingdom Government on the Visit to the United Kingdom Carried Out by the European Committee for the Prevention of Torture and Inhuman or Degrading Treatment or Punishment (CPT) from 13 to 23 May 2019* [Online], available from: https://rm.coe.int/16809e4404 (Accessed: 27th May 2020).

Coyle, A. (2009) *A Human Rights Approach to Prison Management: A Handbook for Prison Staff*. 2nd ed. London: International Centre for Prison Studies.

Crawley, E. (2013) *Doing Prison Work: The Public and Private Lives of Prison Officers*. New York: Routledge.

Crouch, C. (2011) *The Strange Non-death of Neo-liberalism*. Cambridge: Polity Press.

Cullen, F. T. and Gendreau, P. (2001) From Nothing Works to What Works: Changing Professional Ideology in the 21st Century. *The Prison Journal*. 81(3), pp. 313–338.

Daems, T. (2013) Punishment and the Question of Europe. In: Daems, T., van Zyl Smit, D. and Snacken, S., eds. *European Penology*? Oxford: Hart Publishing, pp. 27–52.

Davies, J. (2005) Local Governance and the Dialectics of Hierarchy, Market and Network. *Policy Studies*. 26(3–4), pp. 311–335.

Dawkins, C. E. (2002) Corporate Welfare, Corporate Citizenship, and the Question of Accountability. *Business and Society*. 41(3), pp. 269–291.

Department for Exiting the European Union (2018) *Policy Paper: The Future Relationship Between the United Kingdom and the European Union* [Online], available from: www.gov.uk/government/publications/the-future-relationship-between-the-united-kingdom-and-the-european-union/the-future-relationship-between-the-united-kingdom-and-the-european-union-html-version (Accessed: 25th January 2021).

De Viggiani, N. (2007) Unhealthy Prisons: Exploring Structural Determinants of Prison Health. *Sociology of Health & Illness*. 29, pp. 115–135.

Disability News Service (2019) *Citizens Advice Signed Gagging Clause in Return for Share of £51m from DWP* [Online], available from: www.disabilitynewsservice.com/

citizens-advice-signed-gagging-clause-in-return-for-share-of-51m-from-dwp/ (Accessed: 27th May 2020).

Dodgson, R., Lee, K. and Drager, N. (2002) *Global Health Governance: A Conceptual Review* [Online], available from: https://apps.who.int/iris/handle/10665/68934 (Accessed: 21st February 2020).

Eide, H. M. K. and Westrheim, K. G. (2020) Norwegian Prison Officers' Perspectives on Professionalism and Professional Development Opportunities in Their Occupation. *Journal of Prison Education and Reentry*. 6(3), pp. 316–332.

Exworthy, M. (2010) The Performance Paradigm in the English NHS: Potential, Pitfalls, and Prospects. *Eurohealth*. 16(3), pp. 16–19.

Farnsworth, K. (2013) Bringing Corporate Welfare In. *Journal of Social Policy*. 42(1), pp. 1–22.

Feeley, M. and Simon, J. (1992) The New Penology: Notes on the Emerging Strategy of Corrections and its Implications. *Criminology*. 30, pp. 449–474.

Fidler, D. P. (2007) Architecture Amidst Anarchy: Global Health's Quest for Governance. *Global Health Governance*. 1.

Fitzgibbon, W. and Lea, J. (2018) Privatization and Coercion: The Question of Legitimacy. *Theoretical Criminology*. 22(4), pp. 545–562.

Flinders, M. (2002) Shifting the Balance? Parliament, the Executive and the British Constitution. *Political Studies*. 50(1), pp. 23–42.

Forrester, A., Exworthy, T., Olumoroti, O., Sessay, M., Parrott, J., Spencer, S. J. and Whyte, S. (2013) Variations in Prison Mental Health Services in England and Wales. *International Journal of Law and Psychiatry*. 36(3–4), pp. 326–332.

Foucault, M. (1979) *The Birth of Biopolitics: Lectures at the Collège de France, 1978–79* (translated by Burchell, G.). Basingstoke: Palgrave Macmillan.

Fox, L. (1952) *The English Prison and Borstal Systems*. London: Routledge and Kegan Paul.

Gash, T., Magee, I., Rutter, J. and Smith, N. (2010) *Read Before Burning: Arm's Length Government for a New Administration*. London: Institute for Government.

Gatherer, A. and Fraser, A. (2009) Health Care for Detainees. *The Lancet*. 373, pp. 1337–1338.

Giddens, A. (1984) *The Constitution of Society*. Cambridge: Polity Press.

Ginn, S. (2012) Prison Environment and Health. *British Medical Journal*. 345, p. e5921.

Gramsci, A. (1971) *Selections From the Prison Notebooks of Antonio Gramsci*. London: Lawrence & Wishart.

Grimshaw, D., Johnson, M., Marino, S. and Rubery, J. (2017) Towards More Disorganised Decentralisation? Collective Bargaining in the Public Sector Under Pay Restraint. *Industrial Relations Journal*. 48(1), pp. 22–41.

The Guardian (2019) *John Tizard: I Had to Quit as a Charity Boss to Protest Against Terrible Government Policies* [Online], available from: www.theguardian.com/society/2019/sep/12/quit-charity-boss-protest-against-terrible-government-policies (Accessed: 27th May 2020).

Hacker, J. (2004) Privatizing Risk Without Privatizing the Welfare State: The Hidden Politics of Social Policy Retrenchment in the United States. *American Political Science Review*. 98(2), pp. 243–260.

Hall, S. (2011) The Neo-liberal Revolution. *Cultural Studies*. 25(6), pp. 705–728.

Halsall, J. P., Cook, I. G. and Wankhade, P. (2015) The British Big Society Effect: The Challenges of the Third Sector. *International Journal of Sustainable Society*. 7(4). https://doi.org/10.1504/IJSSOC.2015.073567.

Hansard (1995) *Prison Security: Learmont Report* [Online], available from: https://api.parliament.uk/historic-hansard/lords/1995/oct/16/prison-security-learmont-report (Accessed: 25th January 2021).

Harris, M. and Raviv, A. (1979) Optimal Incentive Contracts with Imperfect Information. *Journal of Economic Theory*. 20, pp. 231–259.

Harvey, D. (2010) *The Enigma of Capital and the Crises of Capitalism*. London: Profile Books.

Hay, C. (2002) *Political Analysis*. London: Palgrave.

Hayton, P. and Boyington, J. (2006) Prisons and Health Reforms in England and Wales. *American Journal of Public Health*. 96(10), pp. 1730–1733.

The Health Foundation (2019) *A Critical Moment: NHS Staffing Trends, Retention and Attrition* [Online], available from: www.health.org.uk/sites/default/files/upload/publications/2019/A%20Critical%20Moment_1.pdf (Accessed: 21st February 2020).

Helboe, H., Halpin, D. and Rasmussen, A. (2015) Who Gives Evidence to Parliamentary Committees? A Comparative Investigation of Parliamentary Committees and Their Constituencies. *Journal of Legislative Studies*. 21(3), pp. 408–427.

Hermann, C. and Flecker, J. (2012) Conclusion: Impacts of Public Service Liberalization and Privatization. In: Hermann, C. and Flecker, J., eds. *Privatization of Public Services. Impacts for Employment, Working Conditions and Service Quality in Europe*. London: Routledge, pp. 192–205.

Hill, M. and Hupe, P. (2015) *Implementing Public Policy*. 3rd ed. London: SAGE.

HM Inspectorate of Prisons (1996) *Patient or Prisoner? A New Strategy for Health Care in Prisons: A Discussion Paper*. London: HM Inspectorate of Prisons.

HM Inspectorate of Prisons (2019) *HM Chief Inspector of Prisons for England and Wales: Annual Report 2018–19* [Online], available from: www.justiceinspectorates.gov.uk/hmi-prisons/wp-content/uploads/sites/4/2019/07/6.5563_HMI-Prisons-AR_2018-19_WEB_FINAL_040719.pdf (Accessed: 25th January 2021).

HM Inspectorate of Prisons (2020) *HM Chief Inspector of Prisons for England and Wales: Annual Report 2019–20* [Online], available from: https://assets.publishing.service.gov.uk/government/uploads/system/uploads/attachment_data/file/927361/hmi-prisons-annual-report-accounts-201920.pdf (Accessed: 25th January 2021).

HM Prison & Probation Service (2017) *Prison Finder A-Z Pages* [Online], available from: www.justice.gov.uk/contacts/prison-finder/prisonfinder-a-z (Accessed: 25th January 2021).

HM Prison & Probation Service (2019) *Her Majesty's Prison and Probation Service Annual Report and Accounts 2018–19* [Online], available from: https://assets.publishing.service.gov.uk/government/uploads/system/uploads/attachment_data/file/818788/HMPPS_Annual_Report_and_Accounts_2018-19__web_.pdf (Accessed: 21st February 2020).

HM Prison & Probation Service (2021a) *About Us* [Online], available from: www.gov.uk/government/organisations/her-majestys-prison-and-probation-service/about (Accessed: 25th January 2021).

HM Prison & Probation Service (2021b) *Become a Prison Officer: One Career, Many Roles* [Online], available from: https://prisonandprobationjobs.gov.uk/prison-officer/ (Accessed: 25th January 2021).

Home Office (1968) *The Treatment of Offenders in Britain*. London: HMSO.

Home Office (1991) *Custody, Care and Justice*. London: HMSO.

Hood, C. (2000) *The Art of the State: Culture, Rhetoric, and Public Management*. Oxford: Oxford University Press.

Hood, C., Scott, C., James, O., Jones, G. W. and Travers, A. (1999) *Regulation Inside Government*. Oxford: Oxford University Press.

House of Commons Health and Social Care Committee (2018) *Prison Health: Twelfth Report of Session 2017–19* [Online], available from: https://publications.parliament.uk/pa/cm201719/cmselect/cmhealth/963/963.pdf (Accessed: 20th April 2019).

House of Commons Justice Committee (2012) *Oral Evidence Taken Before the Justice Committee: The Work of the Secretary of State, Wednesday 28 November 2012: Rt Hon Chris Grayling MP* [Online], available from: https://publications.parliament.uk/pa/cm201213/cmselect/cmjust/c741-i/c74101.htm (Accessed: 25th January 2021).

House of Commons Justice Committee (2019a) *Oral Evidence: Prison Governance, HC 2128* [Online], available from: http://data.parliament.uk/writtenevidence/committeeevidence.svc/evidencedocument/justice-committee/prison-governance/oral/103862.html (Accessed: 25th January 2021).

House of Commons Justice Committee (2019b) *Prison Governance* [Online], available from: https://publications.parliament.uk/pa/cm201919/cmselect/cmjust/191/191.pdf (Accessed: 21st January 2020).

House of Commons Library (2018) *The Prison Estate. Briefing Paper Number 05646, 12 December 2018* [Online], available from: http://researchbriefings.files.parliament.uk/documents/SN05646/SN05646.pdf (Accessed: 19th February 2019).

House of Commons Library (2019) *Briefing Paper Number CBP-04334, 23 July 2019: UK Prison Population Statistics* [Online], available from: http://researchbriefings.files.parliament.uk/documents/SN04334/SN04334.pdf (Accessed: 27th May 2020).

House of Commons Select Committee (2018) *Written Evidence from the Royal College of Nursing* [Online], available from: http://data.parliament.uk/WrittenEvidence/CommitteeEvidence.svc/EvidenceDocument/Health%20and%20Social%20Care/Prison%20health/written/83890.html#_edn1 (Accessed: 27th May 2020).

Hudson, B. (1993) *Penal Policy and Social Justice*. London: Macmillan.

Hulley, S., Liebling, A. and Crewe, B. (2011) Respect in Prisons: Prisoners' Experiences of Respect in Public and Private Sector Prisons. *Criminology & Criminal Justice*. 12, pp. 3–23.

Karamalidou, A. (2017) *Embedding Human Rights in Prison: English and Dutch Perspectives*. London: Palgrave Macmillan.

Kelso, A. (2009) *Parliamentary Reform at Westminster*. Manchester: Manchester University Press.

Kickbusch, I. (2006) The Need for a European Strategy on Global Health. *Scandinavian Journal of Public Health*. 34, pp. 561–565.

Kooiman, J. (2003) Societal Governance. In: Katenhusen, I. and Lamping, W., eds. *Demokratien in Europa*. Heidelberg: Springer, pp. 229–250.

Kooiman, J. and Van Vliet, M. (1993) Governance and Public Management. In: Eliassen, K. and Kooiman, J., eds. *Managing Public Organizations: Lessons from Contemporary European Experience*. London: SAGE, pp. 58–72.

Krachler, N. and Greer, I. (2015) When Does Marketisation Lead to Privatisation? Profit-Making in English Health Services After the 2012 Health and Social Care Act. *Social Science & Medicine*. 124, pp. 215–223.

Krugman, P. (2012) *End This Depression Now*! New York: W.W. Norton & Company.

Leaman, J., Richards, A. A., Emslie, L. and O'Moore, E. J. (2017) Improving Health in Prisons—From Evidence to Policy to Implementation—Experiences from the UK. *International Journal of Prisoner Health*. 13(3/4), pp. 139–167.

Liebling, A. and Arnold, H. (2004) *Prisons and Their Moral Performance: A Study of Values, Quality and Prison Life*. Oxford: Oxford University Press.

Liebling, A. and Crewe, B. (2012) Prisons beyond the New Penology: The Shifting Moral Foundations of Prison Management. In: Simon, J. and Sparks, R., eds. *The SAGE Handbook of Punishment and Society*. London: SAGE, pp. 283–307.

Liebling, A. and Price, D. (2001) *The Prison Officer*. Leyhill: Prison Service and Waterside Press.

Lines, R. (2008) The Right to Health of Prisoners in International Human Rights Law. *International Journal of Prisoner Health*. 4(1), pp. 3–53.

Livingstone, S., Owen, T. and Macdonald, A. (2008) *Prison Law*. Oxford: Oxford University Press.

Loader, I. and Sparks, R. (2002) Contemporary Landscapes of Crime, Order, and Control: Governance, Risk and Globalization. In: Maguire, M., Morgan, R. and Reiner, R., eds. *The Oxford Handbook of Criminology*. 3rd ed. Oxford: Oxford University Press, pp. 83–111.

Marinetto, M. (2003) Governing Beyond the Centre: A Critique of the Anglo-governance School. *Political Studies*. 51(3), pp. 592–608.

Marks, L. (2014) *Governance, Commissioning and Public Health*. Bristol: Policy Press.

Marks, L., Cave, S. and Hunter, D. J. (2010) Public Health Governance: Views of Key Stakeholders. *Public Health*. 124(1), pp. 55–59.

Marsh, D. (2003) *Delivering a New Britain*. London: Palgrave.

Marsh, D. (2011) The New Orthodoxy: The Differentiated Polity Model. *Public Administration*. 89(1), pp. 32–48.

Martikke, S. and Moxham, C. (2010) Public Sector Commissioning: Experiences of Voluntary Organizations Delivering Health and Social Services. *International Journal of Public Administration*. 33, pp. 790–799.

Massey, D. (2011) Economics and Ideology in the Present Moment. *Soundings*. 48, pp. 29–39.

McAnulla, S. (2005) Making Hay with Actualism? The Need for a Realist Concept of Structure. *Politics*. 25(1), pp. 31–38.

McGregor, S. L. T. (2001) Neoliberalism and Health Care. *International Journal of Consumer Studies*. 25(2), pp. 82–89.

Ministry of Justice (2009) *National Offender Management Service Annual Report and Accounts 0809* [Online], available from: https://assets.publishing.service.gov.uk/government/uploads/system/uploads/attachment_data/file/248223/0779.pdf (Accessed: 21st February 2020).

Ministry of Justice (2010) *Breaking the Cycle: Effective Punishment, Rehabilitation and Sentencing of Offenders* [Online], available from: http://webarchive.nationalarchives.gov.uk/20111114164935/www.justice.gov.uk/downloads/consultations/breaking-the-cycle.pdf (Accessed: 2nd March 2018).

Ministry of Justice (2011) *Competition Strategy for Offender Services* [Online], available from: https://assets.publishing.service.gov.uk/government/uploads/system/uploads/attachment_data/file/217248/competition-strategy-offender-services.pdf (Accessed: 3rd July 2018).

Ministry of Justice (2018) *National Partnership Agreement for Prison Healthcare in England 2018–2021* [Online], available from: https://assets.publishing.service.gov.uk/government/uploads/system/uploads/attachment_data/file/697130/moj-national-health-partnership-2018-2021.pdf (Accessed: 12th April 2018).

Ministry of Justice (2019a) *Birmingham Prison Contract Ended* [Online], available from: www.gov.uk/government/news/birmingham-prison-contract-ended (Accessed: 21st February 2020).

Ministry of Justice (2019b) *10,000 Extra Prison Places to Keep the Public Safe* [Online], available from: www.gov.uk/government/news/10-000-extra-prison-places-to-keep-the-public-safe (Accessed: 21st February 2020).

Ministry of Justice (2020) *Prison Service Orders (PSOs)* [Online], available from: www.gov.uk/guidance/prison-service-orders-psos (Accessed: 25th January 2021).

Moore, S. and Stansel, D. (1996) *How Corporate Welfare Won: Clinton and the Retreat from Cutting Business Subsidies*. Washington, DC: Cato Institute.

Morgan, R. (2002) Imprisonment: A Brief History, the Contemporary Scene, and Likely Prospects. In: Maguire, M., Morgan, R. and Reiner, R., eds. *The Oxford Handbook of Criminology*. 3rd ed. Oxford: Oxford University Press, pp. 1137–1195.

Morgan, R. (2011) Austerity, Subsidiarity and Parsimony: Offending Behaviour and Criminalisation. In: Silvestri, A., ed. *Lessons for the Coalition: An End of Term Report on New Labour and Criminal Justice*. London: Centre for Crime and Justice Studies, pp. 18–21.

Morris, T. P., Morris, P. and Barer, B. (1963) *Pentonville: A Sociological Study of an English Prison*. London: Routledge & Kegan Paul.

Murphy, R. (2011) *The Courageous State: Rethinking Economics, Society and the Role of Government*. London: Searching Finance Ltd.

National Audit Office (2017) *Mental Health in Prisons* [Online], available from: www.nao.org.uk/wp-content/uploads/2017/06/Mental-health-in-prisons.pdf (Accessed: 11th January 2018).

National Preventive Mechanism (2021) *OPCAT* [Online], available from: www.nationalpreventivemechanism.org.uk/opcat/ (Accessed: 25th January 2021).

Newburn, T. (2007) "Tough on Crime": Penal Policy in England and Wales. *Crime and Justice*. 36(1), pp. 425–470.

Newman, J. (2012) *Working the Spaces of Power*. London: Bloomsbury.

NHS Improvement (2019) *Performance of the NHS Provider Sector for the Year Ended 31 March 2019* [Online], available from: https://improvement.nhs.uk/documents/5404/Performance_of_the_NHS_provider_sector_for_the_quarter_4_1819.pdf (Accessed: 21st February 2020).

O'Connell, C., Aizpurua, E. and Rogan, M. (2021) The European Committee for the Prevention of Torture and the Gendered Experience of Imprisonment. *Crime, Law and Social Change*. 75, pp. 445–468.

O'Hara, M. (2014) *Austerity Bites: A Journey to the Sharp End of Cuts in the UK*. Bristol: Policy Press.

Osborne, D. and Gaebler, T. (1992) *Reinventing Government: How the Entrepreneurial Spirit is Transforming the Public Sector*. New York: Penguin Books.

Padfield, N. (2018) Monitoring Prisons in England and Wales: Who Ensures the Fair Treatment of Prisoners? *Crime, Law and Social Change*. 70, pp. 57–76.

Payne, S. (2008) Globalization, Governance and Health. In: Kennett, P., ed. *Governance, Globalization and Public Policy*. Cheltenham: Edward Elgar Publishing, pp. 151–172.

Peck, J. and Tickell, A. (1994) Jungle Law Breaks Out: Neoliberalism and Global-Local Disorder. *Area*. 26(4), pp. 317–326.

Plugge, E., Stürup-Toft, S., Møller, L. and O'Moore, E. (2017) Worldwide Prison Health Research and Engagement Network: A Vehicle for Capacity-Building in Prison Health. *Public Health Panorama*, pp. 483–488.

Pratt, J. (2007) *Penal Populism*. London: Routledge.

Prison Officers' Association (2021) *Welcome to the POA* [Online], available from: www.poauk.org.uk/ (Accessed: 25th January 2021).

Prison Reform Trust (2019) *Bromley Briefings Prison Fact File: A Winter 2019* [Online], available from: www.prisonreformtrust.org.uk/Portals/0/Documents/Bromley%20Briefings/Winter%202019%20Factfile%20web.pdf (Accessed: 1st February 2020).

Prisons & Probation Ombudsman (2017) *Annual Report 2016–17* [Online], available from: https://s3-eu-west-2.amazonaws.com/ppo-prod-storage-1g9rkhjhkjmgw/uploads/2017/07/PPO_Annual-Report-201617_Interactive.pdf (Accessed: 27th May 2020).

Prisons & Probation Ombudsman (2019) *Annual Report 2018–19* [Online], available from: https://s3-eu-west-2.amazonaws.com/ppo-prod-storage-1g9rkhjhkjmgw/uploads/2019/10/PPO_Annual-Report-2018-19_WEB-final-1.pdf (Accessed: 27th May 2020).

Prisons & Probation Ombudsman (2021) *About the PPO* [Online], available from: www.ppo.gov.uk/about/vision-and-values/brief-history/ (Accessed: 25th January 2021).

Pusey, M. (1991) *Economic Rationalism in Canberra: A Nation-building State Changes Its Mind*. Cambridge: Cambridge University Press.

Rhodes, R. A. W. (1996) The New Governance: Governing Without Government. *Political Studies*. 44(4), pp. 652–667.
Rogers, R. and Walters, R. (2006) *How Parliament Works*. 6th ed. Abingdon: Routledge.
Rusche, G. and Kirchheimer, O. (1939) *Punishment and Social Structure*. New York: Columbia University Press.
Sachdev, S. (2004) *Paying the Cost? Public Private Partnerships and the Public Service Workforce*. London: Catalyst.
Sasse, T., Guerin, B., Nickson, S., O'Brien, M., Pope, T. and Davies, N. (2019) *Government Outsourcing: What Has Worked and What Needs Reform*. London: Institute for Government.
Scharpf, F. W. (1997) *Games Real Actors Play: Actor-centered Institutionalism in Policy Research*. Colorado: Westview Press.
Scholte, J. A. (2011) *Building Global Democracy? Civil Society and Accountable Global Governance*. Cambridge: Cambridge University Press.
Sim, J. (1990) *Medical Power in Prisons: The Prison Medical Service in England 1774–1989*. Milton Keynes: Open University Press.
Sim, J. (2002) The Future of Prison Health Care: A Critical Analysis. *Critical Social Policy*. 22(2), pp. 300–323.
Smart, B. (1985) *Michel Foucault*. London: Tavistock.
Snacken, S. and Dumortier, E., eds. (2012) *Resisting Punitiveness in Europe?: Welfare, Human Rights and Democracy*. Abingdon: Routledge.
Sparks, R. and Bottoms, A. E. (1996) Legitimacy and Order in Prisons. *The British Journal of Sociology*. 46(1), pp. 45–62.
Syrett, K. (2011) Health Technology Appraisal and the Courts: Accountability for Reasonableness and the Judicial Model of Procedural Justice. *Health Economics, Policy and Law*. 6, pp. 469–488.
Terry, L. D. (1995) *Leadership in Public Bureaucracies*. Thousand Oaks, CA: SAGE.
Tomczak, P. (2018) *Prison Suicide: What Happens Afterwards*? Bristol: Bristol University Press.
van Zyl Smit, D. and Snacken, S. (2009) *Principles of European Prison Law and Policy: Penology and Human Rights*. Oxford: Oxford University Press.
van Zyl Smit, D., Weatherby, P. and Creighton, S. (2014) Whole Life Sentences and the Tide of European Human Rights Jurisprudence: What is to Be Done? *Human Rights Law Review*. 14(1), pp. 59–84.
Walsh, K. (1991) *Competitive Tendering of Local Authority Services: Initial Experience*. London: Department of the Environment.
Watson, R., Stimpson, A. and Hostick, T. (2004) Prison Health Care: A Review of the Literature. *International Journal of Nursing Studies*. 41(2), pp. 119–128.
Weber, M. (1930) *The Protestant Ethic and the Spirit of Capitalism*. Oxford: Basil Blackwell.
Weber, M. (1978) *Economy and Society: An Outline of Interpretive Sociology*. Vol. 2. Berkeley, CA: University of California Press.
Whitfield, D. (2001) *Private Finance Initiative and Public Private Partnerships: What Future for Public Services*? Kerry: European Services Strategy Unit.
Williams, B. and Matheny, A. (1995) *Democracy, Dialogue, and Environmental Disputes: The Contested Languages of Social Regulation*. New Haven, CT: Yale University Press.

Chapter 4

Current state of health in English prisons

Introduction

In May 2019, judges in the Netherlands refused a UK extradition application for a man suspected of smuggling cocaine and heroin (The Guardian, 2019). The refusal relied on an official report by the HM Inspectorate of Prisons detailing rat infestations in several prisons, squalid conditions, and increasing violence. Such circumstances, the judges believed, meant permitting the extradition would contravene Article 3 of the European Convention on Human Rights, which prohibits torture, inhumane and degrading treatment, and punishment. The refusal came despite assurance from the Director of Prisons that the man would not be subjected to similar conditions.

This chapter details the current state of health in English prisons. It begins by analysing the social determinants of prisoner health, such as poverty, housing, and employment, revealing how poor health is a by-product of a punitive cycle evolved from contemporary neoliberalism. This cycle begins in the community and is reinforced in prisons. The pervasive impact of austerity since 2010—illuminated by the literature on poor access to healthcare, demeaning prison living conditions, and growing violence—has contributed to ongoing prison instability and poor governance for prisons and prison healthcare.

Then the chapter explores the sociological underpinning of prison health using the lenses of habitus (how a social structure influences the attitude and behaviour of prisoners), importation (how prisoners induct their deviant behaviours into prisons), and deprivation (how prisons withdraw basic entitlements of prisoners as an individual as a form of punishment). I consider the worsening prisoner health during post-2010 austerity and the government responses to it. Overall, I demonstrate how the prevailing neoliberalism limits political possibilities for reducing health inequalities among prisoners and the wider population and causes human rights violations. To understand austerity's impact on English prison health governance and delivery of prison healthcare, we must appreciate the context of health in English prisons.

DOI: 10.4324/9781003182337-4

Social determinants of prisoner health

Imprisonment has long been recognised as detrimental to health. As early as the 19th century, Thomas Buxton (1818, p. 19) observed that incarceration "impaired [prisoners'] health, debased [their] intellect and corrupted [their] principles". Relatedly, Jeremy Bentham (1864, pp. 351–352) wrote that prisons comprised "every imaginable means of infecting both body and mind", with "forced idleness" leading to "enfeebled faculties" and loss of "suppleness and elasticity" to prisoners' vital organs. More recently, Spencer (2001, p. 18) argued that "the seeds of poor health are sown for the majority [of prisoners] long before [they] entered the institution"—often they come from the most deprived sections of society and have the greatest health needs (ibid.).

Research has firmly established a link between poverty and social exclusion that compromises health (Marmot, 2005; WHO, 2014). Indeed, an extensive study by George Davey Smith et al. (2001) between 1800 and 2000 demonstrated the long-standing association between poverty and ill-health. People experience health within the settings of their daily life (WHO, 1986), and the unequal distribution of health-damaging experiences is a systemic combination of poor social policies, unfair economic arrangements, and bad politics (Marmot et al., 2008).

Overwhelming evidence has conclusively demonstrated prisoners are more likely than others to suffer physical and mental ailments (Dolan et al., 2016; Fazel et al., 2016; Stürup-Toft et al., 2018). Sunita Stürup-Toft et al. (2018) identified cardiovascular issues as the biggest killer in English prisons, exceeding mental health and substance misuse. In a sample of prisoners diverted from prisons to mental health institutions, over half had comorbidities of mental health and drug or alcohol addiction; HMPPS and NHS England lack accurate data regarding the number of prisoners with mental health needs (House of Commons Committee of Public Accounts, 2017; NHS England, 2017). Many entrants to the criminal justice system have poor educational backgrounds, low incomes, meagre employment opportunities, transient abodes, and unstable family relationships (Prison Reform Trust, 2019). These circumstances may reflect prison conditions or prisoner lifestyles before imprisonment (Baybutt et al., 2014). Indeed, these experiences are cumulative across multiple determinants (ibid.).

Alongside cardiovascular issues, tobacco smoking, substance misuse, poor dietary intake, and physical inactivity are risk factors of ill-health in prison (Fazel et al., 2016; Stürup-Toft et al., 2018). NHS England (2017) also estimate at least 7% of prisoners have learning disabilities, including autism, attention deficit hyperactivity disorder (ADHD), and acquired brain injuries that impede their navigation of the criminal justice system compared to 2% of people in the general population. Notably, populations of older, female, transgender, minority ethnic, religious, and foreign national prisoners are rising in English prisons (Lamble, 2012; Stürup-Toft et al., 2018; Ministry of Justice, 2019a). Considerable progress has been made in raising their health profile, for instance addressing the higher burden of self-harm among female prisoners and the sparsity of social care access in prisons for older prisoners (Hawton et al., 2014; Tucker et al., 2021). However, none of the systems within prisons are designed for these growing cohorts. Such issues exist outside the UK too, in other European jurisdictions adopting austerity. Portugal, Ireland, Italy, Greece, and Spain experience poor prisoner health, and their healthcare systems suffer inertia in tackling these issues (Cheliotis and Xenakis, 2021; Cordeiro-Rodrigues, 2020; Gonnella, 2013; Repullo, 2014; Rogan, 2013).

Austerity makes these experiences of living with ill-health even more pervasive, compounding the population's health and well-being. Many local governments in England have cut their Local Welfare Assistance Schemes, leaving vulnerable people and those facing emergencies without anywhere to turn (UN General Assembly, 2019). Homelessness is up 60%, fitful sleeping 134%, and food bank use has quadrupled between 2010 and 2018 (ibid.).

Progress in reducing preventable disease has flatlined since 2012. The Institute for Public Policy Research (2019) attributes 130,000 preventable deaths in the general UK population to austerity due to a combination of flat line reduction in preventable diseases, significant cuts to local authorities' public health budgets, and increased harmful health behaviour. The Marmot Review: 10 Years On (2020) found life expectancy in England has stalled since 2010, something that has not happened since 1900—a sign society has stopped improving. Moreover, public health epidemiologists Richard Wilkinson and Kate Pickett (2009) argued large income differences have damaging health and social consequences. Such consequential precursors cause neglect, inequality, and discrimination—all of which prisoners cumulatively experience.

Legislation and prison numbers

Discussions of ill-health in prisons often discount living conditions: regime, social environment, and purposeful activities. Yet all are key factors of prisoner health. The relationship between prison environment and prisoner health is straightforward. As early as 1990, the CPT highlighted the problem of overcrowding in English prisons (CPT, 2020a). Six in ten (n=70) prisons in England and Wales were overcrowded at the end of December 2019 (NAO, 2020), with most exceeding their certified normal accommodation level—a measure denoting an acceptable standard (House of Commons Health and Social Care Committee, 2018). The ten most crowded prisons exceeded 147% of their operational capacity, implying many prisoners there shared cells designed for fewer people (NAO, 2020).

Official reports note that legislative changes have increased how many individuals enter prisons and their duration of stay (Figure 4.1). The Ministry of Justice (2013) highlights key reasons for the increase: 1) more offenders entering prison receiving an immediate custodial sentence; 2) larger recall populations who stayed longer in prisons; 3) higher overall average of custodial sentence length; and 4) lower parole rates since 2007.

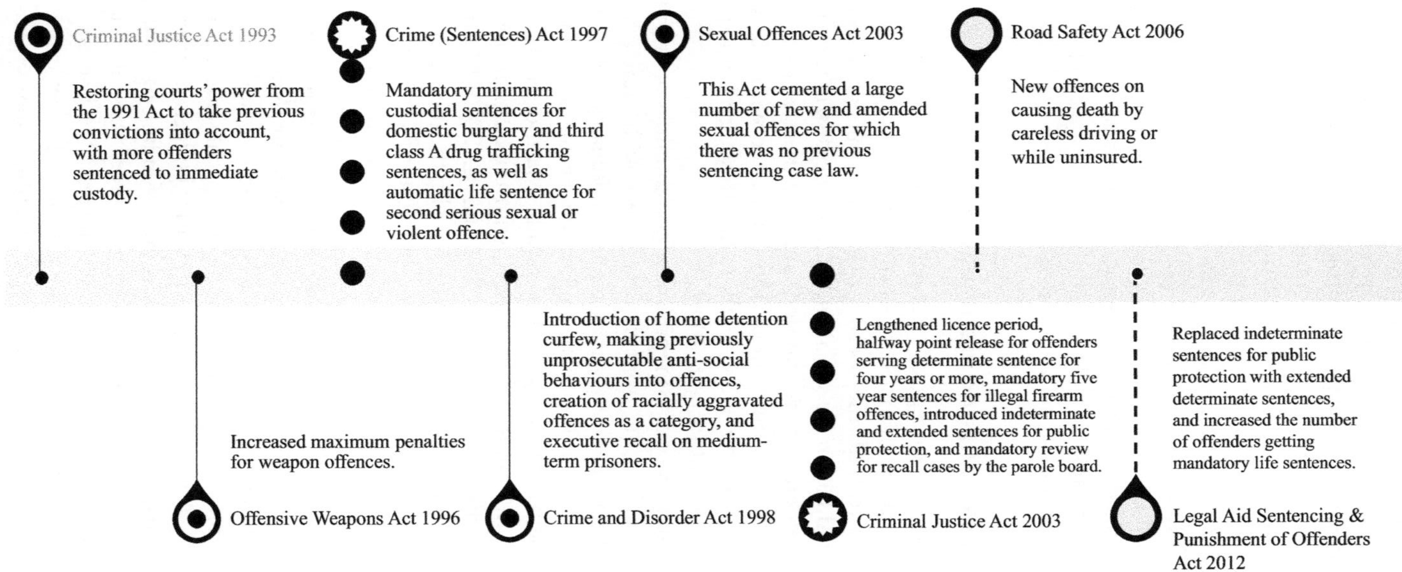

Figure 4.1 Key legislative changes from the 1990s that increased volumes of individuals entering prisons and their length of stay

The Ministry of Justice (2019c) also highlighted that offence groups that rarely receive home detention curfew or release on licence—including those convicted of violence against the person, drug offences, and sexual offenders—had the largest impact on increasing the prison population. Successful prosecutions for sexual offences and continued incarceration of those imprisoned under indeterminate sentences (a total of 2,223 prisoners)—despite being abolished as an option in 2012—also contribute to the rising prison population (Prison Reform Trust, 2020). Given declining crime rates in England and Wales since the mid-1990s, the increase in the average incarceration period reflects not a need. Instead, it reflects an unabated punitive legislative framework, public opinion concerning criminal activities, and politicians eager to please the public through a tough-on-crime policy (Hough and Roberts, 2012).

Habitus, importation, and deprivation

Pierre Bourdieu's (1977) concept of class habitus describes the learned set of dispositions, acquired through socialisation and experience, by which individuals orient themselves towards the social world. The concept reflects how the dispositions of individuals create social and cultural class structure, the impacts of people living in different communities, and how these impacts lead to different lifestyles and life outcomes. Social issues associated with relative deprivation, including imprisonment, are strongly linked to society's unequal income distribution (Wilkinson and Pickett, 2009).

Poor health in prisons derives from prisoners' communities of origin (Spencer, 2001). Prisoners tend to come from deprived areas with entrenched poverty. These experiences determine inequalities in health (Williams, 1995). Indeed, the more deprived the neighbourhood, the higher the chance of having social and environmental problems presenting risks to health (Marmot et al., 2008). Austerity significantly compounds such problems, with implications most severe in deprived areas where the need is greatest (Clifford et al., 2013; Marmot, 2020).

The government's concentrated budget cuts have hit the most deprived regions hardest (Beatty and Fothergill, 2017; Taylor-Robinson and Gosling, 2011). Those include areas that in previous generations depended on employment in mines, steelworks, and shipbuilding. These never fully recovered from the deindustrialisation of the 1980s or the failure of the miners' strike and the long decline of working-class agency through the trade union movement (Milne, 2014). Such areas suffer greater premature mortality (Taylor-Robinson and Gosling, 2011), and much clearer patterns of social deprivation and spatial segregation (Marmot, 2020; Pacione, 1997). A reduction in local authority budgets between 2010 and 2015 and a further 56% reduction in central grant funding to local authorities between 2015 and 2020 (HM Treasury, 2015) reinforced these inequalities.

In the United States, austerity has slowly increased crime in deindustrialised communities. American criminologists have found street crime rises with unemployment; after a lag period of deindustrialisation, more serious criminality develops (Linkon and Russo, 2002). Additionally, between 2001 and 2014, deindustrialisation and incarceration in the United States subtracted roughly two and a half years from the lifespan of the poor, pointing to their role as major health determinants (Nosrati et al., 2018). Furthermore, recessions are cyclical, and each impacts these groups more harshly and makes recovery more difficult (Clark and Heath, 2014). Researchers are yet to replicate these US studies in the UK, but they have linked rising incarceration with government decisions to withdraw from a welfare-based approach to solving social problems (Drake, 2018).

According to Ben Crewe (2005), imprisonment provides an opportunity to improve prisoners' physical and psychological health. This view is consistent with Erving Goffman's (1968) importation theory that prisoners bring their life experiences with them into prison and that these experiences must be addressed during imprisonment. We can see the failure of the welfare state in this situation: citizens' healthcare needs remain so underserved in the community that imprisonment is an improvement.

In his classic study of a maximum-security prison, Gresham Sykes (1958) described imprisonment as the deprivation of physical liberty, goods and services, sexual relations, autonomy, and security. Prisons diminish prisoners' self-worth. Because this deprivation inflicts pain and hardship on prisoners, it contradicts the health values of autonomy, participation, and empowerment (Woodall, 2012). Contrary to the observation that imprisonment merely deprives prisoners of their liberty (Sparks, 1996), deprivation techniques—such as exclusion and social isolation—seek to remove prisoners' individual control and disempowers them, harming mental health and exacerbating feelings of anxiety and hopelessness (Kurki and Morris, 2001). As discussed, prisoners with mental health issues are often criminalised, but the oppressive structure of imprisonment can worsen these issues. Despite the recognition that prisons can improve prisoners' health, these institutions remain unidimensional, existing primarily to punish.

Prison health during the era of austerity

Because prisoners often experience ill-health pre-incarceration, the government imposing strict austerity leads to insensitivity towards prisoners' needs, compounding their pains of imprisonment. This is visible in reports post-2010 that correlate austerity with prison healthcare inaccessibility, degrading living conditions, unavailability of purposeful activities, and rising violence. Collectively, these hinder the aspirations of health and well-being in prisons. Daily healthcare delivery depends highly on a stable prison regime, which is currently deteriorating. This section explores that dynamic.

Impeding access to prison healthcare

Reports by the HMIP, CPT, and Nuffield Trust document the regular cancellation of prisoners' imperative hospital appointments owing to the lack of available discipline officers to escort them to their appointments. Indeed, the reduced number of prison officers has created up to a 12-week delay for the assessment and treatment of prisoners with mental health-related issues in HMP Foston Hall in Derbyshire and HMP Bronzefield in Surrey (HMIP, 2017). Additional observations by the CPT of severe delays in transferring prisoners to psychiatric hospitals and inappropriate placement of acute mental health prisoners in segregation units are rife (CPT, 2017, 2020a). Further, the CPT noted insufficient general healthcare coverage in HMP Doncaster, where a single general practitioner served over 1,000 detainees; there were also several vacant posts within prison healthcare and substance misuse teams (CPT, 2017, 2020a). The Nuffield Trust (2020) stated that 40% of prisoners' outpatient appointments (32,987) were not attended—more than double the number in the general population. Also, over 75% of missed appointments were partly due to lack of staff, costing the NHS £2 million (ibid.).

This inadequate health and social care support risks breaching Article 3 of the European Convention of Human Rights. This article bans torture and inhumane or degrading treatment or punishment. In two cases where a complainant accused the UK of violating Article 3, *McGlinchey v United Kingdom* (2003) 37 EHRR 41 and *Price v United Kingdom* (2001) ECHR 453, the court held that the state has a literal obligation to protect detainees' health and well-being. This is particularly so when a prisoner is at raised vulnerability following severe health concerns—something increasingly prevalent in English prisons. Article 3 describes absolute rights that the government cannot neglect, even in times of war or other public emergencies. Therefore, the principles from *McGlinchey* and *Price* bind national authorities with a duty to develop and apply the common law consistently with the convention. The conditions reported by HMIP, CPT, and Nuffield Trust clearly violated these obligations, though no material improvement has resulted.

Degrading living conditions

Prison overcrowding imposes degrading living conditions on English prisoners. Lengthy confinement within locked and poorly maintained cells can accelerate disease progression. Prisoners in HMP Doncaster and HMP Liverpool suffered from overcapacity: 152% and 112% beyond the certified normal accommodation rate, respectively, along with unsanitary cells (CPT, 2020a). These circumstances included pest and vermin infestations and dilapidated bathroom facilities, with no plans for refurbishment due to inadequate funding (HMIP, 2017). Additionally, at HMP Pentonville, most prisoners live, eat, and sleep in cells designed for single use, with filthy toilets either partially or totally unscreened (CPT, 2017).

Such conditions are evidence that the overall prison regime is inhumane or degrading. Two cases that applied Article 3 in Greece and one in Bulgaria, *Dougoz v Greece* (2002) 34 EHRR 61, *Peers v Greece* (2001) 33 EHRR 51, and *Kehayov v Bulgaria* (application no. 41035/98), suggest such inimical conditions in English prisons also violate Article 3. The point of law in *Karalevicius v Lithuania* (application no. 53254/99) and *Staykov v Bulgaria* (application no.

49438/99) stipulates that a lack of financial resources does not absolve the state from its obligations to protect prisoners from inhumane or degrading treatment.

Lack of access to purposeful activities

Staff shortages limit prisoners' access to purposeful activities. Despite a recommendation that prisoners should spend at least eight hours per day outside their cells, prisoners in HMP Winchester in Hampshire and HMP Wormwood Scrubs in London spent up to 22 hours per day in their cells without opportunity for educational or social activities (CPT, 2017). Additionally, the HMIP has found that prisoners in HMP Full Sutton (York), HMP Elimley (Kent), and HMP Swinfen Hall (Staffordshire) had very limited time outside their cells to demonstrate behavioural improvements (HMIP, 2017). Moreover, in HMP Pentonville, 36% of prisoners struggled to participate in textile and art workshops, sports, and internal employment (CPT, 2017). Although employed prisoners at each prison the CPT visited in 2019 saw improvements in out-of-cell time, unemployed prisoners were spending 21 to 23 hours a day confined to their cells (CPT, 2020a).

Collectively, these incidents contradict the HMIP's expectation that prisoners should be unlocked for at least ten hours a day—indeed, only 3% of prisoners realised this goal (HMIP, 2019). The lack of access to purposeful activities is not inhumane, but it also imperils prisoners' health, especially their mental health. Self-inflicted deaths in prisons per capita increased 37% between March 2010 and March 2020 (Figure 4.2) (House of Commons Library, 2017). Purposeful

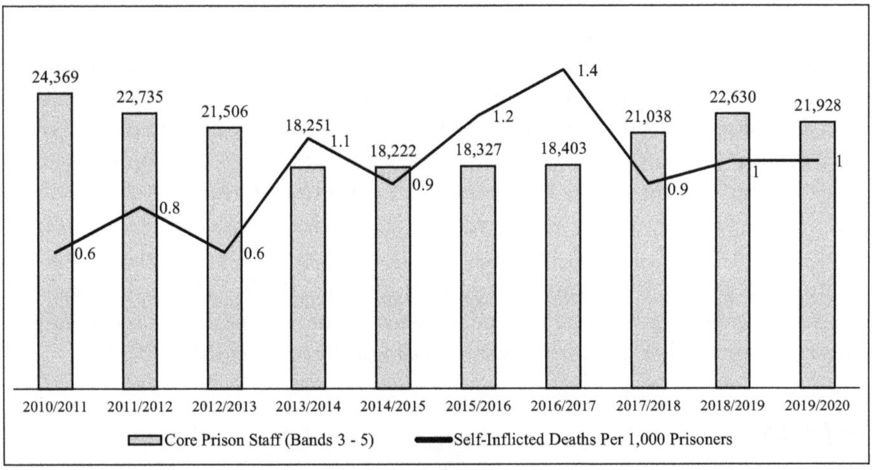

Figure 4.2 Self-inflicted deaths per 1,000 prisoners compared to the number of core prison staff

Source: Ministry of Justice (2020a, 2020c).

activities might help prisoners deal with the boredom and stress of imprisonment productively (HMIP, 2017). The failure to provide opportunities for education, employment, training, and volunteering suggests the government has minimal interest in using rehabilitation to reduce incarceration rates.

Increasing violence

Research directly links the growing number of violent episodes in English prisons with the decreasing staff numbers. The National Tactical Response Group deployed tactical intervention teams in response to hostage-taking and concerted riot incidents, which showed an increase of between 30 and 40 times a month in 2015, and 60 times a month in 2019 (House of Commons Justice Committee, 2016; Parliament UK, 2020a). Also, nearly 2,000 deliberate fires were reported in 2015, a 57% increase from the previous year (Ministry of Justice, 2017). The fires prompted former Prime Minister David Cameron to describe the English prison system as "scandalous", "failing", and "shameful" (Prime Minister's Office, 2016).

Worse, prisoners in both HMP Doncaster and HMP Pentonville complained prison staff responded slowly to violent incidents. Such slow response fuelled an atmosphere of fear and a distrust in the ability of prison management and staff to maintain institutional safety (CPT, 2017). Such distrust may be warranted: several violent incidents were found inadequately reported or reported as less serious than they were (ibid.). As such, a true picture of the situation's severity in English prisons went unrecorded. Essentially, the CPT recommended that the UK government invest more in English prisons to prevent violence from becoming a norm and calibrate strategies to ensure staff can control prisons (ibid.).

Despite some politicians acknowledging the precarious conditions in English prisons, safety in custody measures have continued to deteriorate. According to the HMIP (2017), violent incidents in English prisons have worsened since 2012, both in volume and severity. The number of assaults has increased 53% since 2010 (Figure 4.3): at the end of March 2020, there were 31,568 recorded assaults, including between prisoners and against staff (Ministry of Justice, 2020b). Moreover, this will likely be an underestimate given inadequate reporting practice across prisons (CPT, 2020a), and the number of assaults is rising even with the addition of new staff (Ministry of Justice, 2020a, 2020b, 2020c). Beyond the direct impact on the victims, violent incidents create a general feeling of danger among prisoners that has a negative psychological impact (HMIP, 2017).

Self-harm

The Ministry of Justice Safety in Custody Statistics Bulletins registers incidents of self-harm. It shows a 61% increase in the number of incidents between March 2010 and March 2020 (Figure 4.4, Ministry of Justice, 2020b). Like the assault figures, these are likely underestimations given the poor recording practice across prisons. Self-harm in prison is a risk factor for self-inflicted deaths (Hawton

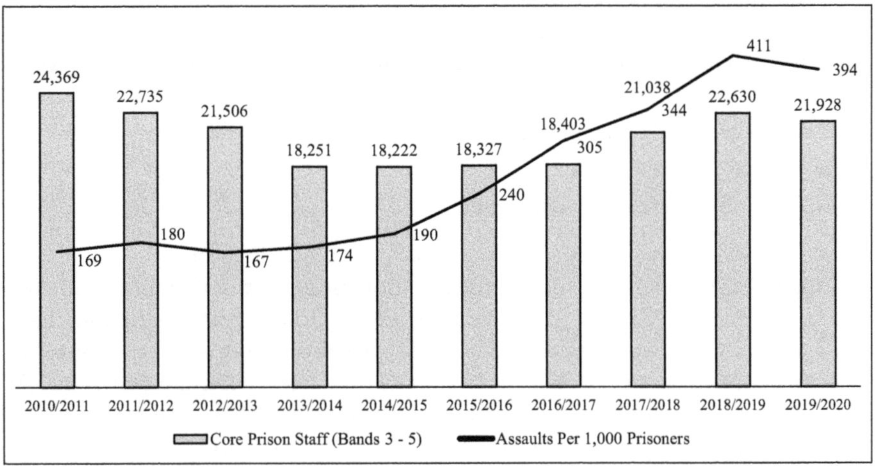

Figure 4.3 Assaults per 1,000 prisoners compared to the number of core prison staff

Source: Ministry of Justice (2020b, 2020c).

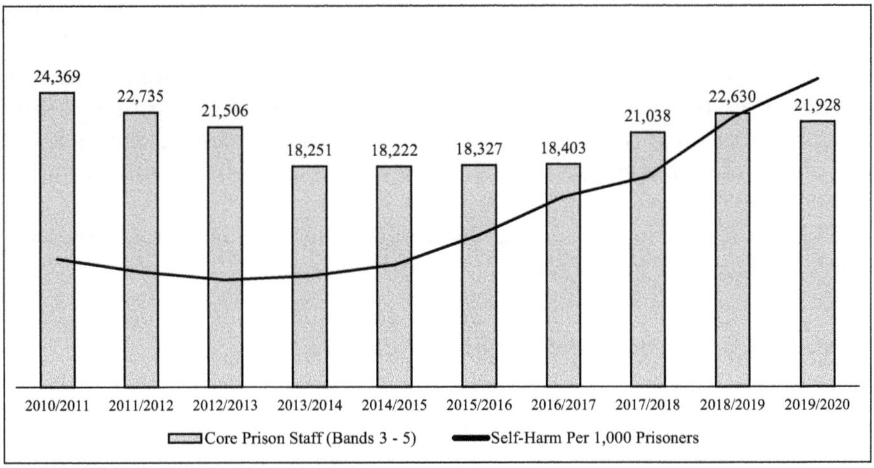

Figure 4.4 Self-harm per 1,000 prisoners compared to the number of core prison staff

Source: Ministry of Justice (2020b, 2020c).

et al., 2014). A systematic review of 34 studies identifying other clinical, psychosocial, and environmental risk factors for suicide in prison determined the following as key precursors: recent suicidal ideation, psychosis, depression, alcohol misuse, a sense of hopelessness, family history of suicide, poor social support, and prior experience of the death of a partner or a child (Marzano et al., 2016).

While the statistics of self-harm, assault, and self-inflicted deaths are routinely grouped together as a coherent whole, this lens has real limitations. It obscures a tremendous diversity in how different prisons and different groups of prisoners experience austerity. Without this knowledge, there is a danger we will treat prisoners as homogenous and pigeonhole them into a category.

Novel psychoactive substances

Drug use has long been a central feature of prison life. Reasons for use include prolonged engagement with drug use pre-imprisonment, self-medication, and as a time "killer" (Crewe, 2005; Penfold et al., 2005). Staff reductions have also hampered the policing of illicit drugs in prison, and novel psychoactive substances (NPS), such as *Spice* and *Black Mamba*, are becoming prevalent. At the end of the fiscal year 2019, authorities had seized these substances 6,699 times, a dramatic increase from the 15 recorded seizures in 2010 (Ministry of Justice, 2019b).

These drugs have been increasingly linked to medical emergencies and violence, and to increases in organised crime and prison gangs operating both within and without the prison walls. In his transnational study, David Skarbek (2011) reveals that criminal groups create and administer the governance of institutions. Although previous research suggested such groups are less entrenched in English prisons compared with foreign prisons (Maitra, 2010), recent research indicates otherwise. Sophisticated financial trading and easy consumption (Gooch and Treadwell, 2020) have enabled organised crime and prison gangs to engage in coercion, violence, and usury, and facilitate overdoses. This criminal activity decreases the legitimacy of prison authority. Though the National Drug Strategy (HM Government, 2017) created a plan to address the growing presence of NPS in prisons via intelligence, treatment, and legislative measures, it has yet to achieve this aim.

Crisis response under the neoliberal agenda

The government has responded to crises in English prisons through investment, but only when spending coheres with its neoliberal vision of recruiting more prison officers and building more prisons. Following a speech at the Conservative Party conference in 2016, the former Justice Minister Liz Truss allocated £291 million to recruit 2,500 additional prison officers (Ministry of Justice, 2016). This reform was incorporated into the Prison Safety and Reform White Paper 2016, which also sought, among other things, to enhance the commissioning autonomy of prison governors, increase the transparency of prison monitoring, and build new community prisons for women (Ministry of Justice, 2016). While the UK General Election in June 2017 halted most proposals from this White Paper, subsequent justice ministers have advanced the policy implementation on staffing levels.

Former Prison Minister Rory Stewart further allocated £10 million to reduce violence and restrict drugs in ten underperforming prisons (Ministry of Justice, 2018). The government managed to recruit an extra 4,500 prison officers from September 2016 to September 2019 (Parliament UK, 2020b). Although prison officer numbers are nearly at the same level as seven years ago, the workforce is now much less experienced. In March 2019, 50% of prison officers had under five years' experience, compared with 22% in March 2010 (Institute for Government, 2019). Just under half (46%) had at least ten years' experience, down from 56% in 2010 (ibid.). As the HMIP (2019) observed, new and inexperienced staff sometimes struggle to challenge poor prisoner behaviour.

The government responded to the CPT's (2017) statements of concern by unveiling a plan to build enough prisons to house 7,000 additional prisoners (CPT, 2018). Also, a follow-up inspection in 2019 prompted plans for further space to accommodate an extra 20,000 prisoners (CPT, 2020b). In response to the CPT's (2020a) recommendation to reduce the rate of imprisonment, the government asserted it should never be subject to an arbitrary rate. These super-prisons do not seem to eliminate existing overcrowding and degrading living conditions in English prisons. David Garland (2001) argued building new prisons can potentially lead to more imprisonment, which does nothing to address the effect of austerity on prison institutions. Building more prisons signifies a motivation to use imprisonment as a tool of social control and to manage communities perceived as risky. These motives accord with neoliberal ideology but fail to improve the safety of English citizens and the health of prisoners.

For 2020/2021, the government recommended a 4.9% increase (in today's monetary value) in the Ministry of Justice's budget, a commitment of £2.5 billion to build an additional 10,000 prison spaces, and an extra £100 million to introduce body scanners in prisons (HM Treasury, 2019). Although partially seeking to address concerns over drugs and violence, these removed the focus from the existing issue of chronic overcrowding and degrading living conditions in English prisons.

Summary

This chapter highlighted the expanding health disparities within the growing and increasingly diverse prison population in England. Because the current political economic system prioritises neoliberalism over moral and ethical standards, prisoners suffer a lack of access to acceptable healthcare and purposeful activities, substandard living conditions, and increasing and uncurbed violence. This creates ongoing instability in English prisons, hampers the rehabilitation agenda, and increases the likelihood of breaching the principles of the European Convention of Human Rights. The state's inadequate and inept response to the crisis and its limitations, unless vigorously challenged then modified, will continue to support human rights violations against prisoners and their health.

But, to understand more granular patterns of how austerity manifests on prisons and prison healthcare, we require much bigger data than that in the existing research. The current literature explored so far clarifies the effects of the government implementing austerity measures from the top down across the public sector, including prisons, and the potential breach of international obligations that seek to protect prisoners' entitlement to health. However, it does not contextualise austerity's impact on prison health governance and delivery in England. It is towards this black box of explanation that my investigation now turns.

References

Baybutt, M., Acin, E., Hayton, P. and Dooris, M. (2014) Promoting Health in Prisons: A Settings Approach. In: Enggist, S., Møller, L., Galea, G. and Udesen C., eds. *Prisons and Health*. Copenhagen: World Health Organization, pp. 180–184.

Beatty, C. and Fothergill, S. (2017) The Impact on Welfare and Public Finances of Job Loss in Industrial Britain. *Regional Studies, Regional Science*. 4(1), pp. 161–180.

Bentham, J. (1864) *Theory of Legislation*. London: Trubner and Co.

Bourdieu, P. (1977) *Outline of a Theory of Practice* (translated by Nice, R.). Cambridge: Cambridge University Press.

Buxton, T. F. S. (1818) *An Inquiry, Whether Crime and Misery are Produced or Prevented, By Our Present System of Prison Discipline*. London: John and Arthur Arch, Butterworth and Sons, and John Hatchard.

Cheliotis, L. K. and Xenakis, S. (2021) What's Left? Political Orientation, Economic Conditions and Incarceration in Greece Under Syriza-Led Government. *European Journal of Criminology*. 18(1), pp. 74–100.

Clark, T. and Heath, A. (2014) *Hard Times: The Divisive Toll of the Economic Slump*. London: Yale University Press.

Clifford, D., Geyne-Rahme, F. and Mohan, J. (2013) Variations Between Organisations and Localities in Government Funding of Third-Sector Activity Evidence from the National Survey of Third-Sector Organisations in England. *Urban Studies*. 50(5), pp. 959–976.

Committee for the Prevention of Torture and Inhuman or Degrading Treatment or Punishment (2017) *Report to the Government of the United Kingdom on the Visit to the United Kingdom Carried Out by the European Committee for the Prevention of Torture and Inhuman or Degrading Treatment or Punishment from 30 March to 12 April 2016* [Online], available from: https://rm.coe.int/168070a773 (Accessed: 11th January 2018).

Committee for the Prevention of Torture and Inhuman or Degrading Treatment or Punishment (CPT) (2018) *Response of the Government of the United Kingdom to the Report of the European Committee for the Prevention of Torture and Inhuman or Degrading Treatment or Punishment (CPT) on its Visit to the United Kingdom from 30 March to 12 April 2016* [Online], available from: https://rm.coe.int/pdf/168077fa13 (Accessed: 12th April 2018).

Committee for the Prevention of Torture and Inhuman or Degrading Treatment or Punishment (2020a) *Report to the United Kingdom Government on the Visit to the United Kingdom Carried Out by the European Committee for the Prevention of Torture and Inhuman or Degrading Treatment or Punishment (CPT) from 13 to 23 May 2019* [Online], available from: https://rm.coe.int/16809e4404 (Accessed: 27th May 2020).

Committee for the Prevention of Torture and Inhuman or Degrading Treatment or Punishment (CPT) (2020b) *Response of the United Kingdom Government to the Report of the*

European Committee for the Prevention of Torture and Inhuman or Degrading Treatment or Punishment (CPT) on its Visit to the United Kingdom from 13 to 23 May 2019 [Online], available from: https://rm.coe.int/16809e4406 (Accessed: 25th January 2021).

Cordeiro-Rodrigues, L. (2020) Social Justice for Public Health: The COVID-19 Response in Portugal. *Bioethical Inquiry*. 17, pp. 669–674.

Crewe, B. (2005) *The Prisoner Society: Power, Adaptation, and Social Life in an English Prison*. Oxford: Oxford University Press.

Davey Smith, G., Dorling, D. and Shaw, M., eds. (2001) *Poverty, Inequality and Health in Britain: 1800–2000—A Reader*. Bristol: Policy Press.

Dolan, K., Wirtz, A. L., Moazen, B., Ndeffo-Mbah, M., Galvani, A., Kinner, S. A., Courtney, R., McKee, M., Amon, J. J., Maher, L., Hellard, M., Beyrer, C. and Altice, F. L. (2016) Global Burden of HIV, Viral Hepatitis, and Tuberculosis in Prisoners and Detainees. *Lancet*. 388, pp. 1089–1102.

Drake, D. (2018) Prisons and State Building: Promoting "The Fiasco of the Prison" in a Global Context. *International Journal for Crime, Justice and Social Democracy*. 7(4), pp. 1–15.

Fazel, S., Hayes, A. J., Bartellas, K., Clerici, M. and Trestman, R. (2016) The Mental Health of Prisoners: A Review of Prevalence, Adverse Outcomes and Interventions. *Lancet Psychiatry*. 3(9), pp. 871–881.

Garland, D. (2001) *The Culture of Control: Crime and Social Order in Contemporary Society*. Oxford: Oxford University Press.

Goffman, E. (1968) *Asylums: Essays on the Social Situation of Mental Patients and Other Inmates*. Chicago: Aldine Transaction.

Gonnella, P. (2013) Italy: Between Amnesties and Emergencies. In: Ruggiero, V. and Ryan, M., eds. *Punishment in Europe: A Critical Anatomy of Penal Systems*. Basingstoke: Palgrave Macmillan, pp. 226–244.

Gooch, K. and Treadwell, J. (2020) Prisoner Society in an Era of Psychoactive Substances, Organized Crime, New Drug Markets and Austerity. *The British Journal of Criminology*. 60(5), pp. 1260–1281.

The Guardian (2019) *Dutch Court Blocks Extradition of Man to 'Inhumane' UK Prisons* [Online], available from: www.theguardian.com/world/2019/may/10/dutch-court-blocks-extradition-of-man-to-inhumane-uk-prisons (Accessed: 25th January 2021).

Hawton, K., Linsell, L., Adeniji, T., Sariaslan, A. and Fazel, S. (2014) Self-harm in Prisons in England and Wales: An Epidemiological Study of Prevalence, Risk Factors, Clustering, and Subsequent Suicide. *The Lancet*. 383(9923), pp. 1147–1154.

HM Government (2017) *2017 Drug Strategy: July 2017* [Online], available from: HM Inspectorate of Prisons (2017) *HM Chief Inspector of Prisons for England and Wales Annual Report 2016–17* [Online], available from: www.gov.uk/government/uploads/system/uploads/attachment_data/file/629719/hmip-annual-report-2016-17.pdf (Accessed: 11th January 2018).

HM Inspectorate of Prisons (2017) *HM Chief Inspector of Prisons for England and Wales Annual Report 2016–17* [Online], available from: www.gov.uk/government/uploads/system/uploads/attachment_data/file/629719/hmip-annual-report-2016-17.pdf (Accessed: 11th January 2018).

HM Inspectorate of Prisons (2019) *HM Chief Inspector of Prisons for England and Wales: Annual Report 2018–19* [Online], available from: www.justiceinspectorates.gov.uk/hmiprisons/wp-content/uploads/sites/4/2019/07/6.5563_HMI-Prisons-AR_2018-19_WEB_FINAL_040719.pdf (Accessed: 25th January 2021).

HM Treasury (2015) *A Country that Lives Within its Means: Spending Review 2015* [Online], available from: www.gov.uk/government/uploads/system/uploads/attachment_data/

file/447101/a_country_that_lives_within_its_means.pdf www.england.nhs.uk/commissioning/health-just/liaison-and-diversion/ld-faqs/ (Accessed: 12th April 2018).

HM Treasury (2019) *Spending Round 2019* [Online], available from: https://assets.publishing.service.gov.uk/government/uploads/system/uploads/attachment_data/file/829177/Spending_Round_2019_web.pdf (Accessed: 25th January 2021).

Hough, M. and Roberts, J. V. (2012) Public Opinion, Crime, and Criminal Justice. In: Morgan, R., Maguire, M. and Reiner, R., eds. *Oxford Handbook of Criminology*. 5th ed. Oxford: Oxford University Press, pp. 279–300.

House of Commons Committee of Public Accounts (2017) *Mental Health in Prisons: Eighth Report of Session 2017–19* [Online], available from: https://publications.parliament.uk/pa/cm201719/cmselect/cmpubacc/400/400.pdf (Accessed: 11th January 2018).

House of Commons Health and Social Care Committee (2018) *Prison Health: Twelfth Report of Session 2017–19* [Online], available from: https://publications.parliament.uk/pa/cm201719/cmselect/cmhealth/963/963.pdf (Accessed: 20th April 2019).

House of Commons Justice Committee (2016) *Indicators of Prison Safety* [Online], available from: https://publications.parliament.uk/pa/cm201516/cmselect/cmjust/625/62505.htm#footnote-051 (Accessed: 10th August 2018).

House of Commons Library (2017) *UK Prison Population Statistics: Briefing Paper Number SN/SG/04334, 20 April 2017* [Online], available from: http://researchbriefings.files.parliament.uk/documents/SN04334/SN04334.pdf (Accessed: 11th January 2018).

Institute for Government (2019) *Prisons* [Online], available from: www.instituteforgovernment.org.uk/publication/performance-tracker-2019/prisons#:~:text=In%20March%202019%2C%2050%25%20of,high%20of%2066%25%20in%202014 (Accessed: 21st February 2020).

Institute for Public Policy Research (2019) *Ending the Blame Game: The Case for a New Approach to Public Health and Prevention* [Online], available from: www.ippr.org/files/2019-06/public-health-and-prevention-june19.pdf (Accessed: 25th January 2021).

Kurki, L. and Morris, N. (2001) The Purposes, Practices and Problems of Supermax Prisons. *Crime and Justice*. 28, pp. 1–21.

Lamble, S. (2012) Rethinking Gendered Prison Policies: Impacts on Transgender Prisoners. *ECAN Bulletin*. 16, pp. 7–12.

Linkon, S. L. and Russo, J. (2002) *Steeltown U.S.A.: Work and Memory in Youngstown*. Lawrence: University Press of Kansas.

Maitra, D. M. (2010) An Exploratory Study of Prison Gangs in Contemporary Society. In: Harding, S. and Palasinski, M., eds. *Psychological Perspectives on Youth Gang Behaviour*. Hershey, PA: APMHBS Book Series, pp. 1–28.

Marmot, M. (2005) Social Determinants of Health Inequalities. *Lancet*. 365, pp. 1099–1104.

Marmot, M. (2020) *Health Equity in England: The Marmot Review 10 Years On* [Online], available from: www.health.org.uk/sites/default/files/upload/publications/2020/Health%20Equity%20in%20England_The%20Marmot%20Review%2010%20Years%20On_full%20report.pdf (Accessed: 25th January 2021).

Marmot, M., Friel, S., Bell, R., Houweling, T. A. J. and Taylor, S. (2008) Closing the Gap in a Generation: Health Equity through Action on the Social Determinants of Health. *The Lancet*. 372(9650), pp. 1661–1669.

Marzano, L., Hawton, K., Rivlin, A., Smith, E. N., Piper, M. and Fazel, S. (2016) Prevention of Suicidal Behavior in Prisons: An Overview of Initiatives Based on a Systematic Review of Research on Near-Lethal Suicide Attempts. *Crisis*. 37, pp. 323–334.

Milne, S. (2014) *The Enemy Within: The Secret War Against the Miners*. London: Verso Books.

Ministry of Justice (2013) *Story of the Prison Population: 1993–2012, England and Wales* [Online], available from: https://assets.publishing.service.gov.uk/government/uploads/system/uploads/attachment_data/file/218185/story-prison-population.pdf (Accessed: 25th January 2021).

Ministry of Justice (2016) *Prison Safety and Reform* [Online], available from: https://assets.publishing.service.gov.uk/government/uploads/system/uploads/attachment_data/file/565014/cm-9350-prison-safety-and-reform-_web_.pdf (Accessed: 23rd July 2021).

Ministry of Justice (2017) *Ministry of Justice: Written Questions: Written Question—66579* [Online], available from: www.parliament.uk/business/publications/written-questions-answers-statements/written-question/Commons/2017-03-06/66579/ (Accessed: 3rd July 2018).

Ministry of Justice (2018) *Minister Announces' 10 Prisons Project' to Develop New Model of Excellence* [Online], available from: www.gov.uk/government/news/minister-announces-10-prisons-project-to-develop-new-model-of-excellence (Accessed: 21st February 2020).

Ministry of Justice (2019a) *Birmingham Prison Contract Ended* [Online], available from: www.gov.uk/government/news/birmingham-prison-contract-ended (Accessed: 21st February 2020).

Ministry of Justice (2019b) *HMPPS Annual Digest 2018/19* [Online], available from: https://assets.publishing.service.gov.uk/government/uploads/system/uploads/attachment_data/file/821148/HMPPS_Annual_Digest_bulletin_2018-2019.pdf (Accessed: 21st February 2020).

Ministry of Justice (2019c) *Home Detention Curfew (HDC) Policy Framework* [Online], available from: https://assets.publishing.service.gov.uk/government/uploads/system/uploads/attachment_data/file/950856/home-detention-curfew-pf.pdf (Accessed: 25th January 2021).

Ministry of Justice (2020a) *Safety in Custody Summary Tables to December 2019* [Online], available from: https://assets.publishing.service.gov.uk/government/uploads/system/uploads/attachment_data/file/893372/safety-in-custody-summary-q4-2019-tables.xlsm (Accessed: 25th January 2021).

Ministry of Justice (2020b) *Safety in Custody Summary Tables to March 2020* [Online], available from: https://assets.publishing.service.gov.uk/government/uploads/system/uploads/attachment_data/file/905014/Safety-in-custody-summary-q1-2020-final-tables.xlsm (Accessed: 25th January 2021).

Ministry of Justice (2020c) *HMPPS Workforce Statistics Bulletin: 31 March 2020 Tables* [Online], available from: https://assets.publishing.service.gov.uk/government/uploads/system/uploads/attachment_data/file/891138/HR-tables-31-March-2020.xlsx (Accessed: 11th January 2018).

National Audit Office (2020) *Improving the Prison Estate* [Online], available from: www.nao.org.uk/wp-content/uploads/2020/02/Improving-the-prison-estate.pdf (Accessed: 25th January 2021).

NHS England (2017) *About Liaison and Diversion Services* [Online], available from: www.england.nhs.uk/commissioning/health-just/liaison-and-diversion/ld-faqs/ (Accessed: 12th April 2018).

Nosrati, E., Ash, M., Marmot, M., McKee, M. and King, L. P. (2018) The Association Between Income and Life Expectancy Revisited: Deindustrialization, Incarceration and the Widening Health Gap. *International Journal of Epidemiology*. 47(3), pp. 720–730.

Nuffield Trust (2020) *Locked Out? Prisoners' Use of Hospital Care* [Online], available from: www.nuffieldtrust.org.uk/files/2020-02/prisoners-use-of-hospital-services-main-report.pdf (Accessed: 25th January 2021).

Pacione, M., ed., (1997) *Britain's Cities: Geographies of Division in Urban Britain*. London: Routledge.

Parliament UK (2020a) *National Tactical Response Group: Question for Ministry of Justice, UIN HL10159, Tabled on 10 November 2020* [Online], available from: https://questions-statements.parliament.uk/written-questions/detail/2020-11-10/HL10159 (Accessed: 25th January 2021).

Parliament UK (2020b) *Prison Governance: Government Response to the Committee's First Report of Session 2019* [Online], available from: https://publications.parliament.uk/pa/cm5801/cmselect/cmjust/150/15002.htm (Accessed: 25th January 2021).

Penfold, C., Turnbull, P. J. and Webster, R. (2005) *Tackling Prison Drug Markets: An Exploratory Qualitative Study*. London: Institute for Criminal Policy Research, King's College London.

Prime Minister's Office (2016) *Prison Reform: Prime Minister's Speech* [Online], available from: www.gov.uk/government/speeches/prison-reform-prime-ministers-speech (Accessed: 3rd July 2018).

Prison Reform Trust (2019) *Bromley Briefings Prison Fact File: A Winter 2019* [Online], available from: www.prisonreformtrust.org.uk/Portals/0/Documents/Bromley%20Briefings/Winter%202019%20Factfile%20web.pdf (Accessed: 1st February 2020).

Prison Reform Trust (2020) *A Helping Hand: Supporting Families in the Resettlement of People Serving IPPs* [Online], available from: www.prisonreformtrust.org.uk/portals/0/documents/A%20helping%20hand.pdf (Accessed: 25th January 2021).

Repullo, J. R. (2014) Healthcare in Prisons: Reflections on the Inertia of Systems and the Low Effectiveness of Health Policies in Spain. *Revista Española de Sanidad Penitenciaria*. 16, pp. 103–109.

Rogan, M. (2013) Prison Policy in Times of Austerity: Lessons from Ireland. *Prison Service Journal*, pp. 1–17.

Skarbek, D. (2011) Governance and Prison Gangs. *American Political Science Review*. 105(4), pp. 702–716.

Sparks, R. (1996) Penal Austerity: The Doctrine of Less Eligibility Reborn? In: Matthews, R. and Francis, P., eds. *Prison 2000: An International Perspective on the Current State and Future of Imprisonment*. Basingstoke: Macmillan, pp. 74–93.

Spencer, A. (2001) *Removing Bars to Good Treatment*. London: NHS.

Stürup-Toft, S., O'Moore, E. J. and Plugge, E. H. (2018) Looking Behind the Bars: Emerging Health Issues for People in Prison. *British Medical Bulletin*. 125, pp. 15–23.

Sykes, G. (1958) *The Society of Captives: A Study of a Maximum Security Prison*. Princeton, NJ: Princeton University Press.

Taylor-Robinson, D. and Gosling, R. (2011) English North—South Divide. Local Authority Budget Cuts and Health Inequalities. *British Medical Journal*. 342, p. d1487.

Tucker, S., Hargreaves, C., Cattermull, M., Roberts, A., Walker, T., Shaw, J. and Challis, D. (2021) The Nature and Extent of Prisoners' Social Care Needs: Do Older Prisoners Require a Different Service Response? *Journal of Social Work*. 21(3), pp. 310–328.

United Nations General Assembly (2019) *Visit to the United Kingdom of Great Britain and Northern Ireland: Report of the Special Rapporteur on Extreme Poverty and Human Rights* [Online], available from: https://undocs.org/A/HRC/41/39/Add.1 (Accessed: 25th January 2021).

Wilkinson, R. G. and Pickett, K. (2009) *The Spirit Level: Why Equality Is Better for Everyone*. London: Penguin.

Williams, S. J. (1995) Theorising Class, Health and Lifestyles: Can Bourdieu Help Us? *Sociology of Health & Illness*. 17, pp. 577–604.

Woodall, J. (2012) Health Promoting Prisons: An Overview and Critique of the Concept. *Prison Service Journal*. 202, pp. 6–11.
World Health Organization (1986) *Ottawa Charter for Health Promotion*. Geneva: WHO.
World Health Organization (2014) *Prisons and Health* [Online], available from: www.euro.who.int/__data/assets/pdf_file/0005/249188/Prisons-and-Health.pdf (Accessed: 12th April 2018).

Chapter 5

Deconstructing the experimental nature of austerity

Introduction

In the remainder of this book, I draw on the experiences of the 87 study participants to illustrate the impacts of austerity on the prison and the prison health systems, as well as on prisoners. Far from merely reproducing their narrative, I both explain and interrogate their experiences on this topic. An overview of these categories is provided in Figure 5.1.

In this chapter, I explore participants' understanding of austerity. I also explore how austerity measures have been operationalised experimentally, which subsequently impacts the policy and delivery of prison healthcare and prison services. Further, I ask participants about the construction of political narratives that have made austerity economically unavoidable but seemingly necessary, and I evidence this claim. I conclude by unpacking participants' views on the execution of austerity programmes in English prisons.

Participants' understanding of austerity

The first interview question I asked participants was, "What does austerity mean to you?" Almost all of them paused to reflect on it. Comments such as "that is an interesting question" and "I have never thought of that before" were relatively common. Their answers reveal awareness of the political undercurrent of the austerity measures and how these measures have been translated into policymaking and the delivery of prison healthcare and prison services in England. Their accounts depict austerity both as financial cuts and a political ideology, which has been experimentally executed. And they reveal how both perspectives have shaped the policy and delivery of prison healthcare and prison services.

Almost unanimously, participants agreed austerity meant government funding cuts directed at public services. Their definitions included such common phrases as "demand and supply" and "purposeful disinvestments". As illustrated by Participant 43, a research lead of a national think tank:

> We focus on the important relationship between the extent to which demands on the prison service and prison healthcare services have gone

DOI: 10.4324/9781003182337-5

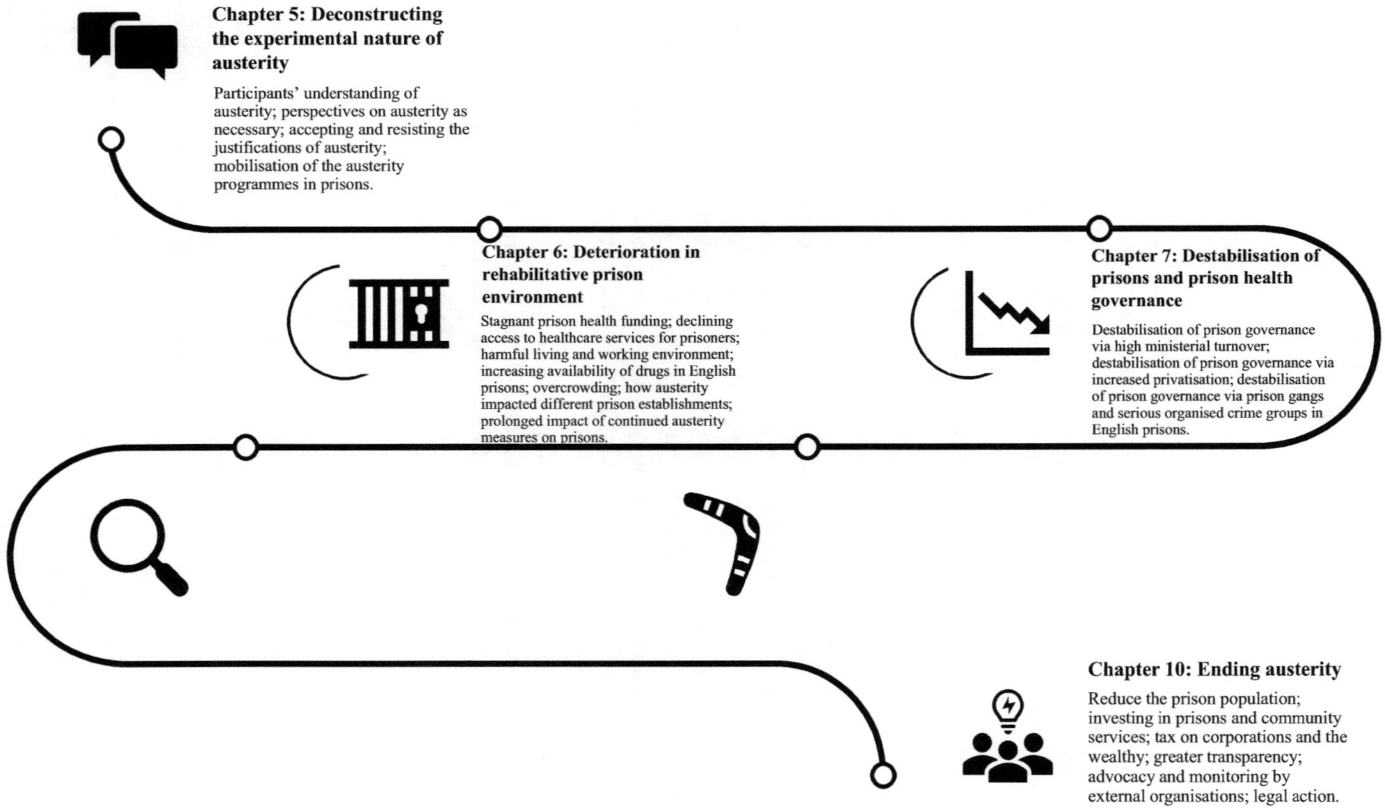

Figure 5.1 Major categories derived from the study analysis

> up at the same rate as, or faster than, the spending they see. To put this in simpler terms, these services have not seen the spending that they need to match the demand at the same time.

To Participant 41, a regional prison director of a justice ministry, austerity meant a tight control of financial expenditures from one year to another:

> I associate austerity with tight control of spending. Usually, in our business, that means that less is spent on running prisons, and that particularly impacted snacking budgets—certainly in the period from about 2012 to 2016 or 2017. That meant we were going to year-on-year producing budgets. That is what austerity meant to me on a practical basis.

Moreover, phrases such as "overstretched and under-resourced services" (Participant 59, senior prison officer of a closed prison with an urgent notification status) and "no flexibility in the budget, compared to the pre-austerity era" (Participant 75, prison governor of a closed prison with an urgent notification status) were common.

Most participants' understanding of austerity paralleled the early definitions of it as strict financial discipline (Anderson and Minneman, 2014; Fontana and Sawyer, 2011; Schui, 2015). These early definitions also intersect with the UK government's claim that decreasing state spending will stimulate economic growth (Gamble, 2014). On the surface, such reasoning appears definitive, pragmatic, and free from ideology, while creating the opportunity to raise doubts about the financial sustainability of the welfare state, which is politically strategic (Farnsworth and Irving, 2018).

Often, participants, irrespective of their governance level, linked the imposition of austerity to the political ideology of the current government. Several participants mocked politicians' justifications of austerity. They referred to such political rhetoric as "maxing out the national credit card" and "the need to balance the economy", as is exemplified by the following excerpts:

> The way in which politicians like George Osborne[1] talk: "We have maxed out the national credit card". That is just economically illiterate. That is a whole pile of bollocks, but, of course, people buy that reason that if we have spent up to the whole limit on our credit card, then we have to pay it back.
>
> (Participant 10, an academic and advisor to a European anti-torture organisation)

> These politicians have never to my satisfaction justified long-term austerity. They tend to revert back to the balancing the books thing that is based on their neoliberal ideology. Now, a well-managed economy is versatile. You can do different things with it depending on the needs of the day and

> also long-term prospects. Balancing the books is such a primitive approach to economic management.
>
> (Participant 15, an academic and former Cabinet Office advisor)

Their cynicism mirrors the extant political economy literature. That literature points to the UK government's voluntary, pre-emptive deflation efforts in contrast to the mandatory deflation that the Troika inflicted on Greece, Ireland, and Portugal as part of their bailout conditions (Gamble, 2014). There was no requirement for the implementation of austerity in the UK (ibid.). Yet, despite lacking any economic evidence, the politicians experimented with their own version of austerity, signalling British exceptionalism. Based on participants' understanding, misleading political narratives focused on the need to balance the economy by allowing the financial market to dictate a decrease in public sector spending that would avoid an increase in taxes to ensure that the government could continue to borrow at reasonable interest rates (Gamble, 2014).

Some participants also ridiculed the claim that austerity reduces debts. Instead, they argued austerity does not reduce debt, and that national debts increased despite austerity. In fact, participants argued that national debts increased despite austerity.

> I am all for living within our means, but this government have actually borrowed more than the previous government ever did. They cut public services, they bring in austerity, they cut benefits, they target the most vulnerable in society, and they are still borrowing more as a government than we ever have. What is going on?
>
> (Participant 64, head of prison officers' union)

This assertion is similar to the observation of how austerity measures in Romania, Estonia, Bulgaria, Latvia, and Lithuania coincided with increasing debt (Blyth, 2013). Likewise, the UK debt ballooned rather than dissipated after a decade of austerity. The debt-to-GDP ratio was 74.7% in 2010 before austerity hit the economy (Office for National Statistics, 2021). By 2019, the ratio had increased to 84.6% (ibid.).

Debt was a vehicle for imposing austerity measures. Yet a decade of austerity has created an annual financial gap in state finances of £180bn per year for the UK government, following several high-profile bank bailouts suggestive of corporative welfare (Farnsworth, 2018). These included the Royal Bank of Scotland, Lloyds TSB, and HBOS. Such a contradiction also exposes the distinctiveness of neo-austerity following the 2008 financial crisis: despite the effort to restrict public spending to prevent burgeoning national deficits, austerity has enabled measures to support and promote private actor interests (Farnsworth and Irving, 2018).

While recognising the economic failings of austerity, participants also saw it as a vehicle to advance a political ideology. Participant 50, head of the legal department of a national penal reform organisation, clarified that economic rationing has always been political:

> So, irrespective of how the economy is performing or ways in which the economy could be managed, the way actually it is being managed, and the way the decisions are made all come down to being political decisions.

Drawing on the participants' understanding of austerity as political ideology, their accounts illustrate how such an ideology has been used as a vehicle to shape the prison healthcare and prison services. This then brings us to the analysis of how austerity has been framed as necessary.

Perspectives on austerity as necessary

The participants recognised that politicians justified austerity politically by saying it was inevitable. Further, they recognised that politicians failed to analyse austerity's impact before implementing it. As Participant 35, a regional health and justice lead of a national health organisation, put it:

> The [politicians] justified it politically, didn't they? They justified it politically on the basis that we have got less money, and we have all got to make sacrifices. They did not justify it on the basis that they could deliver it. They did not do any kind of analysis of what the impact would be. They had no understanding of what the impact of cutting funding would be and what the impact of that would be on life.

Supporting such claims, both HM Treasury (2018) and O'Dea and Preston (2010) found that assessing the robustness of the distributional impact of spending cuts on public services was impossible. The participants believed ideological belief superseded evidence-based policymaking at all levels of government.

> I do not believe that austerity is about making things more efficient. George Osborne, who was basically the architect of all this financial mess, had a target to reduce state spending . . . a decision that was not based upon cost-benefit analysis. It was a priori an ideological decision that he had taken.
>
> (Participant 10, academic and advisor to a European anti-torture organisation)

> [T]he Ministry of Justice gets their big dollop of money from the Treasury. [It] then decides what way that is going to be carved up, between police, prosecution, courts, probation service, youth justice, community safety

> and prisons. It would be absolutely naïve to expect that the Chancellor, or indeed the Treasury, would have sufficient knowledge or detail, nor do they need to within the Ministry of Justice, about what way that's carved up.
>
> (Participant 22, advisor to a European intergovernmental organisation and head of prison service)

The result of this widespread ignorance about the impacts of austerity therefore meant its implementation was purely experimental. Yet in the words of Participant 35 (a regional health and justice lead of a national health organisation), they reasoned that they had "no alternative but to simply go ahead with the austerity plan of the government".

Additionally, some participants also believed that the government tended to blame previous Labour governments (holding office between 1997 and 2010) for leaving the country in a state of debt, thereby making austerity unavoidable (Gamble, 2014). The blame game is a product of the current government aligning itself with many right-wing economists who argued that the state should suffer the consequences of its financial mismanagement in preceding decades (Panitch and Konings, 2009; Thompson, 2013). This alignment gave the government credibility and signalled that it—unlike its predecessors—was capable of managing finances (Gamble, 2014).

Although the government claimed austerity measures would rectify the financial mistakes of its Labour predecessor, such measures remained in place a decade later, though now more draconian, and the country had more debt. Participant 55 (a prison health lead of a national health organisation and magistrate) stated:

> Whenever I have heard government ministers being challenged about austerity, you will hear the same old broken record of "it is because of the previous Labour government leaving us with debt". Actually, there is only so long you can keep saying that. Is that a good enough excuse for allowing everything to fall apart?

Moreover, several participants also considered this "blame game" a public relations exercise to placate the public by highlighting the necessity of austerity.

A few participants had a nuanced view: framing austerity as a technical economic 'fix' limits the public's ability to engage in the austerity debate. They contrasted the UK's situation with that of Iceland, which held a referendum in March 2010 to ratify bailout packages. These participants argued by setting the terms of the debate and framing austerity as economically inevitable, politicians neutralised the public's efforts to scrutinise the austerity programme. For example, Participant 19 observed:

> These austerity measures are presented but not justified. They are framed as unavoidable. [T]his has effects on the participation of people in politics.

> They cannot scrutinise these political strategies, like Iceland. If you present that something is just a technical issue and not a political issue, there is no space for public engagement. Austerity was presented in such a way.

Despite being presented as an economic imperative, participants perceived austerity measures as politically motivated, riddled with experimental traits. In particular, they felt that such action lacked supporting evidence and that current politicians imputed the measures to the previous administration's fiscal ineptness. They questioned the validity of this political framing.

Accepting and resisting the justifications of austerity

The participants reacted variously to the language the government used to justify austerity as necessary. Their responses ranged from positive and passive acceptance to active resistance. Context drove the reactions, and they varied according to participants' location within the governance and delivery structure of prison healthcare in England.

A small group of participants, notably those within civil service, explicitly accepted austerity as necessary. Their responses focused on prison healthcare and prison service policy and delivery. Several understood austerity as a necessary evil: "[it] makes people more aware that whatever they are doing is limited by the resources that are reducing" (Participant 55, a prison health lead of a national health organisation and magistrate). Others viewed it as an opportunity to streamline service delivery: "identifying what is working within the system, and what is not working, [because] austerity exposes gaps much more" (Participant 35, a regional health and justice lead of a national health organisation).

Civil servants' descriptions frequently included phrases like "living within financial means" and "doing things differently" (Participant 34, the head of a national prison health charity) and "becoming more financial[ly] savvy" (Participant 35, a regional health and justice lead of a national health organisation). The response of these individuals revealed that they perceived the government's justifications for the resource reduction were merely semantics. As Participant 56 said,

> We have always been mindful of our finances. Year-on-year, we have been told to find savings in our budget. Frankly, we have run out of creative ideas on how to support the slogan of "delivering more with less". There is just not enough money in the system.

Unlike opponents of austerity measures, however, these participants did not regard the government's actions as politically motivated.

Other participants demonstrated compliance, believing they could not challenge the situation. As Participant 20, a public health specialist at an international health organisation, stated: "There's no money left. Just put up with it . . . people tend to accept it and try to avoid the subject altogether. Because what's the alternative?" Echoing this stance, Participant 22, an advisor to a European intergovernmental organisation and head of prison service, averred:

> I can simply [say], "Oh, economic austerity is terrible. We can't do this; we can't do that". The fact is we have economic austerity. There is less public service. You can either be one of those people that is "I cannot do my job because I do not have enough money", or you keep going. The fact of the matter is we have got to do our job whether we have enough money or less than enough money. You have got to look at how you do things in order to look at what you can do against what are your real priorities and what is the best and most efficient way to do that. That is a fact of life in public service austerity, because there is no cash cow coming to resolve that.

The interviews evidenced that most policymaking participants avoided using the term "austerity". Instead, they used euphemisms, such as a "lack of funding" (Participant 17, an advisor to a European intergovernmental human rights organisation) or "working under financial pressure" (Participant 4, an advisor to a European intergovernmental human rights organisation), to express the continual austerity challenges they faced. Participant 29, an academic and consultant for an international health organisation, acknowledged this behaviour and stated: "[W]e hardly use the word austerity . . ., but we all know we are working in a resource-constrained environment". They seemed to use such language deliberately to maintain their neutrality and avoid political engagement.

Many participants provided more nuance. They argued the catchphrases of 'efficiency', 'economies of scale', and 'doing more for less' mask the reality that prison healthcare and the prison service were eventually compromised. As Participant 32, a regional health and justice lead of a health organisation, expressed, such language avoided confronting an increased demand for prison healthcare during resource reduction.

> [Health organisations] have been given their budgets against the contracts that they have tendered for with the expectation they will deliver those contracts. We have seen a reduction in staffing for services such as drug treatment, and many uses of words such as "efficiency" and "economy". In reality, we have not got the staff on the ground. Demands on health services, on the other hand, are increasing. It means that our services are not going to be as robust as they were before, in terms of those interventions for health.

To some extent, the government's response had become a public relations exercise in framing austerity as improving services.

> The government is packaging [austerity measures] up to make it look like we are improving service. This will make it more efficient. They promise that there will be better communication, that the right people doing the right things and tackling all these complex issues. So, the public feels satisfied: "Good, they are actually going to do something about this now". That is the sell. But the subtext beyond . . . you cannot grow the prisoner population but cut the staff at the same time. You just cannot do that without having a negative impact.
>
> (Participant 44, a criminal justice lead of a nursing trade union)

Some participants dissented, directly refuting austerity's necessity. Although they acknowledged improvement was always possible, participants believed their organisations had always been prudent with their resource allocation. As argued by Participant 55, a prison health lead of a national health organisation and a magistrate: "We were fairly good at [looking for value for money] anyway. It was not like we were wasting resources".

Overall, participants actively resisted, passively accepted, or positively accepted the framing of austerity as necessary. Most felt compelled to agree with the narrative, considering their inability to challenge it.

Mobilisation of the austerity programmes in prisons

Most participants cited the Prison Unit Cost Programme, also known as the Benchmarking Programme, and the Fair and Sustainable Programme as responsible for executing the government's austerity efforts. They concluded these programmes sought to reduce state expenditure in prisons by reducing the workforce size without reducing the prison population, thereby compromising safety in operating the prison regime.

Two participant quotations support this belief:

> I have looked at staff-to-prison[er] ratios in Trinidad and Tobago [and] all the West Indian islands. I have been to prisons in India, Australia, Germany, America, and Canada, the UAE, and Mauritius. All of them had a proper ratio of prison staff to prisoners. They never let the ratio fall between one [staff] to three prisoners. [In England], it is now one to six, which it was in 1960. You do not find a single European country where the staff numbers are so low.
>
> (Participant 18, an academic and advisor to a European administration organisation)

> My establishment [a men's resettlement prison in Midlands] went through a change where the Benchmarking Exercise set the level of staff that we believed was wrong. As a result, we could not run our prison properly. We understand that everybody needs to make cuts. But in places like this, there

> needs to be a minimum of staff for it to be safe, for both the prisoners and the staff, because that is when the frustrations start.
>
> (Participant 74, a senior prison officer of a resettlement prison)

Participant 43 observed a time lag between budget reductions and consequent service reductions:

> They operated on the assumption that there was a lot of fat in public services—"Let's just top-slice all the budgets and let people figure out how to do that". The budget reduction suggests that that did work for a while. The quality of services did not decline in most areas for a while, but that has become harder and harder to sustain as time has gone on and more and more problems bubble up.

This desire to localise the decision-making process of the budget cuts was problematic, according to international and national participants, who thought the UK government failed to thoroughly assess the reductions' practical implications for the prison service. As Participant 49, an investigator for a regulatory organisation, highlighted, the logic of needing to undertake austerity was flawed because the government acted without a sufficient understanding of the budget:

> There are risks to taking a lot of money out of budgets in a very unplanned way. The Ministry of Justice has lost an enormous amount of money. But, it also has fairly fixed costs. Prisons are a massive part of its expenditure; it has to provide prison places for the people who are sentenced to prisons. It is a very difficult financial situation. If you are going to perform radical surgery, you should know where the heart is. This is not the case for this Ministry.

Overall, participants with views against austerity measures noted the direct consequences of austerity measures on prison service. Via the Benchmarking Programme, they observed how the government's unplanned approach in reducing the prison workforce without reducing the prison population compromises the system, even though the impact was not immediately apparent.

Conclusion

In this chapter, I have demonstrated that participants believed austerity has been politically constructed and mobilised throughout the English prison system in three distinct ways. First, they argued austerity was a political choice, despite its reliance on economic measures for justification. Second, recognising the narrative lacked evidence, participants accepted the framing of austerity as necessary. This acceptance was especially apparent among the civil service participants, stemming from a belief that there was no alternative to austerity. Third, participants detailed the implementation of the austerity measures across prisons via the Benchmarking Programme and the Fair and Sustainable Programme. They believed such programmes were not executed in a considered way and compromised system stability. Altogether, their perspectives underscore the experimental nature of austerity.

The next chapter will demonstrate that participants believe implementing austerity policies caused prison governance and prison healthcare delivery in England to deteriorate. I will critically examine participants' views of how prison funding reduction impacted prisoners' access to healthcare services and purposeful activities.

Note

1 Chancellor of the Exchequer under Prime Minister David Cameron from 2010 to 2016, who introduced the programme of austerity post-May 2010 UK General Election.

References

Anderson, B. and Minneman, E. (2014) The Abuse and Misuse of the Term "Austerity" Implications for OECD Countries. *OECD Journal on Budgeting*. 14(1), pp. 109–122.

Blyth, M. (2013) Austerity as Ideology: A Reply to My Critics. *Comparative European Politics*. 11(6), pp. 737–751.

Farnsworth, K. (2018) *The British Corporate Welfare State: Public Provision for Private Businesses*. SPERI Paper No. 24 [Online], available from: http://speri.dept.shef.ac.uk/wp-content/uploads/2018/11/SPERI-Paper-24-The-British-Corporate-Welfare-State.pdf (accessed: 25th January 2021).

Farnsworth, K. and Irving, Z. (2018) Austerity: Neoliberal Dreams Come True? *Critical Social Policy*. 38(3), pp. 461–481.

Fontana, G. and Sawyer, M. (2011) Fiscal Austerity. *Challenge*. 54(2), pp. 42–60.

Gamble, A. (2014) Austerity as Statecraft. *Parliamentary Affairs*. 68, pp. 42–57.

HM Treasury (2018) *The Green Book: Central Government Guidance on Appraisal and Evaluation* [Online], available from: https://assets.publishing.service.gov.uk/government/uploads/system/uploads/attachment_data/file/938046/The_Green_Book_2020.pdf (Accessed: 25th January 2021).

O'Dea, C. and Preston, I. (2010) *The Distributional Impact of Public Spending in the UK: IFS Working Paper W12/06* [Online], available from: www.ifs.org.uk/wps/wp1206.pdf (Accessed: 25th January 2021).

Office for National Statistics (2021) *UK Government Debt and Deficit: September 2020* [Online], available from: www.ons.gov.uk/economy/governmentpublicsectorandtaxes/publicspending/bulletins/ukgovernmentdebtanddeficitforeurostatmaast/september2020 (Accessed: 25th January 2021).

Panitch, L. and Konings, M. (2009) *American Empire and the Political Economy of Global Finance*. New York: Palgrave.

Schui, F. (2015) *Austerity: The Great Failure*. New Haven, CT: Yale University Press.

Thompson, H. (2013) UK Debt in Comparative Perspective: The Pernicious Legacy of Financial Sector Debt. *British Journal of Politics & International Relations*. 15(3), pp. 476–492.

Chapter 6

Deterioration in rehabilitative prison environment

Introduction

One hundred years ago, Yeats (1920) detailed the turmoil across Europe after World War I in his poem "The Second Coming". As he wrote, "Things fall apart; the centre cannot hold;/Mere anarchy is loosed upon the world".

Many writings on societal decline have since adopted Yeats' evocative words. His depiction of turmoil parallels the deterioration in today's rehabilitative prison environment brought on by the political experiments of austerity. As this chapter explores, following the political construction, acceptance, and implementation of these experiments, prisoners are encountering barriers to prison healthcare services and purposeful activities, and contending with the increasing availability of drugs.

The chapter also considers how variably or uniformly austerity measures impacted the delivery of healthcare and supportive prison regimes. Participants' responses revealed that certain types of prison establishments, such as local and closed prisons, suffered a greater impact than conventional male prisons. The chapter further examines the prolonged effect of continued austerity on the government's aspirations for prison rehabilitation. Then, it analyses participants' beliefs about challenges in commissioning and delivering healthcare services across prisons.

Overall, this chapter reflects three strands of political experimentation. The first experiment is this: how long can the delivery of prison healthcare services be sustained when the volume of prisoners and their health are becoming increasingly complex? Second, can we still expect prison healthcare services to maintain an equivalent standard to community ones? And third, to what extent does prison rehabilitation remain viable when the focus on punishment, security, and public protection often trumps health considerations? The outcomes of these three strands of experimentation further reveal the paradoxes of austerity in prisons.

Stagnant prison health funding

Most participants were clear that NHS England's funding of prison healthcare was protected from the government's austerity measures. Indeed, NHS England's funding has been ring-fenced at £400 million per annum since 2013

DOI: 10.4324/9781003182337-6

(NAO, 2017). Yet the participants added a caveat: the strain on services has increased as the volume and complexities of prisoner health have become increasingly intricate. The comment from Participant 36, assistant head of health and justice of a national health organisation, echoed these sentiments:

> Things have changed massively. Six years ago, we did not think about dying well in custody charters. We did not think about palliative care necessarily. We did not think about prisons being old people's homes with a locked door. We did not think about dementia care in the same way that we are having to think about that now. We have now got a huge piece of work going on around acquired brain injury. We have embedded learning disability and difficulties within our primary care specifications to be alert to that. We have not got those nuanced things in place and now we are having to be responsive about that.

Many participants also described making difficult decisions to keep their services afloat. Inescapably, the costs of delivering services frequently trumped quality and best practices, as reflected by Participant 66, a head of a substance misuse service operating in various closed prisons:

> We try to, as far as possible, deliver our mission, which is to help people turn their lives around, keep them alive and help them to move away from drugs and crime. But we are walking a tightrope, between quality and cost, to win healthcare contracts in prisons. It is a constant battle. We always try and come up with more efficient models, but they were rarely driven by evidence and good practice; they were driven by "How do you do this for 30% less?" Constantly, questions such as "Do you pay your staff less?" or "Do you provide a weaker service?" or "Do you rely on volunteers more?" popped up more frequently.

Beyond cost-saving efforts, many participants recognised the political undertones riddling resource allocation for prison healthcare and prison service. They thought these programmes were based on unsound economic decisions. Imposing austerity programmes from the top down upended difficult decision-making processes, with participants witnessing services being scaled back and trade-offs between cost-cutting and delivering quality prison healthcare services.

These descriptions supplement official reports of a real-term decrease in health funding, when accounting for inflation, which simultaneously affects prison health funding (Marmot, 2017; New Economics Foundation, 2018). This situation is occurring even when epidemiological evidence attests to the burden of diseases among prisoners, which is higher compared with the public (Dolan et al., 2016; Fazel et al., 2016; Stürup-Toft et al., 2018).

Several participants also said high staff turnover was an ongoing challenge across prison healthcare services. They believed poor pay and working conditions dampened recruitment and retention of the healthcare workforce within the prison setting. Indeed, most of the healthcare staff in this study said they had to acclimatise to their poor working conditions. Participant 30, a senior commissioning lead of a justice ministry, said:

> Attracting staff to work in the NHS in a prison setting is a massive issue. One of the biggest problems is rate of pay and the working conditions. All of which indicate that usually people are worn out because they are overworked and people feel undervalued.

The recruitment and retention issues of the prison healthcare workforce reflect the general trend in the healthcare system in England. Some participants within the prison healthcare sector argued there was still no systematic workforce planning to continually recruit healthcare staff to work in prisons:

> More people are leaving the system. A significant number of GPs have left the medical profession. Others plan to leave. We have got retirement figures for the next five to ten years and we are going to be left significantly short of prescribing doctors. Those are the people we employ in prisons. We do not have enough nurses. That is nationally. That is not just prison healthcare, that is every healthcare department. There are 40,000 nurse vacancies. Yet, the government removed the training bursary. . . . We have never been more desperate for more nurses and more GPs.
>
> (Participant 55, a prison health lead of a national health organisation and magistrate)

This finding corroborates official statistics that demonstrated a shortfall of 39,520 nurses (NHS Improvement, 2019), with 45% of prison nurses indicating that staff shortages compromised the care they could provide (House of Commons Select Committee, 2018). Also, the most recent CPT inspections of English prisons documented numerous unfilled General Practice positions and healthcare staff posts (CPT, 2020).

Maintaining safe staffing levels within English prisons requires considerably more systematic attention to workplace recruitment than in recent years. As a short-term adaptation, several participants mentioned resorting to agency staff, who were inevitably more expensive. Meanwhile, they acknowledged this alternative contradicts the government's desire to save costs because the practice was common in the health sector in England, prisons included. As Participant 73, the head of a private healthcare organisation at a resettlement prison, explained:

> An agency nurse is far more expensive than even a top band 5 nurse. However, we understand that we need it to run the service. So, [it is a]

> short-term solution . . ., but that short-term seems to creep up to long-term, so that is the problem.

These observations indicate serious inadequacies in prison healthcare. And the trend will likely worsen given the lack of a coherent government approach to recruitment, migration policies, and the uncertainties of Brexit.

Declining access to healthcare services for prisoners

A salutary prison regime that supports prisoners' access to healthcare is critical. But given the real-term decrease in NHS England's funding for prison healthcare, various participants highlighted the decline in the accessibility and quality of services for prisoners. In turn, this deterioration of services has affected the performance of the broader healthcare system in prisons. Prisoners' deteriorating access to healthcare further evidences the paradox of rehabilitation: despite the claim that prisoners can access healthcare interventions to address their health and well-being issues, the decline in healthcare funding hinders access to high quality interventions.

Almost unanimously—regardless of operational level—informants argued that the reduction of prison officers (30% from 2009 to 2017) hindered prisoners from accessing prison healthcare services (CPT, 2017; NAO, 2017). Participant 61, a high-security prison governor, further highlighted the dependency of healthcare services on the availability of prison officers:

> Health services cannot operate in isolation in a prison. Prison officers need to be available in order to supervise clinical deliveries. They are not in the consulting room, but they are waiting outside, and they have to operate in a much tighter way. Sometimes these officers are late getting to the start of the clinics because they have to do a different job first before they go to clinics, whereas previously they would just be allocated to the clinics for the whole of the day. So that causes a lot of disruption and a loss of clinical time.

Some participants at the operational level of prisons observed that health appointments were postponed or cancelled more often after the government implemented the austerity programme. Consequently, it led to backlogs and waste across the prison and community healthcare settings. As Participant 61, the prison governor of a high-security prison, said: "We do not necessarily have people available to supervise escort out of the prison, so that can lead to cancellations or reorganising appointments outside of the prison, which can be problematic for us and the health system outside".

Several healthcare participants mentioned the loss of in-prison clinical time and a ripple effect on the wider NHS performance, as both prison and community healthcare services fall within the same organisational umbrella. For example, Participant 35, a regional health and justice lead of a national health organisation, said:

> NHS trusts that deliver prison healthcare services are struggling more, and the kind of 12-week waits need a turnaround. All performance figures are starting to turn from green to amber to red, and you are seeing that more. That partly has had an impact on prison healthcare and the rest of the system struggles.

The problematic access to healthcare in prison strains the wider NHS, particularly when prisoners must oscillate between prison and community healthcare, since in-prison healthcare services do not provide all services. This situation complemented the Nuffield Trust (2020) study finding that over 75% of missed appointments out of all prison healthcare appointments were partly due to the lack of prison staff and engendered a cost to the NHS of £2m. While extant research evidently idealises prison health in England for embracing the equivalence principle (Gatherer and Fraser, 2009; Leaman et al., 2017), this study finds that austerity and the wider neoliberal preference for punishment challenge the stability of equivalence. Though prison healthcare equivalency has improved following the transition of services to NHS England, austerity impedes such possible achievements. In fact, it worsens healthcare services for prisoners. Prison healthcare services, and thereby prisoner well-being, demand regime stability, which participants often reported to be deteriorating. By uprooting such stability, austerity compromises the governance and delivery of prison health.

Alongside reduced access to healthcare services, many participants observed a decline in the quality of healthcare services. Longer waiting times and insufficient consultation time with medical professionals, they argued, further compromised the quality of prisoner healthcare. Participant 12, an advisor to a European intergovernmental human rights organisation and leader of a national medical organisation, stated:

> We often have just handfuls of sessions of psychiatry. . . . We have three days of psychiatry to manage a caseload of 300 men. The Royal College of Physicians says that we should have 30 sessions to manage that caseload. . . . People often do not get seen or they wait a long time to be seen or they get seen for shorter periods of time than they should be seen. . . . It is really inadequate.

Prison officers, meanwhile, said they often had to trade off healthcare and prison safety due to the lack of staff.

> I have been in charge of the prisoners at night, when we have got absolute minimal staffing levels. I am covering my backside by using the dedicated

> healthcare phone line when prisoners are unwell, and then they cover their backside by saying to me, "Yeah you'd better send them to hospital". Then you are depleting your staffing levels because you have to send two members of staff out with that prisoner. . . . The next thing you know, we cannot even open a door because there are not enough staff now to let prisoners outside their cells. . . . And I am absolutely against there not being 24-hour healthcare. It has made life very, very difficult for us.
>
> (Participant 78, a senior prison officer of a closed prison)

The situation transcends the official reports that detailed the excessive delays prisoners faced in receiving medical treatment (CPT, 2017; HMIP, 2017, 2020). Apart from providing much-needed evidence of how financial cuts impact prison healthcare delivery, this study demonstrates that prison healthcare cannot absorb the effects of austerity on the prison regime, especially when the latter has had a domino effect on the former.

Examples from this study illustrate how the deterioration of prison conditions and the environment under austerity exceed prisoners' deprivation of these materials through obstructed access to healthcare. The decline in prison conditions runs counter to human rights obligations. These responsibilities were proposed by *Kudla v Poland* [2000] ECHR 512: the state ensures that imprisonment does not subject prisoners to distress or hardship surpassing the unavoidable level of suffering inherent in imprisonment. The outcomes of this study highlight excessive punishment through declining access to healthcare services for prisoners, which violates their rights to healthcare.

Harmful living and working environment

Regardless of their governance level, almost all participants stated that the shortage of prison officers had contributed to two problems. These were the decline in access to purposeful activities (sufficient time out-of-cell to engage in activities such as education and employment that support their rehabilitation) and rehabilitative environments in prisons. In particular, they questioned how violent incidents, and the harmful built environment in prisons, could hamper government aspirations for the prison rehabilitation agenda.

First, the participants observed that prisoners had to spend many hours in their cells. This removed the opportunity to socialise with fellow prisoners and participate in purposeful activities that were critical to their health and well-being. Participant 13, a former head of a prison inspectorate, compared the situation in England to his experiences when inspecting prisons in the Middle East:

> I went to inspect the prisons in the United Arab Emirates, where I discovered that they did not have one suicide in Dubai and Abu Dhabi since 1995. They said all landings are locked, but all cells are left unlocked, so by

> day everyone can mix freely with each other. It does not matter if you go and sleep in an overcrowded cell, because that is only by the night. But in England, we insist on separating people by day and doing nothing. That is not natural. I think that if you treat somebody like an animal, that is what you will get.

These observations support a catalogue of failures officials have reported regarding deterioration in the rehabilitation and living environment in English prisons over the last decade (CPT, 2017, 2020). The lack of access to purposeful activities is not only an inhumane condition, but it disproportionately reinforces punishment to imperil prisoner health—especially when seven in ten prisoners suffer from two or more mental disorders (Singleton et al., 1998). Purposeful activities might help prisoners deal with the boredom and stress of imprisonment productively. Previous studies found that lack of access to such activities, segregation, and confinement place prisoners at particular risk (Guenther, 2011). The present study further connects the dots between such conditions and the reduction in prison resources.

Most participants, especially at the national and local levels, observed that being locked in cells for long periods triggered boredom and restlessness. In these instances, they noted minor squabbles among prisoners could become major riots that could halt the delivery of healthcare services. Participant 53, a regional head of health and justice commissioning for the National Health Service, stated:

> The use of the Tornado Team [an elite squad tasked with bringing prison riots under control] has risen enormously. This team moves between prisons. We sometimes need to alert our healthcare providers. Going into prisons like we do, we hear a general alarm bell that [things have] gone through the roof. You just hear it more. You hear, "general alarm, general alarm, general alarm". It is staggering.

Moreover, owing to being locked in cells for too long, most of these participants also cited rising rates of self-harm, suicide, and assaults among prisoners and staff. Participants noted these formerly extreme instances of "lockdowns" were now becoming a daily norm. Despite governing two different institutions with dissimilar security levels, both Participant 81, the governor of an open prison, and Participant 61, the governor of a high-security prison, shared the following similar sentiments, respectively:

> When we do not have enough staff, prisoners cannot get to [engage in] purposeful activity. They are kept in cells longer and therefore frustrations run high. It brings with it reaction and violence amongst the prison population that happens almost every day across the estates, like violence against staff and other prisoners, self-harm episodes, and even suicides.

> Health is not just about a health service. It is about the whole environment supporting people's health and well-being. The deterioration that we have seen in safety is a sign of a much less healthy environment in which people are having to live. They have to live in an environment where there is more violence, more self-harm . . . that is going to affect, not just those individuals involved, but it is going to affect the general health and well-being of everyone who lives and works in a particular prison.

This narrative is consistent with official statistics showing a 37% rise in self-inflicted deaths, 53% increase in assault and a 61% growth in self-harm incidents between 2010 and 2020 (CPT, 2020; House of Commons Library, 2017; Ministry of Justice, 2020a), as well as coordinated riots that took place at least once a day in 2015 (House of Commons Justice Committee, 2016). Given the poor recording practice across prisons, such metrics are likely underestimated.

Beyond the direct impact of such incidents on the targets of violence, they create a general feeling of danger among prisoners, fomenting a negative psychological impact (HMIP, 2017). Because these marked reductions in safety show no sign of abating, interviewees predicted higher rates of such incidents and a rise in reoffending and radicalisation. The climax will be a heightened risk of inflicting torturous, inhumane, and degrading treatment on both prisoners and prison staff.

Many participants questioned how attainable the prison rehabilitation agenda was, owing to the lack of meaningful activities for prisoners.

> But in terms of prisoner well-being, it means that there are a lot more lockdowns, people cannot leave their cells, people have to spend more time in their cells, they have less time outdoors, and they have less meaningful activity. It means that people cannot be escorted to go to training, education, visits, do any kind of meaningful activity, that you would to actually make a prison experience in any kind of way useful.
>
> (Participant 47, a project lead of a national penal reform organisation)

The latest average reoffending rate is surprisingly high: 45% for all those released from custody and 61% of those serving a sentence of fewer than 12 months (Ministry of Justice, 2020b). Despite these figures, the government fails to acknowledge the reduction of purposeful activities for prisoners while still claiming imprisonment reduces reoffending via rehabilitation programmes (ibid.). Participants explicitly recognised this omission, saying that the lack of access to opportunities for education, employment, training, and volunteering infers that the government has minimal interest in using rehabilitation as a core driver for reducing incarceration rates.

Most participants asserted that maintaining order safely and securely in their institutions had become increasingly fraught. Frequently, participants expressed fear and being subject to intimidation. For example, as Participant 78, a senior prison officer of a closed prison, stated:

> When the staffing levels [are] reduced so dramatically now, the prisoners know they can get away with it. They overstep the mark, and they keep pushing, and they keep pushing. Recently, I had a nose-to-nose with a prisoner, because he refused to take his dinner behind his door. He made a stand, and I looked at my watch and I thought, "Right, it is five to five. I want to go home at half past five in one piece". No member of staff was there to back me up, and no-one was watching. The likelihood is, if I [had] carried on and stood my ground, he would either [have] spat [or] punched me, so in the end I just walked away. That is the difference now; you do not have the confidence to deal with the prisoners in the same way.

Like the threats to the frontline prison workforce, Participant 46 also detailed threats to the safety of healthcare staff due to inadequate resources:

> If there was an incident, you pushed an alarm button. There would be a lot of staff come to support you and deal with that situation safely and effectively. Unfortunately, there just are not people there to do that anymore. We have seen nursing and healthcare staff suffer attacks and assaults, and that has got to a point where it is just not acceptable.

Statistics on the prison healthcare staff who have suffered workplace injuries due to prisoner violence are not publicly available. Yet Participant 46's narrative mirrors the Royal College of Nursing's safe and effective staffing review across the NHS, whereby respondents detailed the above-normal aggression that they experienced in prisons (House of Commons Select Committee, 2018). The government then responded by passing the Assaults on Emergency Workers (Offences) Act 2018, which could increase the length of imprisonment terms for individuals who assaulted prison healthcare workers. Yet, these attacks do not happen in a vacuum; they stem from prisoners' frustrations due to the lack of access to out-of-cell activities that could not be delivered due to the shortage of prison staff.

Overall, participants felt that shortages of prison staff contributed to a decline in both access to purposeful activities and to rehabilitative environments in prisons. Following increasingly regular prison lockdowns, most noted that violent incidents against prisoners and staff had become routine. Some questioned the attainment of the prison rehabilitation agenda given this deterioration.

Increasing availability of drugs in English prisons

The availability of drugs is increasingly prevalent in English prisons. There was a 446% increase in the number of seized psychoactive substances in 2019 compared to a similar seizure in 2010 (Ministry of Justice, 2019). Yet, there are too few prison officers to curb the drug supply (e.g., conducting drug searches and intelligence gathering) and an increased demand among prisoners for drugs to cope with their poor living environment. Various participants believed the drug market operating outside the prison was responsible for supplying drugs inside the prison—including novel psychoactive substances. Participants attributed the increase in illicit drug use to an inadequate number of prison officers available to conduct drug searches, perimeter patrols, and intelligence gathering:

> In [our resettlement prison], prison officers were reduced by 40%. Granted, a prison officer is not delivering healthcare. However, if they are not there on the wings or doing searches or finding that people use more and more drugs, that made a huge difference.
>
> (Participant 73, the head of a private healthcare organisation at a resettlement prison)

Many participants believed that a poor living environment had increased prisoners' risk-taking behaviour. Drug use, in particular, had become a coping mechanism. As Participant 40, the head of a national penal reform organisation, explained, "People are being made ill, both mentally, through the stress of living in that environment, and physically, through taking substances to cope with it". Loïc Wacquant (2002) argues that the structure of prisons influences determinants of prisoner health daily. Indeed, the present study agrees, finding a deterioration in prisoners' access to healthcare, purposeful activities, a rehabilitative living environment, and safety.

Rising drug use in prisons has created a ripple effect on internal and external resources. These impacts include preventing healthcare staff from delivering planned activities, attending to medical emergencies, and calling on external healthcare resources (e.g., ambulances). Participant 73, a head of a private healthcare organisation at a resettlement prison, reflected on his team's experience in responding to emergency incidents—'code blues'—that were caused by using *Spice* (synthetic cannabinoids):

> When code blue incidents happened as a result of prisoners using *Spice*, they did not all require [prisoners] to go out to the hospital, but they still interrupted a primary care clinic for hours. When a code blue is activated, an ambulance is automatically called as well. Now, when healthcare staff get to the scene, they will quickly assess the patient, and if they deem that the ambulance is not required, the ambulance stands down. But we had a situation where there were five ambulances a day coming here and then having to turn round. It has a big impact on the community, as well as the prison.

Healthcare services in prisons do not operate 24 hours a day. To attend medical emergencies outside the operational hours of the in-house healthcare services, prisons must still rely on external services. "We are not here 24 hours a day. We are only here during working hours, until half six in the evening. Then, the ambulance service or urgent care GPs take over during the night" (Participant 69, a prison officer at a resettlement prison). Over the four years up to 2019/2020, one in five hospital admissions was related to injury or poisoning, including drug use (Davies et al., 2021). Consequently, prison staff have no other option but to draw on community resources that are already hard-pressed.

Overcrowding

A few participants operating outside the national prison health system expressed concerns about the effects of prison overcrowding and cleanliness in prisons. Although overcrowding is a historical issue pre-dating austerity, they believed periods of austerity exacerbated the deterioration of prisoners' living conditions. They said overcrowding has led to 'warehousing' individuals and more violence among prisoners.

Both Participant 4, an advisor to a European intergovernmental human rights organisation, and Participant 8, a policy lead of a European public-sector trade union organisation, made similar points:

> [T]he single, most corrosive element in any prison system is overcrowding. We end up warehousing people and cannot provide any level of appropriate service when we have overcrowding. What the United Kingdom did in the mid-1980s was a classic mistake—it built more prisons. If you build more prisons, all you are going to do is end up with more prisoners. It's simple.
>
> Prison overcrowding is not getting any better. It triggers violence and aggression, [which contributes to] an aggressive atmosphere. So, austerity is adding salt on a wound. . . . The situation in prison services was certainly not good before 2008, but austerity measures have exacerbated a situation that was already very fragile.

These narratives support the official statistics that six in ten (n=70) prisons in England and Wales were overcrowded, with many prisoners at these establishments sharing cells designed for fewer people (NAO, 2020). The CPT has continually criticised the widespread overcrowding in English prisons, especially when prisoners often spend more than 14 hours daily in their poorly maintained cells (CPT, 2020). Such a degrading living condition triggered boredom and restlessness, and contributed to an increase in self-harm, assault, and self-inflicted death, much of which was underreported (Ministry of Justice, 2019).

Many participants also argued that hygiene in prison has progressively worsened, as prisoners' cells were now harmful living environments. Participant 4, an advisor to a European intergovernmental human rights organisation, believed such poor prison conditions were unacceptable in a developed country:

> I was shown [a category B male prison in North West of England]. I looked at the level of dirt, the level of non-upkeep of material conditions, never

> mind the provision of services. It was really distressing to see. I expect to see conditions like that in some of the Balkan countries I am working in. I do not expect to see conditions like that in England. It is sending a much bigger message than austerity. It is sending the message that we just do not care. That we do not care about prisons; we do not care that they are not viewed as individuals. Then we wonder why they do not respond to our interventions to make them better citizens when we are actually demonstrating to them that society does not care.

These experiences illustrate the prioritisation of punishment over health. The participants' accounts demonstrate how overcrowding imposes degrading conditions on prisoners, and that confinement within poorly maintained cells can accelerate the progression of diseases. Although prison overcrowding has been an issue in England since 1990—and predates austerity (CPT, 2020)—the warehousing of people due to austerity emphasises punishment over rehabilitation. This emphasis is then supported by plans to rebuild the criminal justice system following the COVID-19 pandemic. The plans camouflage neoliberal political rhetoric—more prisoners should spend more time in prisons (Buckland, 2021)—that seeks to warehouse these individuals and thereby perpetuate the cycle of punishment.

The global COVID-19 pandemic has exposed prisons' vulnerabilities to infectious disease outbreaks. Cases and deaths linked to COVID-19 emerged rapidly in English prisons (Ministry of Justice, 2021). Indeed, prisoners remain at considerable risk (Ismail and Forrester, 2020), with the latest statistics revealing 193 deaths and 16,676 positive cases in English prisons through April 2021 (Ministry of Justice, 2021). This study was undertaken prior to the global pandemic in 2020. However, the overcrowding issues, including poor living conditions, that participants highlighted clearly contributed to the spread of the virus. Further, poor resources and rigid security processes doubtless delayed diagnosis and treatment for infected prisoners. Clearly, COVID-19 has been a devastating reckoning of austerity's impact in prisons.

How austerity impacted different prison establishments

We can gain a more nuanced understanding of austerity by examining how it affects different prison establishments. Participants' narratives diverged when asked whether austerity disproportionately impacted healthcare delivery and its enabling prison regime in certain prison establishments. They argued that prison establishments had varying resources, assets, and resilience. As such, austerity effects were inconstant across prisons.

Several participants argued that austerity impacted closed prisons more than open prisons. The reason, they said, was that these establishments already had a fragile workforce following the Benchmarking Exercise in 2012 that reduced prison spending and subsequently reduced prison staff. Participant 40, the head of a national penal reform organisation, named some of these prisons and explained how austerity destabilised the delivery of healthcare services in them:

> The prisons that have always been worrying, such as HMPs Wandsworth [London], Pentonville [London], and Liverpool, all of those well-known Victorian-level prisons, have suffered as much as anybody through austerity and the culture of being incredibly fragile, vulnerable places to begin with. Even more worrying are the prisons in the middle. HMP The Mount [Hertfordshire] is just a classic Category C training prison. Two or three years ago, there were regular riots. If that is happening, then you can absolutely guarantee that basic services, including health services, will not be delivered in the way that they should be.

Participants saw drugs as the main blight on closed prisons: "We are vulnerable to the throw-in of drugs from the outside" (Participant 79, a deputy governor of a closed prison with urgent notification status). In contrast, open prisons were relatively protected from this phenomenon, as "the men are kept busy, everyone has got jobs, everyone has got somewhere to go to, and they have got home leaves or temporary releases to demonstrate compliance and appropriateness of behaviour" (Participant 80, a governor of an open prison). These comments illustrate a novel finding of this study that open prisons were less impacted by austerity compared with closed prisons. The reason is that the greater access to purposeful activities in open prisons served as a protective factor that deterred prisoners from engaging with violence and drug use.

According to other participants, austerity also disproportionately compounded problems in local prisons. They argued that the rapid prisoner turnover in local prisons made it harder to provide health interventions. The turnover highlighted the tension between the long-term view of addressing prisoners' health issues and the short-term perspective of keeping these prisoners safe. Participant 44, the criminal justice lead of a nursing trade union, stated:

> I do see local prisons being directly affected by austerity. Where people come in and move on, that is really a big problem for practitioners and clinical staff. You might need to call up somebody's past history and connect with their community healthcare and housing support teams, so you have got a real short space of time to be able to do something effective before they move on. Where you have a stable population, people who are there for a number of years, you can actually do something more meaningfully, whereas, [with] the former, you can only signpost, and the primary objective is to keep people safe in the short term.

Participant 44's narrative provides further intelligence of how austerity compounds healthcare delivery in local prisons. Recent statistics illustrate that around one in six prisoners, either awaiting trial or sentencing, were housed in local prisons (Ministry of Justice, 2022). Most of them were accused of drug and violence offences, with the highest rates of positive random drug testing coming from these local prisons (ibid.). Tackling their health issues, for instance drug addiction, requires a longer-term rehabilitation programme. Yet these offences often attract short-term imprisonment, which limits the time for rehabilitation. Given the stretched resources of prisons and prison healthcare across English prisons, austerity compounds their inability to improve the health of prisoners in local prisons.

A consensus emerged that financial cuts to high-security prisons could have been less impactful compared with other establishments. Most national and local participants believed high-security establishments were relatively protected from financial cuts, dovetailing with a drive to lock up dangerous detainees for a long period: "[T]he high[-]security prisons already have a lot of staff. . . . My God, they are still throwing money at these places!" (Participant 71, a prison governor of a resettlement prison). Similarly, Participant 28, a former inspector of prisons, argued, "If you look at it on the whole, the staff reductions have not been as great in high-security prisons, like HMP Long Lartin [West Midlands], as they had in other prisons".

However, participants who led and worked at high-security establishments challenged this broader consensus:

> We suffered from austerity too. For others to say, "Well, high-security prisons are unaffected" is untrue. Our prison [a high-security prison in South East London establishment] used to have a budget of £44 million. Now, our annual budget is £29 million, so we have lost the best part of £15 million since 2010. We used to have over 400 prison staff in 2010 and now we only have half of that size.
>
> (Participant 82, a senior prison officer of a high-security prison)

Actual spending data demonstrate that high-security prisons experienced austerity too, albeit less dramatically than other adult prisons. Following the Benchmarking Exercise in 2012, high-security prisons' overall funding was reduced by 4%, from £208m to £199m (Ministry of Justice, 2011, 2012). Then in 2019, their investment increased 8% again to £217m (Ministry of Justice, 2020c). In contrast, other adult prisons experienced an 11% cut, from £2.5 billion to £2.4 billion following the Benchmarking Exercise in 2012 (Ministry of Justice, 2011, 2012), before a 22% increase in investment was allocated for these prisons in 2019, which brings their total funding to £3.1 billion (Ministry of Justice, 2020c). While none of the prisons was insulated from the austerity impact, high-security prisons experienced fewer spending cuts than other adult prisons in England.

Austerity may also inconsistently impact private versus public prisons. As previous chapters have argued, one facet of the neoliberal austerity agenda is the increasing privatisation of public-sector services. As such, understanding whether private-sector prisons are better protected from fiscal cuts can help us judge the logic of the privatisation agenda. Participant 57, a head of a prison governor's union, commented that most private prisons were newer and had better environments conducive to prison rehabilitation. They also, though, believed such institutions were probably afforded more freedom to deal with establishment issues compared with the public-sector prisons:

> Private sector businesses generally have got the new prisons, better accommodations, a more decent environment, and they have got more freedom in how they respond to issues in the private sector. In public[-]sector prisons, we have very little autonomy because we are civil servants, like a big chiming cog that takes forever to change.
>
> (Participant 57, a head of prison governor's union)

While private prisons inherited a lower spending envelope than public prisons, they ran newer establishments and were given the freedom to execute innovation that accounted for their lower funding level. Private prisons absorbed the austerity agenda in their operations, yet they had an unfair advantage in that they were afforded greater discretion in running their establishments. This is unlike public prisons, whose direction was dictated by the central government. As such, we cannot say certainly that private-sector prisons performed better during austerity as the equivalent measures were not given to the public-sector prisons.

Although austerity impacts all prison establishments, some were more resilient in absorbing the government's fiscal cuts. The participants felt austerity affected closed prisons more than others due to their poor staffing. They also discussed how prisoners in closed prisons were vulnerable to supplies of drugs from outside. However, several other participants suggested that local prisons suffered from austerity more than other prisons given the high throughput of prisoners. This, they argued, created difficulties for addressing the health needs of these individuals and providing the support required to ensure a safe custodial environment, and it was detrimental to the long-term functioning of these establishments.

Prolonged impact of continued austerity measures on prisons

Participants were asked to envisage the potential impact of continued austerity measures on prison health. Their responses chiefly focused on four themes: poorer health outcomes for prisoners, increased risk to the health of the community, more violent activities potentially leading to the loss of prison governance, and a rising rate of reoffending.

Some participants suggested prisoners filed more serious health complaints when their access to healthcare services was inadequate. Some of these complaints were so severe that participants believed inadequate access to healthcare had caused disability or even death. Participant 50, the head of legal of a national penal reform organisation, argued:

> The seriousness of the complaints seems to have increased. Heart medication had not [been] provided, and diabetes medications were not available. People could die; it was that serious. They do not happen every week, but they are happening, things that really should not be happening. Massive delays to operations. Or even things like cancer treatment. They are just cancelling appointments. Broken bones not being taken to hospital. A prisoner actually has lost sight in one eye recently because he was not taken promptly to hospital. As healthcare services in prison are inadequate, I anticipate that the seriousness of the prisoner complaints will increase further.

While no systematic data collection illustrates the links between inadequate access to healthcare and disability and deaths in prisons, we must not ignore the participants' suggestion that the situation will worsen. The government has the duty of care to ensure prisoners' safety in custody, and failure to do so can open the floodgate for litigations by prisoners and their concerned others against the government.

A small number of national participants, particularly those dealing with prison health policies, were concerned that reduced access to healthcare in prisons would eventually risk the wider health of society. Their logic was that most prisoners who came from the community would eventually return, yet with poorer health. As Participant 2, a consultant for an international health organisation, stated:

> [P]rison is not an isolated entity. . . . If, as a result of the austerity measures, sexually transmitted diseases or communicable diseases within the prison system [are not] kept isolated only [to] prisons, it will also affect society in general. [I]t also applies to mental disease. If you release people from the prison setting [who] are more mentally ill than they were before, because of insufficient care for them, that has an effect on society.

Indeed, US studies have shown an association between COVID-19 spread in the community and COVID-19 infections that originated from prisons through the release and re-imprisonment cycle (Hooks and Sawyer, 2020; Reinhart and Chen, 2020).

Most participants agreed that prolonged austerity would cause more suicides and violent incidents and heightened reoffending and radicalisation. Participant 18, an academic and an advisor to a European administration organisation, stated, "The ultimate fear is that we reach a stage where we cannot maintain security or order or governance of our prisons". Participant 11, an advisor to a European intergovernmental human rights organisation, made a similar comparison to the Strangeways riot of April 1990. They portrayed it as a consequence of prolonged austerity measures:

> [There] will be higher suicide rates in prisons, more riots, more hostage-taking situations, an increase in re-offending, and an increase in radicalisation. Look at austerity measures in the British prison service, for example, the Strangeways riot in 1990. That was directly due to austerity measures, [with the] lack of staff monitoring the situation; prisoners being locked up for a long period of time, [and] they will eventually explode. The government has not learned from it. If they had, they would not be doing these austerity measures.

Some participants in prison oversight roles believed inadequate access to purposeful activities (designed to foster a beneficial quality of life post-release) would keep the reoffending rate high. As Participant 13, a former head of a prison inspectorate, stated, "[T]hey come out in a worse state of mind then they went in, [and] they are not going to be resettled immediately". Other participants also suggested the offending rate would rise.

> [W]e have a high rank of recidivism in England. Many, many prisoners are recidivists. Very likely the reason is that even when they are released, they do not find a possibility to have a different life, a [different] life from that they had before entering the prison.
>
> (Participant 19, a former president of a European anti-torture committee)

Overall, participants thought prolonged austerity would cause more violence that could lead to the loss of prison governance. The continued impact of austerity, according to participants, could worsen health outcomes by increasing risk-taking behaviours, thus likely placing the health of the broader population in jeopardy and increasing reoffending rates.

Conclusion

The participants reveal that prison health governance and the delivery of healthcare have deteriorated due to austerity. This is despite NHS England retaining the same prison health funding and the equivalency principle that guarantees equal access to healthcare for prisoners and community members. The deterioration is evidenced in the growth of prisoners' health needs; the reduction in the size of the healthcare workforce; prisoners' obstructed access to healthcare; and the declining living environment and safety in prisons.

As examples of the deterioration, participants particularly cited postponement and cancellation of healthcare appointments, increased waiting times, and insufficient consultation time with healthcare professionals. The paucity of access to purposeful activities further adversely affected prisoners' existing rehabilitation. Consequently, violent episodes and risk-taking behaviour—such as self-harm and drug misuse—had dramatically amplified, causing more medical emergencies. Notably, participants' comments varied regarding how austerity impacted certain types of prisons.

Participants also projected more violence, more risk-taking behaviours, more reoffenders, and a higher risk to the broader population's health from continued austerity measures in prisons.

The next section will investigate how austerity destabilises the prison regime. It argues that such destabilisation subsequently affects the delivery of prison healthcare through three developments: constant ministerial turnover, increasing privatisation of prisons and prison healthcare services, and the growth of informal governance via prison gangs and serious organised crime in English prisons.

References

Buckland, R. (2021) Speech: *Lord Chancellor Outlines Government Plans to Rebuild Criminal Justice* [Online], available from: www.gov.uk/government/speeches/lord-chancellor-outlines-government-plans-to-rebuild-criminal-justice (Accessed: 25th January 2021).

Committee for the Prevention of Torture and Inhuman or Degrading Treatment or Punishment (2017) *Report to the Government of the United Kingdom on the Visit to the United Kingdom Carried Out by the European Committee for the Prevention of Torture and Inhuman or Degrading Treatment or Punishment from 30 March to 12 April 2016* [Online], available from: https://rm.coe.int/168070a773 (Accessed: 11th January 2018).

Committee for the Prevention of Torture and Inhuman or Degrading Treatment or Punishment (2020) *Report to the United Kingdom Government on the Visit to the United Kingdom Carried Out by the European Committee for the Prevention of Torture and Inhuman or Degrading Treatment or Punishment (CPT) from 13 to 23 May 2019* [Online], available from: https://rm.coe.int/16809e4404 (Accessed: 27th May 2020).

Davies, M., Keeble, E. and Hutchings, R. (2021) *Injustice? Towards a Better Understanding of Health Care Access Challenges for Prisoners* [Online], available from: www.nuffieldtrust.org.uk/files/2021-10/1634637809_nuffield-trust-prisoner-health-2021-final.pdf (Accessed: 25th January 2022).

Dolan, K., Wirtz, A. L., Moazen, B., Ndeffo-Mbah, M., Galvani, A., Kinner, S. A., Courtney, R., McKee, M., Amon, J. J., Maher, L., Hellard, M., Beyrer, C. and Altice, F. L. (2016) Global Burden of HIV, Viral Hepatitis, and Tuberculosis in Prisoners and Detainees. *Lancet*. 388, pp. 1089–1102.

Fazel, S., Hayes, A. J., Bartellas, K., Clerici, M. and Trestman, R. (2016) The Mental Health of Prisoners: A Review of Prevalence, Adverse Outcomes and Interventions. *Lancet Psychiatry*. 3(9), pp. 871–881.

Gatherer, A. and Fraser, A. (2009) Health Care for Detainees. *The Lancet*. 373, pp. 1337–1338.

Guenther, L. (2011) Subjects Without a World? An Husserlian Analysis of Solitary Confinement. *Human Studies*. 34, pp. 257–276.

HM Inspectorate of Prisons (2017) *HM Chief Inspector of Prisons for England and Wales Annual Report 2016–17* [Online], available from: www.gov.uk/government/uploads/system/uploads/attachment_data/file/629719/hmip-annual-report-2016-17.pdf (Accessed: 11th January 2018).

HM Inspectorate of Prisons (2020) *HM Chief Inspector of Prisons for England and Wales: Annual Report 2019–20* [Online], available from: https://assets.publishing.service.gov.uk/government/uploads/system/uploads/attachment_data/file/927361/hmi-prisons-annual-report-accounts-201920.pdf (Accessed: 25th January 2021).

Hooks, G. and Sawyer, W. (2020) *Mass Incarceration, COVID-19, and Community Spread* [Online], available from: www.prisonpolicy.org/reports/covidspread.html (Accessed: 19th February 2022).

House of Commons Justice Committee (2016) *Indicators of Prison Safety* [Online], available from: https://publications.parliament.uk/pa/cm201516/cmselect/cmjust/625/62505.htm#footnote-051 (Accessed: 10th August 2018).

House of Commons Library (2017) *UK Prison Population Statistics: Briefing Paper Number SN/SG/04334, 20 April 2017* [Online], available from: http://researchbriefings.files.parliament.uk/documents/SN04334/SN04334.pdf (Accessed: 11th January 2018).

House of Commons Select Committee (2018) *Written Evidence from the Royal College of Nursing* [Online], available from: http://data.parliament.uk/WrittenEvidence/CommitteeEvidence.svc/EvidenceDocument/Health%20and%20Social%20Care/Prison%20health/written/83890.html#_edn1 (Accessed: 27th May 2020).

Ismail, N. and Forrester, A. (2020) The State of English Prisons and the Urgent Need for Reform. *The Lancet Public Health*. 5(7), pp. e368–e369. https://doi.org/10.1016/S2468-2667(20)30142-0.

Leaman, J., Richards, A. A., Emslie, L. and O'Moore, E. J. (2017) Improving Health in Prisons—From Evidence to Policy to Implementation—Experiences from the UK. *International Journal of Prisoner Health*. 13(3/4), pp. 139–167.

Marmot, M. (2017) The UK's Current Health Problems Should Be Treated with Urgency. *British Medical Journal* [Online], available from: https://blogs.bmj.com/bmj/2017/09/13/michael-marmot-the-uks-current-health-problems-should-be-treated-with-urgency/ (Accessed: 21st February 2020).

Ministry of Justice (2011) *Costs Per Place and Costs Per Prisoner by Individual Prison: National Offender Management Service Annual Report and Accounts 2010–11* [Online], available from: https://assets.publishing.service.gov.uk/government/uploads/system/uploads/attachment_data/file/218347/prison-costs-summary-10-11.pdf (Accessed: 25th January 2021).

Ministry of Justice (2012) *Costs Per Place and Costs Per Prisoner by Individual Prison: National Offender Management Service Annual Report and Accounts 2011–12* [Online], available from: https://assets.publishing.service.gov.uk/government/uploads/system/uploads/attachment_data/file/218336/prison-costs-summary-11-12.pdf (Accessed: 25th January 2021).

Ministry of Justice (2019) *HMPPS Annual Digest 2018/19* [Online], available from: https://assets.publishing.service.gov.uk/government/uploads/system/uploads/attachment_data/file/821148/HMPPS_Annual_Digest_bulletin_2018-2019.pdf (Accessed: 21st February 2020).

Ministry of Justice (2020a) *Safety in Custody Summary Tables to March 2020* [Online], available from: https://assets.publishing.service.gov.uk/government/uploads/system/uploads/attachment_data/file/905014/Safety-in-custody-summary-q1-2020-final-tables.xlsm (Accessed: 25th January 2021).

Ministry of Justice (2020b) *Proven Reoffending Statistics Quarterly Bulletin, October 2018 to December 2018* [Online], available from: https://assets.publishing.service.gov.uk/government/uploads/system/uploads/attachment_data/file/930446/Proven_reoffending_stats_bulletin_OctDec18.pdf (Accessed: 25th January 2021).

Ministry of Justice (2020c) *Prison Performance Statistics 2019 to 2020* [Online], available from: www.gov.uk/government/statistics/prison-performance-statistics-2019-to-2020 (Accessed: 25th January 2021).

Ministry of Justice (2021) *HM Prison and Probation Service COVID-19 Official Statistics* [Online], available from: https://assets.publishing.service.gov.uk/government/uploads/system/uploads/attachment_data/file/986121/HMPPS_COVID19_Apr21_Pub.pdf (Accessed: 8th November 2021).

Ministry of Justice (2022) *Offender Management Statistics Quarterly: July to September 2021* [Online], available from: www.gov.uk/government/statistics/offender-management-statistics-quarterly-july-to-september-2021 (Accessed: 19th February 2022).

National Audit Office (2017) *Mental Health in Prisons* [Online], available from: www.nao.org.uk/wp-content/uploads/2017/06/Mental-health-in-prisons.pdf (Accessed: 11th January 2018).

National Audit Office (2020) *Improving the Prison Estate* [Online], available from: www.nao.org.uk/wp-content/uploads/2020/02/Improving-the-prison-estate.pdf (Accessed: 25th January 2021).

New Economics Foundation (2018) *Austerity by Stealth? Options for the Chancellor at the Coming Spending Review* [Online], available from: https://neweconomics.org/uploads/files/AUSTERITY-BY-STEALTH-Sep18.pdf (Accessed: 21st February 2020).

NHS Improvement (2019) *Performance of the NHS Provider Sector for the Year Ended 31 March 2019* [Online], available from: https://improvement.nhs.uk/documents/5404/Performance_of_the_NHS_provider_sector_for_the_quarter_4_1819.pdf (Accessed: 21st February 2020).

Nuffield Trust (2020) *Locked out? Prisoners' Use of Hospital Care* [Online], available from: www.nuffieldtrust.org.uk/files/2020-02/prisoners-use-of-hospital-services-main-report.pdf (Accessed: 25th January 2021).

Reinhart, E. and Chen, D. L. (2020) Incarceration and Its Disseminations: COVID-19 Pandemic Lessons From Chicago's Cook County Jail. *Health Affairs*. 39(8), pp. 1412–1418.

Singleton, N., Meltzer, H. and Gatward, R. (1998) *Psychiatric Morbidity Among Prisoners in England and Wales* [Online], available from: www.ons.gov.uk/ons/rel/psychiatric-morbidity/psychiatric-morbidity-among-prisoners/psychiatric-morbidity-among-prisoners--summary-report/psychiatric-morbidity-among-prisoners--summary-report.pdf (Accessed: 11th January 2018).

Stürup-Toft, S., O' Moore, E. J. and Plugge, E. H. (2018) Looking Behind the Bars: Emerging Health Issues for People in Prison. *British Medical Bulletin*. 125, pp. 15–23.

Wacquant, L. (2002) The Curious Eclipse of Prison Ethnography in the Age of Mass Incarceration. *Ethnography*. 3, pp. 371–398.

Yeats, W. B. (1920) The Second Coming. In: *The Dial*. New England: Transcendentalists.

Chapter 7

Destabilisation of prisons and prison health governance

Introduction

In this chapter, I unpack the destabilisation of prisons and prison health governance after the introduction of austerity in 2010. This destabilisation was an unanticipated effect of austerity as a political experiment. I detail participant experiences that revealed discrepancies in 1) legal accountability between ministers and governors; 2) privatisation of some prison establishments as a mode of governance; and 3) the growth of prison gangs and serious organised crime across English prisons.

The accounts reveal how top-down governance shapes and constricts English prison health governance of healthcare delivery. Yet despite the existence of this governance structure, participant accounts also attested to the growth of informal governance via prison gangs and serious organised crime across English prisons. Collectively, these unfolding discrepancies and shifting power dynamics impacted the prison health governance and delivery of healthcare in English prisons both directly and indirectly.

Destabilisation of prison governance via high ministerial turnover

Ministers for the Justice portfolio come and go frequently. This volatility compounds the already problematic command-and-control governance of prisons in England, where the prison regime is steered by the central government through a set of regulations, policies, and standards. The governors are proactively required to interpret these rules for their institutions (Bennett, 2016). However, high turnover compromises their leadership stability. Many policymaker participants observed that the UK had seven justice ministers between 2010 and 2019 (HM Government, 2020a), who created what they called 'butterfly' policies—moving from one policy reform to another. In the interview, Participant 16, the head of a European education association, said, "We have had five justice secretaries in six years, and the sense of no one really wanting to take this on".

DOI: 10.4324/9781003182337-7

These butterfly policies are a form of political experimentation, where policies are often implemented without sufficient prior analysis or due regard for coherence with the previous ministers. Furthermore, the participants observe how ministers often introduce new policies ad hoc, before completing previous reform agendas, contributing to systemic reactivity and further instability. Other portfolios, such as Health, had less than half the turnover in the same period (HM Government, 2020b). Policymaking by Health Ministers has had a more persistent effect because of the stability of the ministers behind it. This includes, for instance, the Health and Social Care Act 2012 under Andrew Lansley (2010–2012) and measures to improve Accident & Emergency Department waiting times and clamp down health tourism under Jeremy Hunt (2012–2018).

Participants viewed these butterfly policies as short term. Participant 33, a regional health and justice lead of a health organisation, echoed this idea:

> David Gauke [Secretary of State for Justice] said short sentences are a nightmare. It sounds fantastic. But is he going to be here in 12 months? Two years? Ten years? What is his legacy? You have got to think about his legacy as well. Governments change. We have got Brexit. There is so much going on. If he is still in, I am sure he will see it through. If he decides to go in a different direction from his current job or things change dramatically with Brexit, who takes forward that legacy, or do we still sit treading water?

Based on their observations of the reforms executed for prisons over the last decade, informants described Gauke (2018–2019) and Gove (2015–2016)—who served as justice ministers, respectively—as more liberal. But they saw Grayling (2012 to 2015) as authoritarian. In fact, their proposed reforms conflicted with each other. During his tenure, Grayling proposed a limit of 12 books for prisoners, a measure Gove swiftly reversed after taking over as justice minister from Grayling. Similarly, Gauke attempted to abolish short sentences under 12 months, contradicting Grayling's tough justice proposal.

As a result, the study shows that given the high throughput of ministerial figures, prison service continues to be ill-equipped to translate vague and conflicting goals into integrated actions. Ministers are typically transient and regularly moved for strategic political reasons, making coordination of governance and delivery challenging (Flinders, 2002). This study builds on Matthew Flinders' (2002) contention by showing how these temporary ministers contribute to the destabilisation of the prison system, following the continual changing policies by the justice ministers over the last decade.

Several participants also questioned the leadership experience of ministers taking Justice portfolios. They perceived a lack of appreciation of the challenges present in delivering prison service.

> They have had cyphers [a person of no credibility, influence, or importance] for too long as Prisons' Ministers. They have just floated in. They

> have never done anything. They have never worked in any organisation. They do not know the stresses and strains; particularly, they do not recognise the need to look after the staff. If things are right for staff, things are going to be right for prisoners. That includes the medical staff. But these ministers do not know anything about the justice system.
>
> (Participant 13, former head of a prison inspectorate)

Despite lacking prison leadership experience, Participant 15 provided a unique insight from his interaction with a former minister who explicitly resisted evidence provided by penal experts simply because it opposed the ministerial agenda.

> I tried to advise [a former minister] about youth offending, mental illness, drugs [misuse] and homelessness. [The Minister] said "We are not interested in experts". Their resistance to evidence of any branch of research was just shocking to me. I do not think the situation has got any better. . . . They are impervious to evidence and that really worries me, because people are dying in prisons all the time.
>
> (Participant 15, academic and former Cabinet Office advisor)

Participants said the political agenda of incumbent politicians also dictated the delivery of healthcare in prisons. This view conforms to a Weberian theory of bureaucracy as an iron cage that denies staff autonomy (Weber, 1930). Specifically, ministers' policies on sentencing, running prisons, increasing the size of prison estates, and lack of scrutiny of the relationships between the UK and the European Court of Human Rights were based on their fickleness.

Despite the lack of prison leadership experience, these ministers have the power and discretion to dictate the running of prison institutions that can often destabilise the system. Participant 75, a prison governor of a closed prison with an urgent notification status, recalled personal frustration when a new minister blocked the 'digitalisation' programme in his establishment. The move was because the minister thought prison amenities should not be better than those on the outside. This accords with the principle of less eligibility, suggesting conditions of life in prison must be set lower than conditions for the poor in the community (Sim, 2002). As Participant 75 said:

> There was a rollout of digitalisation where each prisoner was going to get in-cell computer access. The prisoners could use it to interact with the prison systems, whether that was booking a visit or an appointment to see a doctor, et cetera. One of the ministers, I will not name which one, came in, and he just pulled the plug on that. He argued that not everybody in the community had a computer. Not everybody in the community could book an appointment online. . . . It would have made things much more efficient in the establishment. We have now got a halfway house where

> they have not got a computer, but there are kiosks on the landing. So, that is where the government can impact an establishment's running, an institution, depending on what we might call it.

The descriptions of ministers disbelieving experts and thinking prisoners should experience lower-quality services than the public offer two implications for how their political power and discretion can destabilise prison healthcare and the broader prison regime. First, participants' responses reflected how much the state dictates the minutiae of prison health delivery. Albeit indirectly, this control and volatility in agenda frustrate the principle of equivalence, according to which prison health service provisions should match standards of community health services (WHO, 2014). The problem of equivalency is underscored by the participant's observation earlier of how a minister dismissed evidence on youth offending, mental health, and drug misuse issues among prisoners, whereby the punishment agenda of prison trumps the rehabilitation agenda of prison healthcare services. Second, the state can exercise control over prison health governance according to the prevailing ideology (Peck and Tickell, 1994). This control prioritises the principles of punishment, security, and public protection over rehabilitation.

This study also provides exceptions to the popular social policy literature on 'governance without the government' that purports self-organisation, interorganisational cooperation, fluid interaction with stakeholders, and autonomy (Bevir and Rhodes, 2003; Fidler, 2007; Rhodes, 1996). The government dictates the minutiae of prison activities. Though the concepts of governance without the government were in fashion in the 1990s (Rhodes, 1996), they leave space for domination of one government agency over another, which often leads to adverse outcomes. This study highlights an urgent need for a new definition of governance that meshes the theoretical representation of the prison health system and structure with the empirical manifestation of adaptation towards political activities or pressures. That is, despite the dispersed structure and collaborative nature of prison health governance that permits its actors to organise, protect, and promote the health of prisoners, this governance structure will always be subjected to political power and orientation, with which it is expected to negotiate and align continually.

The findings of this study also challenge the idealistic perception that civil servants are independent from political interference. Several local-level participants accused their senior management of being complicit with ministers. Rhetoric included calling them "a sycophant" (Participant 64, a head of prison officers' union) and "a kiss-ass" (Participant 82, a senior prison officer of a high-security prison), and of having "a yes, sir attitude" (Participant 79, a deputy governor of a closed prison with urgent notification status). In an accusatory tone, Participant 67, the prison governor of an open prison, noted:

> The Chief Executive and her senior management team are always looking up, trying to appease ministers and work with ministers, rather than looking at and trying to take the organisation forward. We are supposed to be

> an executive agency, and we should not have that level of interference from ministers. But we do, and that is hugely frustrating.

The participants criticised the pervasive deference of these officials to the ministers, describing senior management of HMPPS assuaging the ministerial plan rather than honestly describing how austerity affected the ground-level operations. Participants portrayed such managers as being complicit with ministers by legitimising their agenda rather than representing the workforce's views.

Such views oppose Sparks and Bottoms' (1996) theory of a representational dimension: the behaviour of officials typically represents the bureaucrats' view of the prison system as a whole. The failure of the HMPPS upper echelons to manage ministerial expectation aligns with Gramsci's (1971) theory of how elites control state apparatuses to disseminate the values that reinforce their ruling position and the hegemonic project of neoliberalism. By revealing such diverse opinions within one government department, this study demonstrates the destabilising effect of the ministerial agenda.

Many participants spoke about justice ministers' power in dictating policy but escaping the legal responsibility for their decisions. Instead, legal responsibilities rested on the prison governors. Additionally, the ministerial power also perpetuates the irony that prison governors are legally responsible for prison leadership when they merely conform with the justice ministers' political mandates. Section 11 of the 1952 Prison Act holds prison governors as the guarantors for all activities in their establishments. According to the informants, civil servants are expected to obey politicians' objectives. This practice aligns with Gramsci's (1971) hegemony theory of ideological incorporation, as well as with Larry Terry's (1995) and later Arjen Boin's (2001) contextual definition of the autonomy of civil servants, which is highly dependent on the prevailing political values of the government in power.

Critical realists such as Fritz Scharpf (1997), Colin Hay (2002), David Marsh (2003), and Stuart McAnulla (2005) argue structural inequality significantly affects the polity context of the British political system. Specifically, power continues to be concentrated in the hands of central government. This concentration is especially true among those with ministerial control and thus is directly relevant to prisons. Participants averred that policymakers, prison governors, and prison officers cannot be viewed as independent from the state, which plays a key role in running England's prisons.

This research further demonstrates how the prevailing political determinants for prisons will trump the dispersal mode of governance of health services. Like the top-down imposition of the economics of austerity, prison governance has a command-and-control structure. This often collides with the execution of prison healthcare delivery, which uses a more dispersed governance model than prisons. As we have seen, participants mentioned navigating this tension.

We see how the command-and-control prison structure trumps prison health governance and delivery through participants' descriptions of the lack of coherent aims of imprisonment. Rule 3 of the Prison Rules of 1999 states that the purpose of prison service is to encourage and assist prisoners to lead a good and useful life. Being so general, it has faced criticism for providing unfettered discretion for the justice ministers to dictate the purpose of imprisonment (Livingstone et al., 2008). Meanwhile, HMPPS (2021) states imprisonment's functions are to execute court sentences, prevent further victimisation, and reduce reoffending via rehabilitation programmes (e.g., education, employment). None of these official statements acknowledges the need to provision for healthcare and well-being. This omission allows for political experimentation on austerity and the broader prevailing neoliberalism to infiltrate the prison governance.

Furthermore, other aims often precede NHS England's prison health agenda. These include HMPPS priorities around security and public protection, and the managerial emphasis on cost-savings and efficiency to appease taxpayers (Liebling and Crewe, 2012). Clearly at play here is a classical theory on favourable agency myth: politicians can appear to support altruistic goals, yet those goals are impossible to achieve given political preferences and resource constraints (Lipsky, 1980). This study finds a mismatch between what politicians want and what resources public services can offer, with the official goals and practices of the prison health agenda usually portrayed as altruistic and civilised. A misalignment between the policy that recognises rehabilitation as a penal driver and extant resource constraints reinforces the conflict between 'policy-in-form' and 'policy-in-use' enacted on the 'frontstage' and 'backstage' of policy formulation and implementation. Similar to Patrick Diamond et al. (2016) and Jon Pierre and Guy Peters (2020), authoritative and hierarchical governing remains relevant, which has shaped and constricted England's prison health governance and delivery.

Destabilisation of prison governance via increased privatisation

The increased prison and prison healthcare privatisation is a trait of neoliberalism, intersecting with austerity programmes that demand cost savings. As participants reveal, this process of privatisation in the face of resource pressures destabilised prison governance as services were broken up and private agents were introduced piecemeal. Yet study participants also exposed misconceptions about cost savings using private sector providers. They also railed against the moral legitimacy of their delivering punishment on behalf of the state, as well as service efficiency and quality.

Strengthening of privatisation post-2012 programmes

Prison privatisation first occurred in the 1990s as operations transferred to the private sector (Ministry of Justice, 2019a). The Prison Unit Cost Programme of 2012 reinforced further privatisation; it required public prisons to reduce their costs and remain as economically efficient as those in the private sector

(House of Commons Justice Committee, 2012). Participants described how this programme facilitated outsourcing of most services to the private and not-for-profit sectors, leading to a fragmentation of services that affected prisoners' quality of care:

> Chris Grayling[1] privatised different sorts of services. . . . [L]ots of the services within a prison, for instance, estates management, healthcare, [and] substance misuse, were contracted out. [It] was a fragmentation of delivery. The privatisation absolutely affected the throughcare that prisoners might be getting.
> (Participant 28, a former head of a prison inspectorate)

Section 9(4) of the Public Contracts Regulations 2006 requires commissioners to employ competitive bidding in the procurement process for services costing at least €134,000 (or ~£117,552). Moreover, the Health and Social Care Act 2012 allows "any qualified provider" to manage public services. These two statutory instruments mandate that procurement processes provide equal access to all potential bidders and remove bureaucratic obstacles.

National participants, particularly those in a commissioning position, often argued that they had to remain committed, from a legal perspective, to finding the best provider for delivering penal services, irrespective of providers' organisational arrangement. As Participant 55, a prison health lead of a national health organisation and magistrate, stated:

> We do not have a [preference for the services to be delivered by] the public, voluntary, or private sector providers. [The invitation] goes out to open tender. It goes into the Official Journal of the European Union as a tender opportunity. It is made nationally available. People bid against the specification. We then have a process of reviewing all of these bids against the specification, in detail. The most qualified provider within the cost envelope is awarded the contract. If they are the best organisation to provide it, great. They can come in, and they can show their worth, and they can provide it.

Doing so invokes public procurement as part of the competitive and deregulatory processes to permit the government to relinquish its oversight power to the private sector (McGregor, 2001). The outcome has included a 16% increase of £6.8 billion in HMPPS expenditures on private contractors (HMPPS, 2019; Ministry of Justice, 2009) and a 29% rise of £9.2 billion on private health providers in 2018/2019 (Department of Health, 2015; Department of Health and Social Care, 2019). The cost savings agenda during austerity seems to have played a role in this explosion of private contractor involvement in the penal system.

The government framed privatisation as improving efficiency and saving costs, but those who operated outside the government structure disagreed. To them, the government moves were politically motivated. Participant 52, a head of policy of a national penal reform organisation, said the government experiment was about "marketing the criminal justice system and breaking it up so it is possible to sell bits of it off and contract it out". Considering the ideological nature of privatisation of prison healthcare and prison services, most participants objected to the measures on the grounds of morality, quality, and efficiency, as we will explore next.

Participants' objections vis-à-vis morality

Consistent with Mary Corcoran (2014), many participants from different levels of governance and delivery objected on moral grounds to private entities administering punishment. Participant 23, an advisor to a European intergovernmental human rights organisation and an international drug and crime organisation, made a forceful argument. "[I]t was the state who took away the liberty of persons, so it is the state's full responsibility, direct responsibility, to care for prisoners in a direct way and not to outsource it". Moreover, Participant 75, a prison governor of a closed prison with an urgent notification status, believed "there is something morally wrong around making a profit out of people's misery".

However, the government rejects this sentiment, wanting to outsource public services per its neoliberal perspective. Thus, participants in a commissioning position argued earlier in this chapter their only choice was to appoint the best provider for delivering penal services, irrespective of providers' organisational arrangement.

A few participants from the advocacy and monitoring fields observed that privatisation reduces scope for accountability. According to these participants, private contractors typically hide behind the veil of commercial confidentiality to avoid data sharing and consequently scrutiny of their services. Participant 52, the head of policy of a national penal reform organisation, stated:

> The Ministry of Justice will say: "Well, that prison is not run by us. That is run by G4S or Sodexo". These providers, in turn, will say: "We are just following government policy. This is what we have agreed in our contracts regarding how we will deliver services". They just push the responsibility backwards and forwards. So whom do you hold to account?

Fragmented services, according to several participants within the monitoring role, could further sever the chain of accountability of these private businesses. Yet as Participant 37, a health and social care lead of a national social care organisation, reminds us, the government stayed responsible for services despite contracting them out:

> You can contract out provision of services, but you do not contract out your responsibility. You are still responsible for ensuring services are delivered to the quality that is required to deliver the outcomes that are needed. Across health, social care, and indeed prisons and other aspect of public services.

That both the HMPPS and their private contractors shirk accountability is consistent with David Harvey's (2010) contention that neoliberalism leads to the consolidation and centralisation of power in the hands of a few institutions that escape public control. As such, it illustrates a democratic deficit (Chomsky, 1999), representing the fault line in the governance structure. The lack of moral accountability for punishment and the thwart of institutional accountability calls for the government to robustly and continually monitor private-sector providers. These calls signify the omnipresence of the central government's command and control in directing the English prison system. This diametrically opposes the social policy literature that popularises self-organisation and autonomy (Bevir and Rhodes, 2003; Fidler, 2007; Rhodes, 1996).

Some participants who managed private prisons dismissed some of the aforementioned monitoring concerns. For instance, Participant 84, a director of a closed private prison, claimed that the monitoring framework imposed on private prisons was, in fact, more stringent than public sector prisons:

> The governance in a private establishment is huge. We get a lot of scrutiny internally, because it is a risky business, and it can impact the rest of the business units which we provide elsewhere. We have an internal Controller Team. They monitor performance. We are set up against a group of KPIs, which is internal to the contract, but we are also then marked across the national baseline. We are held to account much more than our public sector counterparts in terms of scrutiny and delivery.

Yet the keyword here is 'internal'. This scrutiny was predominantly undertaken by internal audit teams at private prisons, raising questions of objectivity and conflicting interests. This study finds parallels with Australian studies demonstrating that the lack of oversight frameworks and quality control of private security operators can undermine the image of the penal sector among the public (Andrew and Cahill, 2007; Baldino et al., 2010).

The commercialisation of services under the privatisation movement further prompted morality concerns from participants. Markets are not self-correcting and cannot provide appropriate quality control (Fitzgibbon and Lea, 2018). Therefore, many participants operating in a commissioning capacity felt that they had to safeguard prisoner health requirements from private organisations desiring to deliver services commercially. Acting as gatekeepers (Lipsky, 1980), they imposed close monitoring on private contractors, despite recognising this would inevitably increase transaction costs. As Participant 53, a regional head of health and justice commissioning of a national health organisation, said:

> They are always looking at their profit margins. So, there is always that awareness, from a commissioning point of view, that there is an organisation that is not just about making positive outcomes for prisoners, or providing the best[-]quality, high-quality services that are responsive to need. It is constantly in my head that they are also looking at their profit margins.

This behaviour illustrates that, notwithstanding previous research, there are no significant differences in cost savings between public and private prisons (Le Vay, 2015). Indeed, this study offers evidence against austerity's putative cost-saving rationale and the government's desire "to secure new services to improve existing service delivery, encourage innovation and drive value for money" (Ministry of Justice, 2011, p. 4). Quality of care is suffering from a destabilising tension between the political austerity agenda and its implementation in private hands. Most participants considered health a common good. And they felt financial capabilities ought not to dictate access to health provisions. Though access to healthcare was free at the point of access and delivery for prisoners, several participants echoed that introducing financial constraints under a privatisation framework could indirectly limit access to healthcare.

> [H]ealthcare is a public good. Once you put it into a setting where it becomes dependent on a resource, you instantly create a problem where you might have unequal access to that resource. It also changes the way in which medical professionals go about their business: "Have we reached the limit on the scans we can do for this person? What is this person's cover?"
>
> (Participant 18, an academic and advisor to a European administration organisation)

Others had serious doubts about the de-prioritisation of some services over others, depending on the financial interests and capabilities of the private companies, when delivering prison healthcare services. Ironically, their preferences contradict the government's commitment to some areas of prison healthcare that not only makes service delivery rather disjointed but also morally questionable.

> NHS England gives £5 million a year to a private healthcare provider in [a closed male prison near London]. The provider then has to spread all of that money across all the different healthcare functions. Of course, it's sub-contractors, like us, who have the lowest priority. So, they cut our substance misuse services to relieve the pressure on their other healthcare services. The market dictates de-prioritisation of our service, but the policy documents of NHS England and the Ministry of Justice say that responding to substance misuse in prisons is a top priority, and they are committed to reducing drug problems and providing drug treatment. The policy and the commissioning do not fit together.
>
> (Participant 66, the head of a substance misuse service operating in various closed prisons)

A minority of participants spoke of private contractors' superior quality regarding innovation and financial savvy. Yet overall, there remained broader concerns around the harmful impacts on prisoners and prison workforces in private prisons. These concerns extended to service quality and efficiency, which the next section explores.

Quality and efficiency

Although nearly all participants protested privatisation on morality grounds, they blamed quality concerns less consistently. A minority of participants thought the private sector was better at introducing innovation than the government. Participant 84, a director of a private closed prison, substantiated this:

> We are piloting currently a medication locker, so people can collect their medications remotely. It will take the pressure out of the queuing system which is on the in-house doctors. . . . I have seen those queues grow massively. The experience for the clinical staff there is not great and the infrastructure in the rooms means that the amount of medication cannot be dispensed properly. The experience for the prisoners to have to go and stand in those queues and the ability to manage in-possession medics is an absolute nightmare. They have to wait to be unlocked; they have to wait 20 minutes in the queue so you are normally looking on average 40 minutes roughly to get their medications at a time in which you are expected to do all the good things in the regime. We are very good at innovations.

Alongside innovations, some participants argued that the private sector could better contain costs through remuneration packages. Participant 73, a head of private healthcare organisation of a resettlement prison, for example, argued his organisation was more efficient because it refused sick pay and pensions for employees. Private healthcare organisations readily queried the relationship between profit margin and access to prison healthcare delivery. As he asserted:

> We get a set amount of money from NHS England. They will not reduce it year on year; it is just a set amount of funding each month, where with other Trusts you know they are told to save the amount. The benefit for NHS England to have a private provider is that you have not got to worry about NHS pensions or NHS sick pay, because those costs are huge—aren't they? . . . If a nurse here goes off sick, they do not get paid; they will get statutory sick pay after two weeks, which for us does not have any effect really. I think there is more accountability, so we are far more aware that we must fulfil contractual obligations, and we cannot rely on the wider NHS to fund us if we go way over budget.

Those who ran private prison healthcare services explicitly recognised the relationship between cost and profit margin in their daily functioning. Participant 73, the head of a private healthcare organisation of a resettlement prison, illustrated this point:

> We review our budget each year with our finance manager. We have far more hospital escorts that are going out. I can request more money, but it

> obviously reduces any sort of profit margin there. We pay for the prison officers escorting, so if somebody is going out to hospital and the officers that are escorting that patient it comes out of the healthcare budget. For one day, it is a £1000; so, if somebody had one day in hospital just the escorting of themselves, £1000 comes out of the budget. It is a lot of money and that is not to mention anything to do with the hospital and the care that they are getting, just for the two officers to stand there for £1000 for 24 hours.

Participants claimed that penal commercialism and prisoner rehabilitation were contradictory: one was based on financial opportunities, the other on needs. Although prison contractors in England project efficiency by reducing employment costs (Hermann and Flecker, 2012; Sachdev, 2004), this study found no improvement in quality. Discussed elsewhere by Alison Liebling and Amy Ludlow (2017) is how some of the weaknesses inherent in private sector establishments, such as high turnover, lack of loyalty, inexperience, and a drift into criminal justice work rather than a vocation, are underestimated. Participants contended that health is a common good but that privatisation and austerity jeopardise this reality; indeed, they consider it incompatible with market-based distributional strategies.

The transactional nature of this approach prioritises profit over a social agenda; businesses have reduced impetus to rehabilitate prisoners entrusted to them (Andrew and Cahill, 2007; Feeley and Simon, 1992). This finding builds on Saldivar and Price's transatlantic study (2015) that found that privatisation financially benefits private prisons at the expense of prisoners. Privatisation therefore conflicts with the prison rehabilitation agenda. This conflict of interests has materialised as a reduction in quality. For example, in a few private prisons, HMPPS, rather than NHS England, directly commissioned healthcare services (House of Commons Justice Committee, 2019). This meant healthcare provision escaped subjection to the NHS England delivery framework, and indeed, several governors raised concerns about worsening healthcare standards in these prisons (ibid.). Overall, privatisation seemingly serves to depoliticise the use of imprisonment through economic logic, desensitises the state from its welfare obligation, and camouflages health governance and delivery in a commercialised structure.

Some participants exemplified the quality and efficiency failings of privatisation. They cited: 1) the transfer of HMP Birmingham from G4S to public sector prisons due to excessive violence and poor standards (Ministry of Justice, 2019a); 2) the recent inquiry highlighting the poor performance of the Community Rehabilitation Companies in reducing reoffending post-release (Sasse et al., 2019); and 3) the bankruptcy of Carillion, a private sector provider of prison maintenance that was responsible for 50 prisons across southern England in 2018 (House of Commons Library, 2018a).

Finally, Carillion's bankruptcy, as well as failures of the Community Rehabilitation Companies (CRCs) in supervising offenders at low and medium risk of serious harm in the community, concerned most of the policy informants.

Participant 55, a prison health lead of a national health organisation and magistrate, reflected on his experience in dealing with CRCs. They have, he believed, failed to deliver service objectives and left a service gap behind them:

> I have absolutely no confidence in the CRCs at all. For instance, somebody in prison for two years; we have taken every bit of responsibility away from them for those two years. They are not allowed to decide when they go to bed, when they shower, when they eat, when they go to work, everything. That is all decided for them, they have no responsibility. Then we tip them out the door and expect them to all of a sudden be responsible members of society who can find themselves a GP, get themselves to the community drug services, all of those kinds of things—all of those things the CRCs should be doing. Getting a roof over their heads, getting their benefits sorted out. CRCs have done nothing, absolutely nothing. That is my experience from the ones that are local to me that I have had to work with. It is also echoed quite a lot elsewhere and in the official publications. Now that they have gone belly up, we have been left with a massive gaping hole. Well, more so at the end of people's custodial sentences.

Taxpayers paid an estimated £72 million for these services (Sasse et al., 2019). The participants' views here speak to the continued corporate welfare approach, where the state continues to heavily subsidise private businesses (Farnsworth, 2013). These three early debacles—of G4S, CRCs, and Carillion—warn us that privatisation might cost more in the long run, as the government continues to subsidise those firms' failures. They have also diverted public expenditures from entities in need (Dawkins, 2002).

Nevertheless, many participants observed the current government's appetite for contracting out services. This shows it has yet to learn from the evident failings of its continued political experimentation. Despite the poor track record across the English criminal justice system, forecasts indicate private contractors will occupy an increasingly significant role in the penal landscape: at least two out of four prisons that will be built by 2026, HMPs Glen Parva and Wellingborough, have been hypothecated for private contractors (House of Commons Library, 2018b; Ministry of Justice, 2019b).

Participants felt that given the results to date, continued privatisation evidences political irrationality. As reasoned by Participant 64, a head of a prison officers' union, the practice is counterintuitive:

> Birmingham got privatised in 2011, and we have just taken it back in the public sector—we said it would not work; it has not worked. It has not been profitable for G4S. They also have had Medway removed from them, because of the scandal with the juvenile offenders there, as highlighted by the Panorama programme.[2] So, the Medway Youth Offending Institution came back into the public sector, [and] we did a good job there. Then they

> have just announced last week that that is going to be a secure school run by a Christian Charity called Oasis, and we never heard of them before. So, it seems that these private companies can mess up, lose contracts but they are still allowed to bid for new contracts. It does not make sense at all. It is not value for money for the taxpayers.

To summarise, participants observed that outsourcing services (prison healthcare services included) countered the government's objectives of greater service efficiency, quality, and cost savings. Privatisation destabilises the prison governance structure through the questionable legitimacy of punishment being delivered by a business rather than the state, alongside a more fragmented service delivery, inferior service quality, and a higher monitoring requirement than with public-sector providers. All these predicaments could lead to a crisis of legitimation resulting from a loss of confidence in the private institutions running prison healthcare and the whole prison establishment. Yet the continuing desire for increased privatisation signifies political irrationality and supports participants' observations that it was an ideological manoeuvre.

Destabilisation of prison governance via prison gangs and serious organised crime groups in English prisons

Despite prisons' hierarchical nature, prison gangs and organised crime groups are usurping their top-down governance structure. The growth of these informal governance structures has coincided with rising drug use in prisons, a domino effect created via a reduction in prison officers that has weakened the institutional governance structure.

Most participants believed that a continual weakening of institutional governance cumulatively led to a disengaged prison population. For example, Participant 25, a European law and human rights specialist, noted, "[W]hen you have lower staff [levels] and less secure prisons, people start looking to informal structures, i.e. gangs, for their security". Participants viewed this disengagement as significant given the rapid rise of prison gangs and serious organised crime groups who supply illicit drugs into local prisons as part of the informal economy.

Ground-level participants illustrated that these groups could pose insurmountable challenges in maintaining control in these institutions. Gangs also preyed on vulnerable prisoners, according to participants' responses. For example, Participant 57, a head of a prison governor's union, explained, "Strong gangs take control of our prisons. They bully other prisoners, weaker prisoners, and force them into taking drugs".

> Most prisons that have drug issues, there will be serious organised crime involved, because no one throws over drugs worth over £50,000 like a lottery and thinks it will not get there, without having some serious backing.
> (Participant 71, Prison governor of a resettlement prison)

Participant 55's responses also addressed the impact of organised crime on the prison system. The participant stated:

> These organised crime groups ensure that those illegal substances are available within the prison estate. Yes, there are some small local level dealers who will get stuff in. The scale of the supply into the prison system has to indicate that it is a problem of serious organised crime nationally, rather than just looking at small scale individual dealers, or small groups of dealers. Tackling that serious organised crime angle is probably one of the things that would significantly improve the stability of the prison estate. Therefore, the delivery of healthcare.
>
> (Participant 55, prison health lead of a national health organisation and magistrate)

Several participants explained that prison gangs use social media and mobile phones to operate an illicit economy of drugs. They believed gangs sustained this economy through cumulative debts, bullying, and violence. Considering the profits to be made, some local participants said released prisoners would even attempt to get reincarcerated to traffic the drugs back into establishments. Participant 75, the prison governor of a closed prison with an urgent notification status, stated: "We have seen now where individuals are being paid to come back to prison after being released and they are full of drugs, like people who come back from abroad".

Building on previous research (Gooch and Treadwell, 2020; Maitra, 2010; Skarbek, 2011), this study demonstrates the sophistication of the microeconomic structure of organised crime. The findings show how gangs thrive in English prisons and how criminal groups sustain a monopolistic market through coercion and violence. This study also highlights an important new finding: these groups prey on vulnerable staff and traffic drugs via former prisoners. Habermas's (1973) crisis of legitimacy theory explains and conceptualises the lack of detection and enforcement resulting from having fewer prison custodians. A broader crisis of legitimacy of prison governance, resulting in a loss of control of the prison institution, undermines leadership and coordinated action for health delivery. Indeed, this study demonstrates how this conundrum requires a more robust governance of prisons by the government. That is the opposite of social policy literature on governance, which prefers self-organisation among actors and autonomy from the state (Fidler, 2007).

These findings corroborate several participants' fears of the total loss of order and governance in English prisons. They suggested that something like the Strangeways riot of April 1990 (Sim, 2002) might happen again. Several participants portrayed that riot as a consequence of prolonged austerity measures. The present findings are a wake-up call regarding the cumulative effect of disruptions to prison authority. Despite the top-down nature of England's prison governance, which is often hailed as providing predictability, security, and stability of governance structure, evidence shows the opposite.

Conclusion

This study evidences the destabilisation of the top-down governance of prison service that resulted from the political experiment of austerity and neoliberalism. It finds three sources combining to create this destabilisation. First is frequently reactive and short-term ministerial direction of the policies and delivery of prison agenda. Second is the dysfunction of outsourcing of the governance to private sector organisations. And third is the burgeoning prison gangs and serious organised crime across English prisons.

Inevitably, this destabilisation of governance constricts the delivery of prison healthcare. First, the prevailing political structure—with high ministerial authority and turnover—prevents consistent policymaking and implementation. Participants also criticised the intensification of the privatisation of prison healthcare and prison services since 2012. Contradicting the political perception that private-sector organisations delivered cost savings and improved service efficiency, most participants objected to privatisation on the grounds of questionable morality, decreased quality, and reduced accountability. Yet the government appears to be planning augmented privatisation, signifying political irrationality. Finally, destabilisation manifests in the form of prison gangs and serious organised crime groups that supply drugs to prisoners and attempt to corrupt the formal governance structure by inducting prison staff, albeit in small numbers.

The existing prison structure directs prison governance from the central government down to the individual prison establishments. Despite this, the present study also proposes that the examples of destabilisation (through political volatility, increased privatisation, and growth of prison gangs and serious organised crime in prisons) challenged this governance structure's robustness. The central government's dictation of the minutiae does not prevent the prisons from destabilising. Yet these observations also contradict the utility of self-governance that is prevalent in social policy, which prefers fluid interaction with stakeholders and a wide margin of autonomy by stakeholders (Bevir and Rhodes, 2003; Fidler, 2007; Rhodes, 1996).

The next chapter will illustrate participants' perspectives on recent government policies putatively intended to ameliorate austerity's impacts. In particular, it will examine the government's announcement of the recruitment of new prison officers in 2016, the proposals of building more prisons, and the blaming of psychoactive substances such as *Spice* that have intensified incessant prison instability.

Notes

1 The former Justice Secretary between 2012 and 2015 who instituted the Benchmarking Exercise to reduce the number of prison officers.

2 The Ministry of Justice took over Medway Youth Offender Institution from G4S in 2016 following allegations of staff abuse towards the residents (The Guardian, 2016).

References

Andrew, J. and Cahill, D. (2007) *Value for Money? Neoliberalism and New South Wales Prisons*. New South Wales: University of Wollongong.

Baldino, D., Drum, M. and Wyatt, B. (2010) The Privatisation of Prisoner Transfer Services in Western Australia: What Can We Learn from the Ward Case? In: Bennett, J., eds. (2016) *The Working Lives of Prison Managers: Global Change, Local Culture and Individual Agency in the Late Modern Prison*. London: Palgrave Macmillan.

Bennett, J. (2016) *The Working Lives of Prison Managers: Global Change, Local Culture and Individual Agency in the Late Modern Prison*. London: Palgrave Macmillan.

Bevir, M. and Rhodes, R. A. W. (2003) *Interpreting British Governance*. London: Routledge.

Boin, A. (2001) *Public Institutions: Leadership in Two Prison Systems*. Boulder: Lynne Rienner Publishers.

Chomsky, N. (1999) *Profit Over People: Neoliberalism and Global Order*. New York: Seven Stories Press.

Corcoran, M. (2014) The Trajectory of Penal Markets in a Period of Austerity: The Case of England and Wales. *Punishment and Incarceration: A Global Perspective*. 19, pp. 53–74.

Dawkins, C. E. (2002) Corporate Welfare, Corporate Citizenship, and the Question of Accountability. *Business and Society*. 41(3), pp. 269–291.

Department of Health (2015) *Annual Report and Accounts 2014–15* [Online], available from: https://assets.publishing.service.gov.uk/government/uploads/system/uploads/attachment_data/file/447002/DH_accounts_14-15_web.pdf (Accessed: 1st February 2020).

Department of Health and Social Care (2019) *Annual Report and Accounts 2018–19* [Online], available from: https://assets.publishing.service.gov.uk/government/uploads/system/uploads/attachment_data/file/832765/dhsc-annual-report-and-accounts-2018-to-2019.pdf (Accessed: 1st February 2020).

Diamond, P., Richards, D. and Smith, M. J. (2016) Re-centring the British Political Tradition: Explaining Contingency in New Labour and the Coalition's Governance Statecraft. In: Turnbull, N., ed. *Interpreting Governance, High Politics and Public Policy*. Oxford: Routledge, pp. 19–38.

Farnsworth, K. (2013) Bringing Corporate Welfare In. *Journal of Social Policy*. 42(1), pp. 1–22.

Feeley, M. and Simon, J. (1992) The New Penology: Notes on the Emerging Strategy of Corrections and Its Implications. *Criminology*. 30, pp. 449–474.

Fidler, D. P. (2007) Architecture Amidst Anarchy: Global Health's Quest for Governance. *Global Health Governance*. 1.

Fitzgibbon, W. and Lea, J. (2018) Privatization and Coercion: The Question of Legitimacy. *Theoretical Criminology*. 22(4), pp. 545–562.

Flinders, M. (2002) Shifting the Balance? Parliament, the Executive and the British Constitution. *Political Studies*. 50(1), pp. 23–42.

Gooch, K. and Treadwell, J. (2020) Prisoner Society in an Era of Psychoactive Substances, Organized Crime, New Drug Markets and Austerity. *The British Journal of Criminology*. 60(5), pp. 1260–1281.

Gramsci, A. (1971) *Selections From the Prison Notebooks of Antonio Gramsci*. London: Lawrence & Wishart.

Habermas, J. (1973) *Legitimation Crisis*. London: Heinemann Educational Books.

Harvey, D. (2010) *The Enigma of Capital and the Crises of Capitalism*. London: Profile Books.

Hay, C. (2002) *Political Analysis*. London: Palgrave.

Hermann, C. and Flecker, J. (2012) Conclusion: Impacts of Public Service Liberalization and Privatization. In: Hermann, C. and Flecker, J., eds. *Privatization of Public Services. Impacts for Employment, Working Conditions and Service Quality in Europe*. London: Routledge, pp. 192–205.

HM Government (2020a) *Ministerial Role: Lord Chancellor and Secretary of State for Justice* [Online], available from: www.gov.uk/government/ministers/secretary-of-state-for-justice (Accessed: 21st February 2020).

HM Government (2020b) *Ministerial Role: Secretary of State for Health and Social Care* [Online], available from: www.gov.uk/government/ministers/secretary-of-state-for-health-and-social-care (Accessed: 21st February 2020).

HM Prison & Probation Service (2019) *Her Majesty's Prison and Probation Service Annual Report and Accounts 2018–19* [Online], available from: https://assets.publishing.service.gov.uk/government/uploads/system/uploads/attachment_data/file/818788/HMPPS_Annual_Report_and_Accounts_2018-19__web_.pdf (Accessed: 21st February 2020).

HM Prison & Probation Service (2021) *About Us* [Online], available from: www.gov.uk/government/organisations/her-majestys-prison-and-probation-service/about (Accessed: 25th January 2021).

House of Commons Justice Committee (2012) *Oral Evidence Taken Before the Justice Committee: The Work of the Secretary of State, Wednesday 28 November 2012: Rt Hon Chris Grayling MP* [Online], available from: https://publications.parliament.uk/pa/cm201213/cmselect/cmjust/c741-i/c74101.htm (Accessed: 25th January 2021).

House of Commons Justice Committee (2019) *Prison Governance* [Online], available from: https://publications.parliament.uk/pa/cm201919/cmselect/cmjust/191/191.pdf (Accessed: 21st January 2020).

House of Commons Library (2018a) *The Collapse of Carillion: Briefing Paper Number 8206, 14 March 2018* [Online], available from: http://researchbriefings.files.parliament.uk/documents/CBP-8206/CBP-8206.pdf (Accessed: 21st February 2020).

House of Commons Library (2018b) *The Prison Estate. Briefing Paper Number 05646, 12 December 2018* [Online], available from: http://researchbriefings.files.parliament.uk/documents/SN05646/SN05646.pdf (Accessed: 19th February 2019).

Le Vay, J. (2015) *Competition for Prisons: Public or Private?* Bristol: Policy Press.

Liebling, A. and Crewe, B. (2012) Prisons Beyond the New Penology: The Shifting Moral Foundations of Prison Management. In: Simon, J. and Sparks, R., eds. *The SAGE Handbook of Punishment and Society*. London: SAGE, pp. 283–307.

Liebling, A. and Ludlow, A. (2017) Privatising Public Prisons: Penality, Law and Practice. *Australian & New Zealand Journal of Criminology*. 50(4), pp. 473–492.

Lipsky, M. (1980) *Street Level Bureaucracy: Dilemmas of the Individual in Public Services*. New York: Russell Sage Foundation.

Livingstone, S., Owen, T. and Macdonald, A. (2008) *Prison Law*. Oxford: Oxford University Press.

Maitra, D. M. (2010) An Exploratory Study of Prison Gangs in Contemporary Society. In: Harding, S. and Palasinski, M., eds. *Psychological Perspectives on Youth Gang Behaviour*. Hershey, PA: APMHBS Book Series, pp. 1–28.

Marsh, D. (2003) *Delivering a New Britain*. London: Palgrave.

McAnulla, S. (2005) Making Hay with Actualism? The Need for a Realist Concept of Structure. *Politics*. 25(1), pp. 31–38.

McGregor, S. L. T. (2001) Neoliberalism and Health Care. *International Journal of Consumer Studies*. 25(2), pp. 82–89.

Ministry of Justice (2009) *National Offender Management Service Annual Report and Accounts 0809* [Online], available from: https://assets.publishing.service.gov.uk/government/uploads/system/uploads/attachment_data/file/248223/0779.pdf (Accessed: 21st February 2020).

Ministry of Justice (2011) *Competition Strategy for Offender Services* [Online], available from: https://assets.publishing.service.gov.uk/government/uploads/system/uploads/attachment_data/file/217248/competition-strategy-offender-services.pdf (Accessed: 3rd July 2018).

Ministry of Justice (2019a) *Birmingham Prison Contract Ended* [Online], available from: www.gov.uk/government/news/birmingham-prison-contract-ended (Accessed: 21st February 2020).

Ministry of Justice (2019b) *10,000 Extra Prison Places to Keep the Public Safe* [Online], available from: www.gov.uk/government/news/10-000-extra-prison-places-to-keep-the-public-safe (Accessed: 21st February 2020).

Peck, J. and Tickell, A. (1994) Jungle Law Breaks Out: Neoliberalism and Global-Local Disorder. *Area*. 26(4), pp. 317–326.

Pierre, J. and Peters, B. G. (2020) *Governing Complex Societies: Trajectories and Scenarios*. Basingstoke: Palgrave Macmillan.

Rhodes, R. A. W. (1996) The New Governance: Governing Without Government. *Political Studies*. 44(4), pp. 652–667.

Sachdev, S. (2004) *Paying the Cost? Public Private Partnerships and the Public Service Workforce*. London: Catalyst.

Saldivar, K. M. and Price, B. E. (2015) Private Prisons and the Emerging Immigrant Market in the US. *Central European Journal of International & Security Studies*. 9(1), pp. 40–65.

Sasse, T., Guerin, B., Nickson, S., O'Brien, M., Pope, T. and Davies, N. (2019) *Government Outsourcing: What Has Worked and What Needs Reform*. London: Institute for Government.

Scharpf, F. W. (1997) *Games Real Actors Play: Actor-centered Institutionalism in Policy Research*. Boulder, CO: Westview Press.

Sim, J. (2002) The Future of Prison Health Care: A Critical Analysis. *Critical Social Policy*. 22(2), pp. 300–323.

Skarbek, D. (2011) Governance and Prison Gangs. *American Political Science Review*. 105(4), pp. 702–716.

Sparks, R. and Bottoms, A. E. (1996) Legitimacy and Order in Prisons. *The British Journal of Sociology*. 46(1), pp. 45–62.

Terry, L. D. (1995) *Leadership in Public Bureaucracies*. Thousand Oaks, CA: SAGE.

The Guardian (2016) *Independent body to oversee scandal-hit Medway youth facility* [Online] available from: https://www.theguardian.com/society/2016/jan/26/medway-bosses-failed-to-protect-young-inmates-from-staff (Accessed: 2nd September 2022).

Weber, M. (1930) *The Protestant Ethic and the Spirit of Capitalism*. Oxford: Basil Blackwell.

World Health Organization (2014) *Prisons and Health* [Online], available from: www.euro.who.int/__data/assets/pdf_file/0005/249188/Prisons-and-Health.pdf (Accessed: 12th April 2018).

Chapter 8

Deflection of political responsibility

Introduction

"When the facts change, I change my mind". This familiar wisdom is usually attributed, apocryphally, to John Maynard Keynes or Winston Churchill. And while we might expect such logical thinking from political leaders, the UK government has demonstrated otherwise when faced with the facts of austerity's failure.

Even when implementing potential solutions to overcrowding, instability, and high reoffending rates, the government refuses to recognise that the austerity programme was the cause. This amounts to a political paradox: the government deflects responsibility for its neoliberal agenda while attempting to ameliorate its consequences. Furthermore, many of these solutions, according to participants, have failed to reduce the impacts of austerity. I will discuss participants' responses towards two key experimental efforts to ameliorate the impact of austerity that is linked to prison instability: 1) recruiting new prison officers to stabilise the English prison regime; and 2) blaming prison instability on the rise of *Spice*, claiming that the profile of prisoners is changing in an attempt to individualise the explanation.

I will also describe participants' scepticism of recent political announcements that the era of austerity is finally ending. They were sceptical because they observed the continual impoverishment of public sector services, which contradicts the idea of austerity ending. Here, the participants witnessed a deflection of political responsibility where the government attempted to distance itself from the impact of austerity. Finally, I analyse participants' beliefs about how long Brexit will prolong austerity for, at least in its immediate aftermath, following the predicted decline in economic growth.

The paradox of the government's solution towards prison instability

Responding to the rising violence in English and Welsh prisons, the government allocated £291 million and launched a nationwide campaign in 2016 to recruit 2,500 new prison officers—a move that was part of the Prison Safety

DOI: 10.4324/9781003182337-8

and Reform White Paper 2016 (Ministry of Justice, 2016). Participants were asked whether these new prison officers improved prison safety and whether they facilitated prison healthcare governance and delivery. Many directly involved in the campaign's delivery considered it a success. Per Participant 30, a senior commissioning lead at a justice ministry:

> We have successfully recruited 2,500 prison officers. The government did invest in new officers. We are now reaping the benefits of them coming online. It is heart-warming to see the number of new officers on the landings.

Some frontline participants—particularly new prison staff members—believed the new prison staff had brought complementary skills to the existing workforce (e.g., IT skills) and values (e.g., concerns for diversity, regard for rehabilitation) that were reflective of the outside world. Participant 72, a prison officer of a resettlement prison, said:

> We bring in new skills that we need. We are quite savvy about using computers. We have got a different way of thinking. We have open minds. Our mindsets are open to divisive issues, for example, the issues of equality and prisoner rehabilitation. We have been exposed to a lot of things outside prisons, so it does help.

A few participating prison governors believed that linking the new officers to the necessary cultural change and values connected to prisoner rehabilitation was more important than merely having enough officers working on the grounds. For example, Participant 58, a prison governor of a closed prison with an urgent notification status, said:

> You can have a lot of officers swarming around, but if they are not interacting with our men, they do not know why they are there. If they are just standing around in huddles, it changes nothing. It makes them feel better, but it does not necessarily improve things. Recruitment has been massively pivotal . . . but the fundamental message has to be that "You are not just there to turn and un-turn, lock and unlock those people. You are there because you have got a purpose". That is really important.

While the government managed to recruit 4,500 new prison officers between 2016 and 2019 (Parliament UK, 2020), most participants operating at all prison levels challenged these positive narratives. Participant 64, a head of a prison officers' union, for instance, argued the recruitment campaign had not reinstated the number of prison officers present during pre-austerity measures:

> We do not have the investment we would like. When austerity first came in, we lost over 7,000 front line prison officer posts. They were all

> experienced staff. Since that time, we have saved over £900 million for the taxpayers, but cuts have dire consequences because we have never been in such a poor state. So, we want that reinvestment. We want those pre-austerity staffing levels reinstated. We want that £900 million reinvested because, so far, despite the bold announcements from the government on the prison officers' recruitment, we have only had about £300 million put back in. It is simply not enough. You cannot run justice on the cheap.

Additionally, many participants working in operational capacities commented on the perpetual cycle of recruitment and retention. Participant 78 (from earlier) explained, "It is just a constant cycle of getting new [officers]. Some will just resign in the first week; some will just do the training then resign. It never ends".

Participants argued it has created ongoing operational uncertainty amid institutional crises. And they believed this cycle stemmed from dangerous working environments (as discussed in Chapter 7) and a dearth of employment benefits. For example, Participant 36, an assistant head of health and justice of a national health organisation, stated:

> When Michael Spurr (the then Chief Executive Officer of HMPPS) said to me before he left [in March 2019], "Well, now we have recruited 2,000 people". What he failed spectacularly to tell me was that 45% of those people had left after the first week. You do not think you will get knifed with a sharpened toothbrush every time you go to work. Let's face it. We are not talking about pink, fluffy bunnies here. There are some nasty bastards in our prisons. What you do need to be is risk-aware and not be a puppy, thinking you are going to save the world. And you have had just six weeks of training, which amounts to nothing because actually, you have not got the life skills to manage somebody.

We can substantiate Participant 36's report: 38% of departures in 2019 were officers who had served less than one year, up from 31% the previous year (HMPPS, 2019). This high attrition continues to destabilise prison health governance and delivery. Participants' descriptions also corroborated the official report that in March 2019, half of prison officers in England had under five years of experience, a large decline from 22% in March 2010 (ibid.). Forty-six percent had at least ten years of experience or more, down from 56% (HMPPS, 2019), reflecting the culling associated with the Benchmarking Exercise in 2012. This high turnover rate is inconsistent with the government's claim that these new prison officers will instil prison stability.

Several participants observed that, due to the low retention among prison officers, the rate of registered overtime across institutions remained high. This has affected delivery of the prison regime and supporting services, including healthcare. As Participant 78, a senior prison officer of a closed prison, asserted, "In every prison, there is a ridiculous amount of overtime. Even though the numbers have gone up, there is still not enough staff to cover the work. This has adversely impacted other services, including healthcare".

Beyond recruitment and retention, most interviewed prison governors and officers commented on these officers' want of jailcraft. Prison officer numbers are nearly the same as seven years ago, but the workforce is now much less experienced. Indeed, most participants said new prison officers lacked the physical and emotional agility or soft skills needed to perform their duties effectively (e.g., communicating with and befriending prisoners) for prisoner rehabilitation and the broader prison regime. As Participant 63, a prison officer at an open prison, explained:

> Some of the new officers have not got the physical ability [yet], and they are being passed through the training. We have to do some remedial training with them, which we are not meant to do, because we do not have the extra training resources. When you ask them the sports they have done at school and college, many of them have not done any kind of physical activity, so they are a lot less confident in doing physical interventions. So, having somebody my size come up threatening them might seem intimidating. . . . They only get 37 hours of Control and Restraint Training. They do not have the physical and mental confidence to challenge prisoners, and they will not challenge the prisoners. . . . [Furthermore,] a lot of the newer staff also do not know how to have a talk with the prisoners. There is a joke that they need emoji cards to talk to some prisoners! They prefer to work behind the screen, behind their phone and do not like to do much one-to-one engagement with individuals. We do not have many screens in the prison; it is all personal face-to-face contact.

This quote illustrates how staff lacked the training to act as prisoners' mentors, counsellors, and social workers, despite the government requiring them to provide such support (HMPPS, 2021). This study thus adds evidence to the phenomenon of deskilling. Participants also highlighted that new and inexperienced staff sometimes struggled with challenging disobedient prisoners, leading them to question the legitimacy of prison governance.

In summary, several national participants felt that the initial recruitment campaign for new prison officers (beginning in 2016) was a success. Yet most participants thought that it failed to stabilise prisons. Many questioned the calibre of new prison officers, recognised a low retention rate among them, and attributed that low rate to insufficient training.

Denial through the blaming of *Spice*

Several participants also mentioned how politicians opportunistically experimented with the narrative that *Spice* was to blame for the rising prison instability. Participant 65, the service manager of an NHS Trust in a closed prison, was one. To her, blaming the drug failed to address the core problem of austerity:

> Not admitting how austerity impacts prisons is bloody outrageous. Prison officer numbers went down, and, at the same time, the suicide rate was going up. It is an undeniable connection, and the government did not want to admit the harm that they inflicted. I hear political bollocks that the increased suicide rate is attributed to the availability of *Spice* in prisons, but that is a really good excuse and a really good smokescreen for not acknowledging what drastic impact the reduction in prison funding has had on the well-being of prisoners.

Blaming drugs seemed like an attempt to individualise the discourse on the existing prison instability. As Christina Pantazis (2016) argues, politicians frame public issues, such as health, social care, poverty, homelessness, and social welfare, as individual choices rather than a collective responsibility, with the intention of allowing the state to relinquish its moral obligations. This leaves prisoners in a precarious position: they are disproportionately sick, and confinement leaves them no alternative but to depend on the state provisions to improve their health and occupy their minds with purposeful activities that divert them from risk-taking activities. Framing *Spice* as a cause of prison instability positions individualism as an artificial barrier that deflects the state responsibility from engaging in structural interventions that would improve prisoners' lives. Indeed, this example illustrates a longer-term shift towards neoliberalism.

Additionally, attributing problems to *Spice* rather than austerity resembles interpretive denial (Cohen, 2001). This is a form of denial where one accepts the facts but rejects the meaning. In this case, the government accepts that prison instability exists while eschewing responsibility and blaming drug use. This narrative is safer to them than acknowledging that austerity hindered purposeful activities and reduced workforce capacity to conduct drug searches and safeguard prisoners.

Extending Cohen's sociology of denial theory, Copes (2003) suggested that deniers often use denial techniques to justify their actions and simultaneously cleanse their consciences. Here, the government dispensed £10 million to reduce violence and restrict drugs in ten underperforming prisons via x-ray body scanners, metal-detecting equipment, drug trace detection machines, and toilet traps to collect flushed substances (Ministry of Justice, 2018).

In a noteworthy response, a prison policymaker participant argued that austerity did not exacerbate prison instability. Contrasting the majority opinion, Participant 31, a head of custodial services at a justice ministry, said such a claim lacked evidence:

> I do not think it is all negative. I think some of it has been extremely challenging, things like the arrival of psychoactive substances. It probably has

> been as impactful on health as a range of other things. We do not have a clear evidential [base] that says the financial reduction causes instability. . . . It is very difficult to attribute certain effects that you might see to a particular cause, because there are so many other contextual and multiple factors going on that you cannot necessarily know.

This response is an example of literal denial (Cohen, 2001). Unlike interpretive denial, literal denial is a simple, outright rejection that something happened. Here, the participant suggests that there is no evidence linking instability and health problems to austerity. By denying the link between austerity and prison instability and calling for more evidence, Participant 31 is manufacturing doubt about the validity of the relationship (Magnus, 2008). Such denialism is agnotologic—that is, it promotes ignorance and indifference—and it illustrates how those in power attempt to gaslight or manipulate the public by fragmenting the reality of austerity (Proctor and Schiebinger, 2008).

In suggesting a need for more evidence, Participant 31 was an outlier. Other interviewees overwhelmingly thought such dismissal amounted to "living in denial" (Participant 36, an assistant head of health and justice of a national health organisation), was simply "a lazy way out", (Participant 70, a healthcare manager of an NHS Trust in a resettlement prison), or sounded "outrageous" (Participant 40, the head of a national penal reform organisation). They explicitly rejected the minority claim that additional evidence was needed to prove austerity had contributed towards current prison instability.

The rhetoric that austerity is ending

At the time of this study's fieldwork, the government announced the end of the era of austerity (HM Treasury, 2019a, 2019b). Nearly all national and local participants were either unconvinced or sceptical about the announcement. They said it was a "soundbite" (Participant 35, a regional health and justice lead of a national health organisation), "rhetoric" (Participant 80, a governor of an open prison), and a "political sell" (Participant 44, a criminal justice lead of a nursing trade union).

This study's findings support existing academic and policy observations (Farnsworth and Irving, 2015; The Conservative and Unionist Party, 2017). Eleven months apart in 2018 and 2019, two different chancellors announced that the austerity era was ending (HM Treasury, 2019a, 2019b), without any alteration to prison and prisoner health resources. They felt that austerity's end date would vary as it approached and that general elections will continually motivate politicians to postpone the end of austerity.

The UK's economy has been growing for years. It had not returned to the recession lows of 2009, plus growth had exceeded 2% since 2013 (OECD, 2018). Typifying Naomi Klein (2007) and Mark Blyth (2013), the economic growth is evidence that politicians fabricated the crisis, experimented with narratives to justify austerity's implementation, and resorted to neoliberal adjustments as solutions.

Since austerity served politicians' neoliberal ideology, one might be sceptical they would relinquish it. Indeed, many participants doubted it had ended. For example, Participant 56, a regional head of health and justice commissioning for a national health organisation, asked, "If austerity is truly coming to an end, why have we not seen more prison officers and new prison buildings so that we can deliver modern prison healthcare in a truly 21st century way?"

Similarly, several participants also noted the government was borrowing more than pre-2010. Participant 35, a regional health and justice lead of a national health organisation, stated: "NHS funding is still below the level of demand. To me, that is still austerity. We are still working within a very tight budget to deliver the services that people want".

Several participants also discussed political speeches that implied austerity was ingrained in daily operations across English prisons. This entrenchment of austerity solidified their belief that spending on prison health would not increase. Even if spending was increasing, alleviating austerity's impact on prisons would take time. Participant 66, a head of a substance misuse service operating in various closed prisons, argued:

> What does that mean "austerity coming to an end"? The level of expenditure is not returning to its pre-austerity levels, so only in that circumstance could we say austerity is coming to an end. Of course, it can come to an end, but the damage is done. You cannot reverse all those years of austerity.

Through exhaustive analyses of HMPPS spending, Participant 42, the chief economist of a national think tank organisation, deduced that HMPPS was still experiencing a cycle of financial cuts. It had used funding allocated for capital spending on operations, which, she maintained, demonstrated declining financial support from the central government:

> One thing that eventually emerged in the last two years is that the Ministry of Justice has started transferring some money from its capital investment budget into seed level to day-to-day spending. In 2018/2019, it moved around and was only roughly recorded. The point being that one strategy the Ministry seemed to have employed involved transferring some money that was going to be used for investment into running day-to-day services. This is the same as dealing with austerity. It is shelving some problems for later if you are investing in things that you thought were important to begin with.

Indeed, official data show £235 million was transferred from the capital to the operational budget between 2017 and 2018 (House of Commons Scrutiny Unit, 2018). Capital spending on prisons has focused on "improving statutory compliance and addressing issues such as fire safety, water hygiene, and asbestos" (NAO, 2020); this suggests austerity remains in place. Indeed, these examples refute the political claim that austerity is abating and suggest a political attempt to divert attention away from the impact of austerity as it depletes prison services.

A series of reforms that the government executed—intended to signify the end of austerity—has only reorganised the existing funding allocation. Participants observed three moves that challenged the idea that the era of austerity was ending.

First, participants perceived that the single funding injection by the former Prisons Minister Rory Stewart (2018–2019) toward ten underperforming prisons (Ministry of Justice, 2018) was withdrawn from other prison establishments' budgets by stealth. Participant 67, a prison governor of an open prison, alleged:

> The "ten prisons project"[1] has taken all of the money. I am sure I am not the only one who feels a little bit hard done by because of that . . . I understand why they were the most problematic and worst prisons. But it does feel like the rest of us are not getting access to some of the resources that would be massively helpful.

Second, many prison officers expressed cynicism about the announcement by the erstwhile Prime Minister Theresa May that civil servants would receive a 2% pay increase in 2019 (Ministry of Justice, 2019a). For the prison workforce, the raise depended on prison governors finding 1% from their internal budget, to be matched by the government for another 1% (ibid.). Participants described the measure as "peanuts" (Participant 82, a senior prison officer of a high-security prison), "pittance" (Participant 63, a prison officer of an open prison), and "tokenistic" (Participant 74, a senior prison officer of a resettlement prison). Furthermore, Participant 82, a senior prison officer of a high-security prison, viewed the pay rise as austerity in disguise:

> Theresa May announced that civil servants are going to get a 2% pay rise before she departed. She also said that the Treasury could only fund 1%, and the rest will have to be found from within existing prison budgets. This means each prison governor, up and down the country, will have to cut budgets by 1% to give the staff a pay rise. So, the budget cuts are still there. They just come in a different disguise.

Third, many participants did not believe that austerity was ceasing in the community due to shrinking community resources. The outcome was more homelessness and higher dependency on food banks—both indicators that austerity persists as a policy (UN General Assembly, 2019). For example, a provocative account by Participant 64, a head of a prison officers' union, revealed:

> If the politicians are telling us austerity is coming to an end, why have we got an increased number of food banks and an increased level of people accessing them? The two do not marry up. If austerity is coming to an end, food bank usage would be diminishing, but it is not. In fact, it is increasing. You only have to walk through any city centre and see the number of people begging and living on the streets. So, if austerity is coming to an end, why are these people still living on the streets? It is just a myth, where we are getting sold a lie by the government.

Additionally, to evidence austerity persists, some participants reasoned that the NHS funding remained below the level of demand. The government promised a funding increase of £20.5 billion for the entire NHS by 2023/2024, funded through a combination of tax increases and a Brexit dividend (Prime Minister's Office, 2018). To the participants, NHS funding was meant for all parts of the organisation. They felt that prison healthcare funding risks being jettisoned in favour of more politically popular services. Participant 37, a health and social care lead for a national social care organisation, stated:

> The NHS has received more money year-on-year, but it has never received as much money as we actually need year-on-year. They have always played with the numbers and the arguments and the way they presented them. They have basically passed the problem back down to NHS England: "You have got to manage this". There are important things, the high-profile political things that you have got to deliver, such as responding to people in Accident and Emergency and making sure people are not detained in hospitals longer than they need to be. Because prison healthcare is a bit of a Cinderella aspect of what we do, it has not got the attention that it should have had because other things have been of a much higher physical profile. [They are] not going to invest in prison healthcare; they will just pass the problem down, and it will be quietly ignored.

Finally, informants were tentative at best about the recent promise of a cash injection because Brexit—which was to fund this injection—was expected to reduce trade flows and stall economic growth (Erken et al., 2017; Mion and Ponattu, 2019; PricewaterhouseCoopers, 2016). Participants viewed Brexit as a political force that would throw the future of prison and prison healthcare services into further uncertainty. Participant 40, a head of a national penal reform organisation, further explained this viewpoint:

> [Austerity] is about to get a whole lot worse. Brexit is coming up. We are still wildly over-borrowed as a nation, and demand is growing in all sorts of areas, especially health. You have got an ageing population. The number of people who pay taxes is diminishing. The number of people who consume services paid for by taxes is increasing. The circle has not gotten any more square.

Participants' predictions on how Brexit could lessen economic growth ring true. In October 2021, the UK goods trade with the EU was 15.7%, or £12.6 billion lower than it would have been if the UK stayed in the EU single market and customs union (Centre for European Reform, 2021). This figure was worse than UK government projections of a 10% decrease in trade following Brexit (HM Government, 2018).

The global COVID-19 pandemic subsequently masked the economic cost of leaving the EU. The Bank of England (2020) predicted that Britain would experience its worst recession in 300 years and that its economy would likely suffer the most extreme damage of any country in the developed world from the COVID-19 crisis (Bank of England, 2020). The latest data demonstrate that the UK's gross domestic product surpassed pre-COVID levels for the first time in November 2021 (Office for National Statistics, 2021a). However, concern over slow growth remains following the spread of the Omicron variant, as well as rising taxes and borrowing costs, increased inflation, supply chain blockages, and a persistent shortage of labour (ibid.). All suggest an uncertain future.

In fact, the UK is set to weather another austerity era. The current Chancellor of the Exchequer, Rishi Sunak, announced a decrease of more than £10 billion per year from departmental spending plans next year and for subsequent years (HM Treasury, 2020). In five years' time, departments' daily budgets will be £13 billion lower than planned in March (ibid.). This contradicts the political rhetoric that austerity is ending.

In summary, most participants rejected political announcements of austerity's imminent end. Their evidence was the reorganisation of funding to accommodate ten underperforming prisons and the modest pay increase for prison officers. A belief that the increase in NHS funding might not benefit prison health compared with other more pressing and politically popular measures further fuelled their scepticism. Moreover, Brexit and, more recently, COVID-19 continue to impact economic uncertainty, implying austerity is not ending.

The paradox of political rhetoric: tough on crime and 'we are all in this together'

Over the past few decades, politicians have experimented with the tough-on-crime agenda through sentencing policies. Participants argued that being tough on crime requires considerable resources. These sentencing policies will require enormous financial support, undermining the political narrative of austerity that requires spending cuts on public sector services.

This section will also detail participants' disbelief in the political slogan that 'we are all in this together' (Cameron, 2010), orchestrated during the austerity period. The burden of austerity, according to them, has ironically impacted the marginalised and excluded the most vulnerable via the visible loss of welfare services and deindustrialisation processes that push some of these individuals into the criminal justice system. This example also reinforces the neoliberal principle that expects individual responsibility to allow the state to relinquish its responsibility.

The paradox of tough on crime

Participants traced the tough-on-crime movement to the 1990s. It marked an increased use of prison as a sentencing option—a policy that still fuels political debate. The UK's major political parties have committed unwaveringly to being tough on crime (Reiner, 2011), and politicians have repeated the message (Hough and Roberts, 2012). As participants observed, penal politics are increasingly responsive to punitive and retributive public opinion.

Several participants suggested that historical statutory obligations, particularly those pre-2010, maintained the high imprisonment rate. They cited the Criminal Justice Act 2003 and the Indeterminate Sentences for Public Protections, arguing prison sentence lengths for several serious crimes had dramatically increased despite a diminishing crime level and police resources. As Participant 40, a penal reformist, explained:

> We performed an analysis of what the prison population would be if you did not have the mandatory minimum and increased maximum sentences in the 2003 Criminal Justice Act, including tariffs for indeterminate sentences. The prison population would now be 16,000 fewer than it currently is if the 2003 Act had not been passed. The courts did what they were told. That is why we have got the prison population we have got. The number of people getting short prison sentences has fallen dramatically. Crime overall has been falling for most of the last three decades. Police resources in the last few years have dropped. Courts have closed. All of these are substantial brakes on the increase of the prison population, but the foot on the accelerator is sentencing.

Several participants also cited successful prosecutions of sexual offences under Operation Yewtree as contributing to longer incarceration terms. To them, this was partly behind the failure to reduce the prison population despite the sizeable cut to prison funding. Participant 30, a senior commissioning lead of a justice ministry, noted:

> We are bringing in a new wave of longer-term prisoners with longer sentences. . . . One needs to be reminded that more serious crimes are taking place [and that is] why people are getting much longer sentences. It is also worthy to note that historical child sex offences and paedophile rings, who have been brought to justice, quite rightly, have spiked our prison population, as there are an awful lot of people coming into custody. I think all of those things contribute to why the prison population is not reducing dramatically despite lesser budgets.

The high rate of imprisonment in England has also been maintained by the incentivised recall policy of the now-defunct Community Rehabilitation Companies. It was invoked for released prisoners not complying with the terms of their releases and because of a decrease in the use of community sentences (Ministry of Justice, 2013). As Participant 36, the assistant head of health and justice for a national health organisation, explained:

> The CRC contracts and managing people in the community are really problematic. You give your contracts the financial incentive to send people back to prison, and you wonder why your prison numbers shoot through the roof. It is because you have given CRCs a financial incentive to simply go back on a 28-day recall, so people are in and out for 28 days. Somebody was supervising them in the community previously, whereas now that is not the case. So that is why we see a growth in people being recalled for not complying with the licence as well. Go figure.

This example demonstrates how statutory commitments run counter to austerity's intentions: austerity demands reductions in public sector spending, yet the unabated imprisonment rate serves to do the opposite. These examples reveal the paradox of austerity by illustrating the government's prioritisation of spending only when it coheres with their neoliberal vision of being tough on crime.

This study tracks the drift in imprisonment, although existence of short sentences, criminal cases, and declining police resources are not yet systematically understood. The imprisonment rate stands at 174 prisoners per 100,000 people in England and Wales, far higher than the European average of 132 per 100,000 (House of Commons Library, 2019). Although remaining high, the rate of imprisonment has stabilised over the last decade, partly because the backlog of court cases—currently at 45,500 cases—has prevented a surge (Crest Advisory, 2020).

A few participants believed that the magistrates and judges could have resisted sending people to prisons. However, Participant 55, who also worked as a justice of the peace, provided a nuanced perspective on sentencing practices. This informant's experience suggested that judges and magistrates were inevitably constricted by sentencing guidelines—despite their best intentions to avoid awarding custodial sentences. He further explained how the sentencers were obligated to follow the government's will:

> Some of it comes down to the understanding and attitude of sentencers. Some sentencers will have been in a prison once in their entire life, as a part of their recruitment to the magistracy, when they will have been required to carry out a prison visit. I am fortunate as a magistrate in that, as a commissioner, I am in prisons two or three times a week, so I get to see a lot of different prisons. I bring that perspective to the bench as a sentencer. Additionally, magistrates always work from the starting point of what the sentencing guidelines say; if the sentencing guidelines say this

> would normally be a custodial sentence, you have got to have a really good reason not to follow that through. Often, there is no good reason why people still tend to get sent to prison, even for short sentences.

The current UK Prime Minister announced in 2019 that police resourcing would increase by 2022, that police would extend stop and search, and that officials would review sentencing for serious offenders (Ministry of Justice, 2019b). Given this announcement, the imprisonment rate will conceivably continue to grow.

Some insinuated that the expense of punitive politics had not yet translated into political realisation. For instance, Participant 50, the head of legal for a penal advocacy organisation, said sending people to prisons aligned with the political promises of being tough on crime but cost a lot:

> Quite a lot of [Ministry of Justice] policies cost money. Locking up so many people is very, very expensive. All research shows that community punishments actually work much better to prevent re-offending and keeping down crime. Governments are spending much more money than they need because of this punitive agenda; they want to be seen as very tough.

Politicians assert that 'prison works' (Parliament UK, 1993) and that crime is falling because prison incapacitates criminals (Green et al., 2003). Yet reoffending rates remain high: 45% for all those released from custody and 61% for those serving a sentence of fewer than 12 months (Ministry of Justice, 2020). Despite the absence of evidence demonstrating that imprisonment reduces crime rates and reoffending, the government continues to advance penal drift by stating that "there are no plans to end short term prison sentences" and that "sentencing must match the severity of the crime" (CPT, 2020). Additionally, the government responded to the condemnation of the CPT after its inspection of England's prison in 2019 by stating that it "does not propose to set arbitrary targets for reducing the prison population" (ibid.). This defensive response signals the continuation of tough-on-crime policies that herald further expansion of imprisonment despite evidence that it fails to lower crime and deflects the government responsibility from addressing the root cause of offending.

Overall, participants observed historical and recent legislation, which had mandated increasingly lengthier and more punitive sentences—as well as the subsequent Yewtree Operation for historical sexual crimes in 2012. They noted how this legislation ensured a high incarceration rate in England and Wales. A few participants also blamed the CRC's incentivised sentencing policy for England's high incarceration rate, as well as political resistance to avoiding imprisonment despite the high reoffending rates. Despite the desire to appear tough on crime, these examples point to the paradoxical nature of austerity: finance is dissipating for other public sector services, yet it is available to expand prisons to support the political rhetoric of tough on crime, despite evidence that prisons work.

The irony that 'we are all in this together'

Despite then-Prime Minister David Cameron's claim that 'we are all in this together' (Cameron, 2010), this research demonstrates that the burden of austerity is experienced unequally. This inequality manifests in two ways: 1) the withdrawal of welfare services from the community and 2) deindustrialisation processes during the austerity period. Both signal a state withdrawal from the economy to allow the market to dictate the fate of the population—a key feature of neoliberalism—by pushing the penal system to become the safety net for vulnerable individuals. The irony is that the very people who claimed *equality* of experience were the ones who engineered its *inequality*, profiting from the asset bubbles while the poor suffered most (Callinicos, 2012).

Some participants who developed prison health policies believed that prisons were increasingly becoming first responders when community provisions were no longer available to vulnerable individuals. Although this trend pre-dated austerity, participants perceived that austerity exaggerated it since community services were also affected by adverse fiscal measures. Participant 32, a regional health and justice lead of a health organisation, painted the following picture:

> You think about the criminal justice system, the number of people who have mental health problems, and who live in poverty and their childhood experiences. Austerity is going to affect all the services that they would have gone to for support. People who slipped through the net will end up going to prison now, whereas before, there might have been a bit more support around to help them. Once that gets cut back or taken away, it leads to more problems. You just have to look at the homeless people in the street to realise there is an issue, and a lot of those homeless people would have been in and out of custody.

These remarks support the conclusion that the poor health of prisoners is partly a by-product of their experiences before entering incarceration. Prisoners predominantly come from the most deprived sections of society, and they bring their poor health into prisons (Marmot, 2005; Spencer, 2001). Many entrants to the criminal justice system have little education, low incomes, meagre employment opportunities, transient abodes, and unstable relationships (Prison Reform Trust, 2019). These experiences are even more pervasive and compound the population's health and well-being during austerity, when government measures withdraw community assistance. This leads to neglect, inequality, and discrimination—all of which prisoners have cumulatively experienced. As Wacquant (2000) argued, neoliberalism doubly regulates the poor: by welfare conditions and sanctions and through the criminal justice system. When the welfare state withers, the penal state flourishes instead (ibid.). Participants described a closer meshing of conditional welfare and criminal sanctions over time, where most English prisoners come from deprived areas and have experienced unemployment, homelessness, and poor health and well-being. The examples of the withdrawal of the state provisions support Wacquant's proposition by demonstrating how the government attempts to disconnect its moral responsibility to address the social needs of socially marginalised and excluded populations.

Parallel scholarship notes that imprisonment is an opportunity to improve prisoner health (Crewe, 2005). This view is consistent with Goffman's (1968) importation theory. It proposes that prisoners bring their life experiences into prison and that these experiences must be addressed during imprisonment. However, the findings of this study show that this opportunity for health improvement is being missed, with austerity creating significant barriers to healthcare in prisons.

Participants particularly noted that these institutions are inappropriately committed to deal with social issues: "The government is committed to this kind of notion that we can imprison our way out of our social problems" (Participant 52, a head of policy of a national penal reform organisation). Similarly, due to declining community provisions, Participant 65, an NHS Trust service manager for mental health, illustrated how institutions could not divert these vulnerable individuals from prisons, despite opportunities to do so:

> We are seeing an increase in the number of people that need to be sectioned, for example, into the Mental Health Act, coming into prison. [They] potentially would have been diverted out of the criminal justice system at the police custody stage. Now, that is muddied because only those who are eligible for Psychiatric Intensive Care Unit (PICU) beds—charged with lower-end offences—would be eligible for that. But you will get some that are clearly mentally unwell and are charged with quite serious offences, and we have never been able to access that directly.

Leaving a citizen's need for healthcare to imprisonment is illogical given studies indicate that prisons currently exist to punish, not rehabilitate. Penal institutions lack the moral and financial means to provide welfare, with access to healthcare and decent living provisions deteriorating across English prisons. That they are poor guarantors of crime prevention and reduction further compromises hope for rehabilitation (Downes, 2001).

Participants working across English prisons talked about the visibility of austerity's impacts on the community in their daily operations. Participant 58, a prison governor of a closed prison with an urgent notification status, reported:

> A lot is going on, which means that we are throwing more and more people into prison, and it was always the case that austerity affected services on the outside. Probation officers are stretched. Social workers are stretched. Health visitors are stretched. We all know that when those services are stretched, the default position becomes prison. When people end

> up in prison, it is because all of those areas outside have failed. And the reason that they are failing more is that those services are stretched and un-resourced and all that kind of stuff. It is easier to send someone to prison, and we then end up looking after more and more complicated and challenging people. The vulnerability from outside is simply imported inside, making our jobs really, really tough.

These examples point to how the failure of the welfare state in the community leaves prisons as the safety net for these individuals. There was a one-third reduction in local authority budgets between 2010 and 2015 and another 56% decrease in central grant funding to local authorities between 2015 and 2020 (HM Treasury, 2015). This reveals the established link between poverty and social exclusion that compromises health (Davey Smith et al., 2001; Marmot, 2005). Social issues associated with relative deprivation, including imprisonment, are strongly linked to society's unequal income distribution. The UK's Gini coefficient, Palma Ratio, Top 1% share, S80/S20 ratio, and P90/P10 ratio point to an increase in income inequality between 2010 and 2019 (Office for National Statistics, 2021b). Homelessness is up 60%, fitful sleeping has risen 134%, and use of food banks has increased four-fold between 2010 and 2018 (UN General Assembly, 2019). The social gradient in health illustrates that the lower a person's social position, the worse his or her health (Marmot, 2020; Wilkinson and Pickett, 2009).

Participants argued that these individuals arrive at penal institutions possessing extraordinarily complex health and social needs that have gone unmet owing to diminished community services from austerity. A combination of deflecting the government's moral responsibility to address the social needs of the marginalised population and the belief that society experiences austerity equally underscores that we are *not* all in this together.

Alongside degrading social services, austerity's unequally experienced burden is evident in the process of deindustrialisation in communities that were highly dependent on manufacturing industries. Several participants observed how the deindustrialisation of the 1980s, the failure of miners' strikes, and the long decline of working-class agency through the trade union movement have left them vulnerable (Milne, 2014).

Participant 15, an academic and former Cabinet Office advisor, linked economic downturns to increased crime rates and incarcerations. In particular, he discussed ex-servicemen who had no employment following their deployment overseas. This was due in part to the closure of manufacturing industries following government austerity measures, which reduced employment opportunities:

> In Cambridgeshire and Essex, we have a lot of ex-military servicemen. They lost all sense of purpose in life coming back from the wars. They do not go straight from military service to prison; their life unravels over a

> year or two. Drinking heavily, battering their wives and children, becoming homeless, and eventually ending up in prisons. They were overwhelming in prison for violent offences while drunk. When you are a fit, young twenty-four-year-old who has had army training and you get drunk outside a pub and hit somebody, you are likely to do actual bodily harm, so you are going to get a custodial sentence. Similarly, we saw [the closure] of many traditional industries, like the steel industry in South Wales and North Lincolnshire. Around 11,000 young men were laid off by Ford in one year. Guess what? Problems of domestic violence, alcohol, and drug use in the same year went through the roof. This is how austerity at a national level can contribute to offending.

This observation supports existing research that suggests austerity's impact is severest in areas of high deprivation (Beatty and Fothergill, 2017; Clifford et al., 2013; Taylor-Robinson and Gosling, 2011). Here, we see neoliberalism at work: it allows the market to dictate outcomes, leading to deindustrialisation and the withdrawal of social assistance. These are both processes that disproportionately affect vulnerable members of society. Furthermore, the discovery of a relationship between economic downturns and increased crime rates and incarcerations among former military and those who were affected by the steel industry closures across England advances extant, but currently limited, work by Michael Pacione (1997) and later Michael Marmot (2020). This work examined latent links between the effect of austerity on areas of high deprivation and the diminishing social and welfare services in these areas across England.

With inadequate community provisions for vulnerable individuals, these processes have left prisons as first responders. Although American criminologists have evidenced how austerity and deindustrialisation in the United States reduce the lifespan of those living in poverty and exacerbate crime—thus leading to imprisonment (Linkon and Russo, 2002; Nosrati et al., 2018)—these findings have yet to be replicated in the UK. This present research represents a starting point that illustrates the paradox of the political rhetoric that 'we are all in this together'. It shows the burden of austerity has disproportionately impacted marginalised and vulnerable populations and communities that depend heavily on state provisions.

Conclusion

This chapter has demonstrated participants' qualms about the government responses (since 2016) to improve safety across English prisons. Although the government attempted to manage prison instability by mobilising nationwide recruitment for new prison officers in 2016, many participants questioned the calibre of new prison officers recruited via this scheme. Additionally, participants linked poor retention rates among new prison officers to insufficient training, low salaries, and dangerous working environments.

Prison instability continues. Simultaneously, politicians blamed *Spice*, which impacted the stability of the overall prison regime and the delivery of services, including healthcare. More broadly, these two strategies reflect a deflection from admitting that austerity has been the root cause of the ongoing prison instability.

Notably, most participants contested the end of the austerity era. Their scepticism was due to the lack of improvement in the operation of English prisons. Despite the promised cash injection for the NHS, participants from prison healthcare services felt that the prison health agenda was a low priority compared with other politically popular metrics, such as improving access to Accident and Emergency departments. These examples signify that austerity remains in the background, implying Brexit and the COVID-19 pandemic will further heighten economic uncertainty for years to come.

Finally, the paradox of being tough on crime encourages harsher statutory commitment, which maintains a high imprisonment rate. This tough-on-crime stance exposes the paradox of austerity: as funding for other public sector services dissipates, more money is allocated to imprison individuals. Equally, the logic that 'we are all in this together' has been exposed via the visible loss of welfare services and deindustrialisation processes that inevitably targeted poor people as the ideal candidates for imprisonment. Altogether, these examples illustrate the deflection of governmental responsibility to address the need of marginalised and excluded populations that tend to depend on the state welfare provisions. This observation, then, links to the individualism that is the crux of neoliberalism: individual action is prioritised over collective action, which allows the state to sever its moral obligations.

Note

1 Following an announcement by the former Prison Minister Rory Stewart (2018–2019), ten prisons were selected to benefit from additional £10 million of funding to improve security, address drug issues, and improve governors' leadership capabilities through new training schemes (Ministry of Justice, 2018).

References

Bank of England (2020) *Monetary Policy Report and Interim Financial Stability Report—May 2020* [Online], available from: www.bankofengland.co.uk/report/2020/monetary-policy-report-financial-stability-report-may-2020 (Accessed: 1st September 2020).

Beatty, C. and Fothergill, S. (2017) The Impact on Welfare and Public Finances of Job Loss in Industrial Britain. *Regional Studies, Regional Science*. 4(1), pp. 161–180.

Blyth, M. (2013) Austerity as Ideology: A Reply to My Critics. *Comparative European Politics*. 11(6), pp. 737–751.

Callinicos, A. (2012) Contradictions of Austerity. *Cambridge Journal of Regions Economy and Society*. 36(1), pp. 65–77.

Cameron, D. (2010) *Press Conference on the Coalition: Our Programme for Government: 20 May 2010*. London: HM Government.

Centre for European Reform (2021) *The Cost of Brexit: October 2021* [Online], available from: www.cer.eu/sites/default/files/insight_JS_costbrexit_oct_13.12.21.pdf (Accessed: 25th January 2022).

Clifford, D., Geyne-Rahme, F. and Mohan, J. (2013) Variations Between Organisations and Localities in Government Funding of Third-Sector Activity Evidence from the National Survey of Third-Sector Organisations in England. *Urban Studies*. 50(5), pp. 959–976.

Cohen, S. (2001) *States of Denial: Knowing about Atrocities and Suffering*. Cambridge: Polity Press.

Committee for the Prevention of Torture and Inhuman or Degrading Treatment or Punishment (CPT) (2020) *Response of the United Kingdom Government to the Report of the European Committee for the Prevention of Torture and Inhuman or Degrading Treatment or Punishment (CPT) on Its Visit to the United Kingdom from 13 to 23 May 2019* [Online], available from: https://rm.coe.int/16809e4406 (Accessed: 25th January 2021).

The Conservative and Unionist Party (2017) *Forward, Together: Our Plan for a Stronger Britain and a Prosperous Future* [Online], available from: www.conservatives.com/manifesto (Accessed: 25th January 2021).

Copes, H. (2003) Societal Attachments, Offending Frequency, and Techniques of Neutralization. *Deviant Behavior*. 24, pp. 101–127.

Crest Advisory (2020) *Impact and Legacy of Covid-19 on the CJS: Modelling Overview* [Online], available from: https://b9cf6cd4-6aad-4419-a368-724e7d1352b9.usrfiles.com/ugd/b9cf6c_e16b3e351b12430bb79cd6a2830f88f3.pdf (Accessed: 25th January 2021).

Crewe, B. (2005) *The Prisoner Society: Power, Adaptation, and Social Life in an English Prison*. Oxford: Oxford University Press.

Davey Smith, G., Dorling, D. and Shaw, M., eds. (2001) *Poverty, Inequality and Health in Britain: 1800–2000—A Reader*. Bristol: Policy Press.

Downes, D. (2001) The Macho Penal Economy, Mass Incarceration in the United States—A European Perspective. *Punishment and Society*. 3(1), pp. 61–80.

Erken, H., Hayat, R., Heijmerikx, M., Prins, C. and de Vreede, I. (2017) *Assessing the Economic Impact of Brexit: Background Report by Rabobank* [Online], available from: https://economics.rabobank.com/publications/2017/october/assessing-economic-impact-brexit-background-report/ (Accessed: 21st February 2020).

Farnsworth, K. and Irving, Z. (2015) Austerity: More Than the Sum of its Parts. In: Farnsworth, K. and Irving, Z., eds. *Social Policy in Times of Austerity: Global Economic Crisis and the New Politics of Welfare*. Bristol: Policy Press, pp. 9–42.

Goffman, E. (1968) *Asylums: Essays on the Social Situation of Mental Patients and Other Inmates*. Chicago: Aldine Transaction.

Green, D. G., Grove, E. and Martin, N. A. (2003) *Civitas: The Institute for the Study of Civil Society Final Report for the Rethinking Crime and Punishment Project How Can the Criminal Justice System Reduce the Criminal Activities of Known Offenders?* [Online], available from: www.civitas.org.uk/pdf/CivitasRCP_Report.pdf (Accessed: 25th January 2021).

HM Government (2018) *EU Exit: Long-term Economic Analysis* [Online], available from: https://assets.publishing.service.gov.uk/government/uploads/system/uploads/attachment_data/file/760484/28_November_EU_Exit_-_Long-term_economic_analysis__1_.pdf (Accessed: 25th January 2021).

HM Prison & Probation Service (2019) *Workforce Quarterly: March 2019* [Online], available from: https://assets.publishing.service.gov.uk/government/uploads/system/uploads/attachment_data/file/801838/hr-publication-tables-march-2019.xlsx (Accessed: 21st February 2020).

HM Prison & Probation Service (2021) *Become a Prison Officer: One Career, Many Roles* [Online], available from: https://prisonandprobationjobs.gov.uk/prison-officer/ (Accessed: 25th January 2021).

HM Treasury (2015) *A Country that Lives Within Its Means: Spending Review 2015* [Online], available from: www.gov.uk/government/uploads/system/uploads/attachment_data/file/447101/a_country_that_lives_within_its_means.pdf www.england.nhs.uk/commissioning/health-just/liaison-and-diversion/ld-faqs/ (Accessed: 12th April 2018).

HM Treasury (2019a) *Spring Statement 2019: Philip Hammond's Speech* [Online], available from: www.gov.uk/government/speeches/spring-statement-2019-philip-hammonds-speech (Accessed: 25th January 2021).

HM Treasury (2019b). *Spending Round 2019: Chancellor Sajid Javid's Speech* [Online], available from: www.gov.uk/government/speeches/spending-round-2019-sajid-javids-speech (Accessed: 25th January 2021).

HM Treasury (2020) *Policy Paper: Spending Review 2020* [Online], available from: www.gov.uk/government/publications/spending-review-2020-documents/spending-review-2020 (Accessed: 25th January 2021).

Hough, M. and Roberts, J. V. (2012) Public Opinion, Crime, and Criminal Justice. In: Morgan, R., Maguire, M. and Reiner, R., eds. *Oxford Handbook of Criminology*. 5th ed. Oxford: Oxford University Press, pp. 279–300.

House of Commons Library (2019) *Briefing paper Number CBP-04334, 23 July 2019: UK Prison Population Statistics* [Online], available from: http://researchbriefings.files.parliament.uk/documents/SN04334/SN04334.pdf (Accessed: 27th May 2020).

House of Commons Scrutiny Unit (2018) *2017/18 Supplementary Estimates: Overview of In-year Budget Revisions* [Online], available from: www.parliament.uk/documents/commons/Scrutiny/Supp_estimates_all_17_18.pdf (Accessed: 1st December 2019).

Klein, N. (2007) *The Shock Doctrine: The Rise of Disaster Capitalism*. Toronto: Random House of Canada.

Linkon, S. L. and Russo, J. (2002) *Steeltown U.S.A.: Work and Memory in Youngstown*. Lawrence: University Press of Kansas.

Magnus, D. (2008) Risk Management Versus the Precautionary Principle: Agnotology as a Strategy in the Debate Over Genetically Engineered Organinsms. In: Proctor, R. N. and Schiebinger, L. A., eds. *The Making & Unmaking of Ignorance*. Stanford: Stanford University Press, pp. 250–265.

Marmot, M. (2005) Social Determinants of Health Inequalities. *Lancet*. 365, pp. 1099–1104.

Marmot, M. (2020) *Health Equity in England: The Marmot Review 10 Years On* [Online], available from: www.health.org.uk/sites/default/files/upload/publications/2020/Health%20Equity%20in%20England_The%20Marmot%20Review%2010%20Years%20On_full%20report.pdf (Accessed: 25th January 2021).

Milne, S. (2014) *The Enemy Within: The Secret War Against the Miners*. London: Verso Books.

Ministry of Justice (2013) *Story of the Prison Population: 1993–2012, England and Wales* [Online], available from: https://assets.publishing.service.gov.uk/government/uploads/system/uploads/attachment_data/file/218185/story-prison-population.pdf (Accessed: 25th January 2021).

Ministry of Justice (2016) *Prison Safety and Reform* [Online], available from: https://assets.publishing.service.gov.uk/government/uploads/system/uploads/attachment_data/file/565014/cm-9350-prison-safety-and-reform-_web_.pdf (Accessed: 23rd July 2021).

Ministry of Justice (2018) *Minister Announces' 10 Prisons Project' to Develop New Model of Excellence* [Online], available from: www.gov.uk/government/news/minister-announces-10-prisons-project-to-develop-new-model-of-excellence (Accessed: 21st February 2020).

Ministry of Justice (2019a) *Pay Rise for Prison Officers 2019: Statement by Robert Buckland* [Online], available from: www.gov.uk/government/news/pay-rise-for-prison-officers-2019-statement-by-robert-buckland (Accessed: 21st February 2020).

Ministry of Justice (2019b) *10,000 Extra Prison Places to Keep the Public Safe* [Online], available from: www.gov.uk/government/news/10-000-extra-prison-places-to-keep-the-public-safe (Accessed: 21st February 2020).

Ministry of Justice (2020) *Proven Reoffending Statistics Quarterly Bulletin, October 2018 to December 2018* [Online], available from: https://assets.publishing.service.gov.uk/government/uploads/system/uploads/attachment_data/file/930446/Proven_reoffending_stats_bulletin_OctDec18.pdf (Accessed: 25th January 2021).

Mion, G. and Ponattu, D. (2019) *Estimating the Impact of Brexit on European Countries and Regions Policy Paper* [Online], available from: www.bertelsmann-stiftung.de/fileadmin/files/user_upload/EZ_Estimating_the_Impact_of_Brexit_2019_ENG.pdf (Accessed: 21st February 2020).

National Audit Office (2020) *Improving the Prison Estate* [Online], available from: www.nao.org.uk/wp-content/uploads/2020/02/Improving-the-prison-estate.pdf (Accessed: 25th January 2021).

Nosrati, E., Ash, M., Marmot, M., McKee, M. and King, L. P. (2018) The Association Between Income and Life Expectancy Revisited: Deindustrialization, Incarceration and the Widening Health Gap. *International Journal of Epidemiology*. 47(3), pp. 720–730.

Office for National Statistics (2021a) *Coronavirus and the Impact on Output in the UK Economy: August 2021* [Online], available from: www.ons.gov.uk/economy/grossdomesticproductgdp/articles/coronavirusandtheimpactonoutputintheukeconomy/august2021/pdf (Accessed: 19th February 2022).

Office for National Statistics (2021b) *Household Income Inequality, UK: Financial Year Ending 2020* [Online], available from: www.ons.gov.uk/peoplepopulationandcommunity/personalandhouseholdfinances/incomeandwealth/bulletins/householdincomeinequalityfinancial/financialyearending2020 (Accessed: 25th January 2021).

Organisation for Economic Co-operation and Development (2018) *Quarterly GDP* [Online], available from: https://data.oecd.org/gdp/quarterly-gdp.htm (Accessed: 25th January 2021).

Pacione, M., ed. (1997) *Britain's Cities: Geographies of Division in Urban Britain*. London: Routledge.

Pantazis, C. (2016) Policies and Discourses of Poverty During a Time of Recession and Austerity. *Critical Social Policy*. 36(1), pp. 3–20.

Parliament UK (1993) *Home Affairs and Education* [Online], available from: https://publications.parliament.uk/pa/cm199394/cmhansrd/1993-11-23/Debate-2.html (Accessed: 25th January 2021).

Parliament UK (2020) *Prison Governance: Government Response to the Committee's First Report of Session 2019* [Online], available from: https://publications.parliament.uk/pa/cm5801/cmselect/cmjust/150/15002.htm (Accessed: 25th January 2021).

PricewaterhouseCoopers (2016) *Leaving the EU: Implications for the UK Economy* [Online], available from: www.pwc.co.uk/economic-services/assets/leaving-the-eu-implications-for-the-uk-economy.pdf (Accessed: 21st February 2020).

Prime Minister's Office (2018) *PM Speech on the NHS: 18 June 2018* [Online], available from: www.gov.uk/government/speeches/pm-speech-on-the-nhs-18-june-2018 (Accessed: 21st February 2020).

Prison Reform Trust (2019) *Bromley Briefings Prison Fact File: A Winter 2019* [Online], available from: www.prisonreformtrust.org.uk/Portals/0/Documents/Bromley%20Briefings/Winter%202019%20Factfile%20web.pdf (Accessed: 1st February 2020).

Proctor, R. N. and Schiebinger, L. (2008) *Agnotology: The Making and Unmaking of Ignorance*. Stanford: Stanford University Press.

Reiner, R. (2011) *Policing, Popular Culture and Political Economy: Towards a Social Democratic Criminology*. London: Routledge.

Spencer, A. (2001) *Removing Bars to Good Treatment*. London: NHS.

Taylor-Robinson, D. and Gosling, R. (2011) English North—South Divide. Local Authority Budget Cuts and Health Inequalities. *British Medical Journal*. 342, p. d1487.

United Nations General Assembly (2019) *Visit to the United Kingdom of Great Britain and Northern Ireland: Report of the Special Rapporteur on Extreme Poverty and Human Rights* [Online], available from: https://undocs.org/A/HRC/41/39/Add.1 (Accessed: 25th January 2021).

Wacquant, L. (2000) The New "Peculiar Institution": On the Prison as Surrogate Ghetto. *Theoretical Criminology*. 4(3), pp. 377–389.

Wilkinson, R. G. and Pickett, K. (2009) *The Spirit Level: Why Equality Is Better for Everyone*. London: Penguin.

Chapter 9

The failure to scrutinise

Introduction

Both internal and external inquiry mechanisms exist in England to hold the government accountable. Yet participants across all levels uniformly believed these mechanisms—particularly internal forums, trade unions, the HMIP, parliamentary inquiries, and third-sector organisations—had failed to mitigate austerity's effects on prison health governance and healthcare delivery. I will explore these views in detail, especially the failure to exercise scrutiny.

Such failure is due to a conflict of interests. The monitoring organisations lack sufficient power and independence to instigate reforms with independent organisations—such as voluntary ones—because they are increasingly subjected to a gag clause in return for continued funding. Therefore, these institutions cannot effectively remedy any violation of prisoners' human rights. And their inability to challenge austerity means its effects on prisons and prison healthcare go unmitigated.

Internal forums

Some civil service participants explained they would escalate issues resulting from austerity measures via their line management. In particular, policymakers reported to high-level partnership boards across governmental departments, such as the National Partnership Board (Ministry of Justice, 2018). Ostensibly, such interdepartmental crosscutting (between health and justice sector partners) opened up potential resolutions to specific prison healthcare issues. Participant 34, the head of a national prison healthcare charity who also chaired the NHS England board for prison healthcare, explained:

> The NHS England Clinical Reference Group has been used to take on specific areas and challenges in delivering healthcare services across prisons. Discussion at that level can obviously fuel strategic thinking for policymakers, who have that line of sight into the ministers and can create compelling cases to unlock funding and resources. There is a route through there

DOI: 10.4324/9781003182337-9

> to get some agenda service. We have also had some interesting dialogue through round tables with HMPPS. There is something about those cross-cutting areas, involving the Home Office, Ministry of Justice, and NHS England via the National Partnership Board.

Similarly, as civil servants, prison governors and officers typically raised issues concerning the unsustainable resource reduction to their line managers, usually in their monthly supervision meeting. Participant 74, a senior prison officer of a resettlement prison, explained, "I could raise it to my line manager and governor, and then it is up to them to take it forward". Broadly, their activities of escalation mirror Goffman's (1968) traditional portrayal of the carceral state of hierarchical, top-down leadership, where operations are highly dependent on the prevailing stance of the government. As civil servants are expected to remain apolitical, they lack the authority to challenge austerity's impact directly.

Like several policymakers who avoided the word 'austerity' in their interview responses (see section 5.1), most participants working at the operational level across English prisons avoided the term when discussing delivery issues with their line management. They recognised it had political undertones. Instead, they self-censored, relating how reductions in resources had impeded their daily governance and the prison regime's delivery. This was because they felt adopting a neutral tone was more appropriate for the discussion with their senior managers. For example, Participant 71, a prison governor at a resettlement prison, said:

> I cannot start making career-defining arguments with my boss! So I have to be very diplomatic in talking about austerity. I do not make any argument that says I am making excuses for poor performance. We all have a sense of duty to do the best we can, so austerity is never discussed directly. But we have always discussed its impact, using examples of staffing issues, for instance . . . I pick my battles to appear as though I am never unreasonable.

Repackaging political language as managerial depoliticises the construct of austerity. Further, it embodies the sociological theory of implicatory denial (Cohen, 2001). That is, officials act as ordered, and their duty to obey supersedes their moral principles. Routinisation (the normalisation of catastrophic events) occurs, and subjects (in this case, prisoners) are dehumanised when deemed undeserving members of the community.

Participants illustrate how they have reluctantly accepted the neoliberal hegemony in a flawed narrative that austerity has streamlined prison service. Such acceptance has depoliticised austerity, as participants felt they have no alternative but to use politicians' flawed economic logic. Because austerity is depoliticised, it is difficult for them to politically oppose it and openly criticise it through their internal platforms.

A few participants compared prison with other public services, such as the police, whose voice they considered more independent and transparent in publicising the fiscal cuts. Participant 67, a prison governor of an open prison, said such opacity allowed austerity measures to be imposed without proper scrutiny. He stated:

> Unlike the police, we are a greatly hidden department. We are an easy target for the government in terms of austerity. The risk is that the damage caused by that [austerity] was predominantly behind closed doors and was not seen by the public. Only in the last year or so did the public start to wake up to the fact that the staff are subject to increasing levels of violence and issues within prison, such as drugs and mobile phone smuggling. Health, safety, and employment problems are all wrapped up into one.

These participant narratives contradict the prevailing literature, which mostly argues that civil servants enjoy a high degree of independence. Social policy scholars (e.g., Gash et al., 2010) theorised that public bodies depoliticise political decision making, improve the independence of the civil service to make decisions, and allow the government to access bureaucrats' skills and expertise. However, several participating governors described thraldom to their superiors. They selected their battles carefully and trod cautiously between conformity and resistance to the prevailing political power, which might go against their aims as leaders.

Austerity reduces the perceived power of prison governors, contradicting a previous perception that prison governors enjoy a degree of discretion in running their establishments (Cheliotis, 2006; Liebling and Arnold, 2004). As early as 1984, Chapman argued that prison leadership should be reserved for ministers, as ministers expect civil servants to execute the ministerial visions. Per the Learmont Report in 1995, ministerial involvement will typically be relatively high compared to other public sector areas—a situation that continues today—which contradicts Gash and colleagues' (2010) theory on the autonomy of the civil servants.

The depoliticisation of austerity and the thraldom of civil servants to their ministerial superiors combine to prevent internal regulation. As policies are implemented and prisoners increasingly subjected to the effects of austerity, the neoliberal ideology is able to infiltrate the prison system via a series of dehumanising resource restraints disguised and reluctantly accepted by civil servants as economic necessities.

Trade unions

Several participants said being part of the Prison Governors' Association and the Prison Officers' Association afforded them more opportunity to question austerity compared to those who operated at the national level—and thus had to remain visibly neutral.[1] Participant 78, a senior prison officer in a closed prison, explained:

> [The POA] does a lot of publicity in the media. We also have good relationships with a lot of the Labour politicians and some of the Tory ones as well. We have done parliamentary drop-ins. A few weeks back, we invited all the staff who have been assaulted to tell politicians their story, and there were some really, really powerful stories. A younger female prison officer from [a Category B prison in Lincolnshire] stood up in a room full of people and told everyone about her assault when she had urine and faeces thrown at her because she dared to say no to a prisoner. Another male prison officer, in tears, said how he was assaulted really badly, ending up in the hospital, with his children visiting him and asking whether he was going to die.

A minority of participants mentioned the close links between these unions and politicians (irrespective of party politics). Yet most were sceptical that these groups could have any effective influence on overturning the austerity measures harming prison governance. As an example, Participant 86, a prison governor of a women's prison, asked:

> Have they made any difference? Not really! [laughs] They are not effective. They will appear on the media occasionally, but I am not sure what impact that actually has. I am not sure whether their voice is heard or taken any notice of in the right places.

Other participants believed that unions were campaigning for austerity issues situated in broader political discussions. The effects of such efforts were felt across the public sector rather than the prison service alone. To these participants, austerity issues affected public services. Therefore, it rendered the unions' activism futile as they only represent one part of the civil service: "Austerity issues are political decisions. They affect all public services and not just us. It is not within our immediate control, and there isn't much that the union activism can do about them" (Participant 72, a prison officer of a resettlement prison). This attitude reflects those in previous studies illustrating how union members are more concerned with their work and immediate environment, which simultaneously projects the level of disinterest in national issues (Bennett and Wahidin, 2008).

Parliamentary inquiries and prison oversights

Just as internal forums and trade unions are unable to challenge austerity, this study reveals parliamentary inquiries and other external scrutiny mechanisms are also ineffective. Despite continual parliamentary inquiries, participants argued that their barrage of reports and the colossal number of recommendations have yet to engender effective reform across English prisons. As Participant 12, an advisor to a European intergovernmental human rights organisation, exemplified:

> In 2017, the UK Human Rights Select Committee focused on the prisons' operation. . . . [T]hen there was the Public Accounts Committee, which considered prisons and their problems. There were also National Audit Reports [highlighting issues] in prisons. But the question is, do they make a difference to the Treasury? And the answer seems to be no.

Although the government has promised many reforms over the last decade, it has made no real effort to fulfil them effectively. As Participant 12 further explained:

> So, the question I have would be, why not? [T]here is an ideological reason why the government has decided not to spend more money on prisons. It has the money; it can spend it. It is just that it chooses to spend it in other areas. They chose to spend it propping up the banks rather than on marshalling up disadvantaged populations.

This belief aligns with the literature, which finds issues of government compliance with parliamentary committees (Brazier and Fox, 2011; Rogers and Walters, 2006). This study provides initial evidence that parliamentary committees are ineffective at improving prisons and prison health.

As with parliamentary committees, participants believed external scrutiny mechanisms struggled to address the impacts of austerity on the prison regime. Most recognised the HMIP and the IMBs as key scrutiny mechanisms for prisons, designed to support prison healthcare governance and delivery. As Participant 81, a governor of an open prison, explained:

> Nationally, we have the HMIP, which would come and inspect our prisons, either announced or unannounced. On a local level, there is an independent body called the IMB. The IMB members write directly to the Secretary of State and produce a report annually. Matters such as poor infrastructure or resource difficulties affecting delivery could be in there. So, matters could naturally escalate that way.

A minority of prison governor participants recognised the value of HMIP for accountability: "They have got a critically important role to do, and they are responsible for driving up standards" (Participant 83, a governor of a high-security prison).

However, most prison governor and officer participants lacked enthusiasm for HMIP. The perceived effectiveness of HMIP was deeply polarised in local participants' narratives. Many felt frustrated that the HMIP—despite having the independence to do so—failed to use its authority to highlight how austerity impacted prison operations. Several participating prison governors believed HMIP ignored their inability to improve prison conditions because of declining resources while refraining from commenting on the government resource allocation issues since they were perceived as political. Participant 58, a prison governor of a closed prison with an urgent notification status, asserted:

> Independent bodies like the HMIP are not concerned enough about austerity, although they know it is there in the background. On the other hand, their standards and CPT standards have not changed. So, I am still being judged, measured, and inspected on a set of standards that do not change. In contrast, my ability to influence those standards is severely limited.

Participants believed HMIP inspectors blamed governors incorrectly due to a detachment from political issues. Participant 57, the head of a prison governor's union, said blaming the governors' leadership was fruitless because they were affected by financial constraints over which they had no control:

> What has irritated me is an agenda to shift the blame onto the quality of institutional leadership. But these are the same leaders we had when we performed the best we ever have. The majority are still the same people. They have not suddenly all had some catastrophic failure in their ability to lead. The fact is that they have had so much money taken away from them. Our prisons' demographics have changed: they are more violent, they are younger, and they are disrespectful. The government knows they have spent no money on improving our prisons. It is very easy for HMIP to blame governors' leadership. They do not blame the fact that the HMPPS has taken 25% of the budget out of the prisons but not reduced the population by one prisoner.

While these participants felt that the HMIP did not fully utilise its independence to challenge the imposition of austerity on prisons, the lack of challenge is partly due to the lack of legal authority to do so. Despite the HMIP's independence guaranteed by the statutory provision of section 5A of the Prison Act 1952 (as amended) and were directly answerable to the UN OPCAT (NPM, 2021), HMIP reports the organisation's inspection of prisons findings to the justice minister, who indeed has the power to sustain the implementation of austerity

By examining the effectiveness of external monitors in impacting those who work and live in prisons, this study fills the scholarly gap identified by Nicola Padfield (2018). It reveals that, like the UN OPCAT, the PPO and IMBs have failed to challenge the governance and commissioning of prison healthcare to ensure prisoner health and well-being. In revealing these failures, the current study contradicts earlier investigations presenting a more favourable view of these institutions' role in highlighting and preventing institutional abuse and upholding accountability (Bennett, 2016; Ramsbotham, 2003).

Recent studies indicate that these agencies have a more managerial than monitoring agenda. As such, the failures of the prison service have become management summaries because the agencies lack power to challenge deterioration in prisons compared with when they were initially established (Behan and Kirkham, 2016; Bennett, 2016; Padfield, 2018). At times, reports have led to negative media publicity. Yet action and meaningful change have been absent: the latest HMIP report explains that half of the HMIP recommendations for improvement have not been achieved in 2019/2020 (HMIP, 2020). This suggests that inspections of prisons and their healthcare services have failed to ensure prisoner health and well-being. This study provides an alternative explanation for why organisations have failed to act on evidence of poor performance, despite a continual level of monitoring.

Participant 52, a head of policy of a national penal reform organisation, argued for additional oversight:

> We see recommendations being made all the time, from the Chief Inspector, from the PPO, from IMBs. Recommendations are made, and then they are not implemented. There is no national oversight mechanism. There is no independent organisation that is (a) tracking what the recommendations are and (b) tracking whether they have been implemented properly or enforcing them or holding anyone to account.

This study also reveals that different monitoring agencies have contradicted each other. HMIP, CQC, PPO, and IMBs have expressed serious concerns about prison staff's failure to implement improvements following their reports (House of Commons Library, 2019). Although these organisations have evaluated prison conditions and fostered indispensable political, policy, and public conversation about them, their conclusions have not necessarily aligned with their findings. For instance, HMIP undermined its criticism by stating that the English prison service is not entirely in crisis, pointing to the minority of prisons that were relatively safe, calm, and professional, and where staff were caring (HMIP, 2019). In contrast, in its annual report, the PPO described the prison system as in crisis (PPO, 2017). Critically questioning why these oversight mechanisms were not in unity in challenging the government is important.

Scrutiny by third sector organisations

Finally, several participants who operated in the advocacy sphere—particularly at the national and operational levels of prisons—spoke of their campaigns for improvement in prison conditions. According to these participants, lobbying politicians and providing evidence to parliamentary committees are the primary routes for raising political awareness of austerity's impact on prisons and beyond. As Participant 39, a policy lead for a penal reform organisation, reasoned:

> We have got good relations with members of Parliament and some parliamentarians. We respond to consultations. We have got an All-Party Parliamentary Group for Women in the Penal System. Even without austerity, we are always trying to talk about improving prison conditions.

Analysis of the participants' comments revealed that some prison healthcare providers often embraced advocacy. They did so despite gagging clauses in their contractual documents. Such clauses were designed to prevent them from speaking against government policies, including austerity. Grounded in the Lobbying Act 2014, interviewees' descriptions of the language of the gagging clauses ranged from the need to observe 'confidentiality' and 'secrecy' to more specific instructions, such as 'use of appropriate channels of communication' and 'consequences for breaching the terms of the contract', including service termination.

Nevertheless, participants felt the current prison conditions outweighed their obligations to obey these restrictive clauses. They remained careful not to offend those who funded their services, however. As Participant 66, the head of a substance misuse service operating in various closed prisons, said:

> We are not an organisation that keeps quiet about austerity. There are organisations in the third sector with a campaigning culture that decides to be quiet about it because of the contractual gagging clause. They do not want to offend the people who control their income. We are not one of those organisations. Of course, we have to be careful what we say, but we do not keep quiet about our causes. In fact, I do not take those seriously because it is basically a political decision for a commissioner to challenge what I am saying. Of course, they have the legal power to force me to stop saying certain things that could bring their organisations into disrepute . . . they can also take my contract away, but they would only do that if they had the moral high ground, and they do not.

This finding adds evidence from the penal sector to the existing consensus among social policy theorists that dependencies on a state's extensive resources and political power can force voluntary organisations to conform to a top-down agenda and solidify principal-agent relationships that could stymie their advocacy arm (Baggott, 2013; Martikke and Moxham, 2010). As such, their ability to gain consensus from those in government could be limited and the scope of negotiations for ameliorating issues concerning prison and prison health could be constricted.

However, Participant 76, a head of a social services charity covering various closed prisons, spoke at length about how the size, status, and reputation of the organisation might work in their prisons' favour when raising negative issues without fear of legal repercussions:

> [Our organisation] is a campaigning organisation as well as a service provider. We have a universal credit campaign, and one of our mantras is that our enemy is social injustice. And austerity helps create social injustice. . . . There is a gagging clause in our contract, but it has not stopped us. Many of our contracts now have this gagging clause, so we just ignore it. . . . If we feel that we need to challenge anything, then we will challenge it. We are big enough to do that, so that is one of the benefits of being a big, longstanding, respected charity.

This ability to defy gag clauses and reject conformity to the top-down agenda was only possible for such large bodies, however. A few participants from smaller, regional charitable organisations merely saw themselves as service providers, expressing concern about contractual repercussions. For example, some cited operational boundaries: "We are not set up to advocate for prisoners. We are more of a self-management programme. . . . We have to have really strong boundaries in this sort of work" (Participant 77, a manager of a mental health charity covering various closed prisons). To maintain their legitimacy as a service provider, these participants resorted to internal channels of communications, as outlined in their contractual obligations, which they perceived to be more appropriate: "I will escalate to my commissioner if I am really concerned about issues, such as treatment delays. The commissioner then has to go and have an arm-wrestle with the other bit of NHS England" (Participant 65, a service manager of an NHS Trust in a closed prison).

This behaviour among smaller organisations fits within what Hall (2011) termed 'disaffected consent'. Such organisations present themselves as a legitimate partner in delivering state services, refraining from challenging their funder (Newman, 2012). This collusion reflects an abandonment of equality and justice and a mutation of these values into consumerist logic. It reproduces neoliberalism in ways that conform to the hegemonic process (Clarke, 2008; Hall, 2011; Newman, 2012). This discourse illustrates the potential loss of the sector's critical voice and autonomy.

Conclusion

Overall, this chapter fills the research gap on the effectiveness of internal and external monitoring to mediate austerity's impact on prison healthcare and the prison system in England. Many participants from various governance levels openly contested the effectiveness of internal and external scrutiny mechanisms. They perceived internal scrutiny as ineffective because civil servants were expected to remain apolitical. They considered external oversight mechanisms—such as the HMIP and the IMBs—as they misdirected their scrutiny towards governors in the form of management critiques. The depoliticisation of austerity, alongside monitoring organisations' lack of authority to challenge its political imposition, sustain its acceptance and implementation and violate prisoners' human rights.

Reflecting on the gagging of charitable organisations, as well as the statutory obligations under the Lobbying Act 2014, this study provides preliminary indications that gag clauses have increasingly crept into the work of prison health charities. It identifies a trend that can be generalised to charitable sector operations across the UK, whereby the work of members of such organisations reflects the viewpoint of their funders. Consequently, the voices of these voluntary organisations are muted, concealed, and obscured.

The next chapter will explore participants' views of the options to improve prison healthcare governance and delivery, as well as its supportive prison regime, in the near future.

Note

1 For instance, in 2018, national prison officers called for a strike because of unsafe working conditions.

References

Baggott, R. (2013) *Partnerships for Public Health and Well-being: Policy and Practice*. London: Palgrave Macmillan.

Behan, C. and Kirkham, R. (2016) Monitoring, Inspection and Complaints Adjudication in Prison: The Limits of Prison Accountability Frameworks. *The Howard Journal of Crime and Justice*. 55(4), pp. 432–454.

Bennett, J. (2016) *The Working Lives of Prison Managers: Global Change, Local Culture and Individual Agency in the Late Modern Prison*. London: Palgrave Macmillan.

Bennett, J. and Wahidin, A. (2008) Industrial Relations in Prisons. In: Bennett, J., Crewe, B. and Wahidin, A., eds. *Understanding Prison Staff*. Cullompton: Willan Publishing, pp. 117–131.

Brazier, A. and Fox, R. (2011) Reviewing Select Committee Tasks and Modes of Operation. *Parliamentary Affairs*. 64(2), pp. 354–369.

Cheliotis, L. (2006) How Iron is the Iron Cage of New Penology? The Role of Human Agency in the Implementation of Criminal Justice Policy. *Punishment and Society*. 8(3), pp. 313–340.

Clarke, J. (2008) Living With/in and Without Neoliberalism. *Focaal: European Journal of Anthropology*. 51, pp. 135–147.

Cohen, S. (2001) *States of Denial: Knowing about Atrocities and Suffering*. Cambridge: Polity Press.

Gash, T., Magee, I., Rutter, J. and Smith, N. (2010) *Read Before Burning: Arm's Length Government for a New Administration*. London: Institute for Government.

Goffman, E. (1968) *Asylums: Essays on the Social Situation of Mental Patients and Other Inmates*. Chicago: Aldine Transaction.

Hall, S. (2011) The Neo-liberal Revolution. *Cultural Studies*. 25(6), pp. 705–728.

HM Inspectorate of Prisons (2019) *HM Chief Inspector of Prisons for England and Wales: Annual Report 2018–19* [Online], available from: www.justiceinspectorates.gov.uk/hmi-prisons/wp-content/uploads/sites/4/2019/07/6.5563_HMI-Prisons-AR_2018-19_WEB_FINAL_040719.pdf (Accessed: 25th January 2021).

HM Inspectorate of Prisons (2020) *HM Chief Inspector of Prisons for England and Wales: Annual Report 2019–20* [Online], available from: https://assets.publishing.service.gov.uk/government/uploads/system/uploads/attachment_data/file/927361/hmi-prisons-annual-report-accounts-201920.pdf (Accessed: 25th January 2021).

House of Commons Justice Committee (2019b) *Prison Governance* [Online], available from: https://publications.parliament.uk/pa/cm201919/cmselect/cmjust/191/191.pdf (Accessed: 21st January 2020).

Liebling, A. and Arnold, H. (2004) *Prisons and Their Moral Performance: A Study of Values, Quality and Prison Life*. Oxford: Oxford University Press.

Martikke, S. and Moxham, C. (2010) Public Sector Commissioning: Experiences of Voluntary Organizations Delivering Health and Social Services. *International Journal of Public Administration*. 33, pp. 790–799.

Ministry of Justice (2018) *National Partnership Agreement for Prison Healthcare in England 2018–2021* [Online], available from: https://assets.publishing.service.gov.uk/government/uploads/system/uploads/attachment_data/file/697130/moj-national-health-partnership-2018-2021.pdf (Accessed: 12th April 2018).

National Preventive Mechanism (2021) *OPCAT* [Online], available from: www.nationalpreventivemechanism.org.uk/opcat/ (Accessed: 25th January 2021).

Newman, J. (2012) *Working the Spaces of Power*. London: Bloomsbury.

Padfield, N. (2018) Monitoring Prisons in England and Wales: Who Ensures the Fair Treatment of Prisoners? *Crime, Law and Social Change*. 70, pp. 57–76.

Prisons & Probation Ombudsman (2017) *Annual Report 2016–17* [Online], available from: https://s3-eu-west-2.amazonaws.com/ppo-prod-storage-1g9rkhjhkjmgw/uploads/2017/07/PPO_Annual-Report-201617_Interactive.pdf (Accessed: 27th May 2020).

Ramsbotham, D. (2003) *Prisongate: The Shocking State of Britain's Prisons and the Need for Visionary Change*. London: The Free Press.

Rogers, R. and Walters, R. (2006) *How Parliament Works*. 6th ed. Abingdon: Routledge.

Chapter 10

Ending austerity

Introduction

We have seen, of course, austerity implemented in the UK before. More than eight decades ago, Keynes (1936) argued that the free market economy showed no signs of correcting negative externalities. Consequently, if we are to reverse the effects of austerity, we require corrective interference.

Yet questions of resource allocation are too important for politicians and economists alone to determine. This chapter therefore considers six measures participants suggested to undo austerity's effects on prison healthcare over the last decade: reducing the prison population, maintaining recurrent funding for prisons, taxing corporations and wealthy individuals, improving political accountability through transparency, using external organisations to call for a reduction in imprisonment and monitoring recommendations for prisons, and holding the government accountable for their austerity measures over the last decade via legal challenges.

Reduce the prison population

First, despite varying professional backgrounds, all participants argued for a reduction in the current prison population, albeit in different ways. Participating international policymakers reasoned that reducing the prison population would align the prison estate with the reduction of prison staff. As they reiterated, imprisonment is expensive:

> There is pressure to have fewer prisoners. Look at what has happened in America, where suddenly even the Republicans realised, "Oh gosh, we have been doing mass incarceration all this time, we cannot pay for it". People do not like having their taxes going up. So, if they spend money properly, things can be done differently.
>
> (Participant 17, advisor to a European intergovernmental human rights organisation)

DOI: 10.4324/9781003182337-10

Considering the annual average cost per prison place is £38,042 (Ministry of Justice, 2017), the state should consider alternatives to imprisonment. Lord Bradley's review on mental health in the criminal justice system and the Corston Review on vulnerable women in the criminal justice system reinforced this point since community alternatives to prison are both effective and cost effective (Bradley, 2009; Corston, 2007).

Similarly, Participant 2, a consultant for an international health organisation, and Participant 39, a policy lead for a penal reform organisation, respectively, used hospitals and motorways as similes for prisons in calling for a reduction in the current prison population in England:

> Prisons, like hospitals, are expensive. Prison health is best served when the general principle of avoiding sending people to prisons is applied. In England and several other Western European countries, many people are sent to prison who should not be sent to prison, which could be looked after much better by the health and welfare system.

> You cannot build your way out of a prison crisis. You cannot build another prison because you are overcrowded. It is like a motorway; it just fills up with cars.

A clear consensus emerged that reducing the incarceration rate would help tackle austerity. Yet participants differed on how to practically do this.

Overall, participants offered three starting points. First, international and national policymaking participants argued for abolishing short sentences; this would reduce the current prison population. Several participants cited the examples of Scotland, France, and Norway, which had reviewed their sentencing policies and decided only those posing a threat to security and the public would face imprisonment. Participants said the UK could adopt the same policy. As Participant 5, a member of a European anti-torture committee, explained:

> In Scotland, there is a presumption against any sentence less than three months. In fact, the Scottish and French Parliament considered a presumption against any sentence of less than one year because prisons should be reserved for those people who are imprisoned for reasons of public protection. That is why we send them to prison, because they are a risk to society on account of their crime.

Second, some participants suggested alternative community sanctions for prisoners not posing a public threat. Participant 2, a consultant for an international health organisation, questioned: "Why is it possible that in Finland, so few people are landing in prisons, and in England, so many people are coming into prison? [The Finnish] have undertaken many measures, from financial fines to the electronic tagging".

Many policymaking participants also favoured community-based interventions. Instead of confinement, they cited distinct examples, such as extended fostering, early intervention, diversion from the courts for those with mental health issues, and mentoring of at-risk youth. For instance, Participant 13, a former head of a prison inspectorate, explained:

> In Germany, they have always identified community services as needing fostering to reduce the imprisonment rate. A prisoner could be put with a family on release, so there is extended staffing outside the prison wall.

Consistent with scholarship arguing that prisons should house those who threaten public safety (Mills and Kendall, 2018), participants believed that fines, community service, and diversion of prisoners with acute mental health problems to a hospital or community-based treatment are less costly, more proportionate to criminal harm, more responsive to prisoners' needs (especially for those with mental health issues), and less disruptive to prisoners' families and social networks.

Considering alternatives to imprisonment, these participants frequently mentioned the need to influence judges and magistrates. For example, Participant 38, a policy lead at a health and social care department, asserted: "We have got to tell [sentencers] what the alternatives to imprisonment are. We have got to give them confidence in these alternatives. Then, they may not use short-term sentences as much as they are doing now". Apart from being more financially sustainable than extant efforts, such options are safer, especially for reducing COVID-19 transmissions (and other potential pandemics) among prisoners and staff (Ismail and Forrester, 2020b).

However, like Participant 38, Participant 47, a project lead of a national penal reform organisation, argued that sentencers must be given confidence in such alternative community sentences, subject to the permitting sentencing guidance. This, argued Participant 47, would require supporting infrastructures to deliver them. He further stated that "the magistrates could, in theory, sentence people to community services, like women's centres, but they can only do that if community services exist". Some participants noted a closure of these services because of receding funding during austerity and urged more should be provided to improve sentencing practices that prevent imprisonment.

Finally, participants suggested a more immediate solution to reduce imprisonment could be to encourage sentencers to make greater use of suspended sentences. As such, imprisonment could become a deterrence tool for potential repeat offenders. As Participant 55, who worked as a magistrate, argued:

> Sentencers often feel more comfortable providing a community order instead of a custodial order, perhaps by looking at things like suspended sentences. They will give somebody, in theory, a custodial sentence of six months, but they will suspend it for two years. That person has that hanging over them for the next two years, so they have to keep their nose clean.

In summary, all participants proposed downsizing prison populations via abolishing short sentences, reserving prisons only for those who present genuine security and public protection threats. In addition, they suggested that using more community sentences with adequately funded infrastructures and more suspended sentences could further decrease dependencies on the prison system.

Investing in prisons and community services

Second, 87 participants across all three levels of prison health governance and delivery urged the government to provide more resources to prisons and community services to prevent individuals from being sent to institutions. Their arguments are detailed next.

The participants reported that the cost-saving measures in the name of lean and efficient operations should be halted. As Participant 17, an advisor to a European intergovernmental human rights organisation, said, "We are now at a level where we cannot even think of saving money because there really is no money to save".

All participants also emphasised that more resources should be provided to the English prison system to assuage the current institutional instability and, in turn, improve healthcare delivery. As Participant 12, an advisor to a European intergovernmental human rights organisation and leader of a national medical organisation, suggested:

> All we need to do is switch on the tap of expenditure again, and things will improve. It is literally as simple as that. The government just needs to choose it, and it can be different.

Several participants working across English prisons discussed how investments could improve existing prison buildings to create more rehabilitative environments. Notably, some participants were careful in their arguments about obtaining additional resources for prisons. They suggested that increased funding should be used to improve prisons' living conditions rather than to build more prisons. For example, Participant 41, a regional director for the National Prison Services, said:

> If we can invest in our prisons to make them safer and more stable, then they would also become more rehabilitative, and we could then release people who are less likely to commit a crime. If they still get involved with prisons, it would be at a less serious level. We do need investment to do that.

Beyond providing additional resources to prisons, many participants also stressed the importance of ensuring recurrent spending across the community to address social issues there rather than in the carceral setting. As Participant 30, a senior commissioning lead of a justice ministry, explained:

> Stop austerity measures in prison altogether. Stop it in the community, too, so there will be better mental health services, better early interventions in the community, people being able to get GP appointments, people being able to get medication, and people not having to live on the street. Certainly, there should be a huge investment in mental health services and investment in our local authorities to provide wraparound care for individuals to keep people safe.

Likewise, additional resources for community services would ensure early support for individuals and prevent them from entering the criminal justice system. As Participant 7, an advisor to a European intergovernmental human rights organisation, suggested:

> Apart from diverting people out of the justice system, fund preventative programmes properly, such as early years interventions. Ensure more social support at early stages, parenting skills for new parents and identify the people with behavioural problems through schools. Prevent them from coming into the criminal justice system.

Apart from improving prisoners' living conditions to mitigate current prison instability, the recurring spending could address potential risk factors at early stages—for instance, via early years' interventions and mentoring of at-risk youths—which might well provide further evidential support for existing work (UN General Assembly, 2019). Doing so would also inspire sentencers' confidence in awarding non-carceral sentences subject to the permitting sentencing guidance.

Tax on corporations and the wealthy

Third, to improve the government's fiscal position, some policymaking participants suggested imposing a tax increase on profitable corporations and wealthy individuals to pay for more prison health investment. Participant 35, a regional health and justice lead of a national health organisation, said that the public's expectations need adjusting:

> People have expectations for high-quality services but also expectations of low taxes. Politicians should tackle this issue by saying either if you want to pay less, you are getting less, or if you want a really high-quality world-class service, you need to pay more.

Similarly, Participant 29, an academic and a consultant for an international health organisation, argued for the need to tackle tax avoidance among individuals and corporations. She also argued for reframing the narrative around taxation to one of purchasing services:

> We need a big social conversation about taxation. We view taxation in the same way as the United States views taxation—as a dreadful imposition by the government. Actually, it is a resource. We are buying into a fairer society. We are buying lots and lots of services. Taxation is effectively good. People should be paying their taxes. Corporations should be paying their taxes. We should not be encouraging people to avoid them in any way. To me, it is fundamentally about what is the purpose of taxation and kind of reframing it, not as an imposition on individual freedom, but actually a resource for the whole of society and something we all benefit from.

Echoing Arne Ruckert and Ronald Labonté (2017), reinforcing more progressive taxation among multinational corporations, tackling tax avoidance and evasion, and addressing discrepancies in corporate tax rates would address the actual root of the financial crisis. For instance, a negligible recovery rate of 0.05% (five pence per pound sterling) for the £5.8 billion tax evasion by multinational companies (Financial Times, 2017) could raise £29 million. This runs parallel to the most recent iteration of the British Social Attitudes survey, which found that support for 'tax more, spend more' is at 60%—the highest level in 15 years (National Centre for Social Research, 2018). The additional funding could be invested in critical services while ensuring that it fits the pattern of discourse established by the UK media and opinion leaders concerning taxation and the broader issue of resource allocation. Simultaneously, the need for additional financial support should highlight that being tough on crime is financially unsustainable.

Greater transparency

Fourth, participants emphasised the need for greater transparency in economic data behind penal policy to expose the paradox of austerity. To embrace improved transparency in penal policy in England, some national participants recommended integrating prison spending data into public discussions. They argued that ensuring more transparent data would allow the public to be informed about how their money is spent on prisons:

> The more we involve communities in how prisons are run or even just having them know about how prisons are run, the better. I think that it has to be a good thing to get people to understand what is being done in their name, what is being done in the name of the public.
>
> (Participant 18, an academic and advisor to a European administration organisation)

Consistent with Ha-Joon Chang (2010), improving the public's political literacy will help reclaim the narrative that austerity is a political, rather than economic, imperative, and that living in conditions of economic scarcity and extreme inequality is unacceptable. The public's ability to scrutinise data will reveal the austerity fallacy: while austerity means less money is available for prisons, prisons are increasingly being used, which is an expensive option to combat crime.

It would also highlight the role of private prisons and expose their actual costs to the public purse. Future studies are needed to determine the costs of corporate welfare for prisons and the broader criminal justice system in England. Such research would warn government actors not to accept the promises of private companies at face value but to reduce corporate welfare and help end private sector operations in prison health and prison service.

Participants also recognised that populist politicians and the public may reject enhanced prison funding. As Participant 25, a European law and human rights specialist, stated, "Prisoners' human rights tend to have a less positive reaction". To dispel this stereotypical perception, participants proposed messages could be framed better. For example, they could focus on how spending can reduce reoffending and lessen the demands on health and law enforcement services. As Participant 21, a regional lead of an international health organisation, said:

> This country spends £15 billion a year on the criminal justice system. A significant proportion of that budget goes to support the prison system. But the people that go through the prison system generate spending across law enforcement services, health services, social services, etc. . . . Not just because it is a benefit to those individuals, but also because it may have a community dividend. We all have a stake in driving down rates of offending and reoffending, getting the best value for our tax money, and reducing the demands on health and law enforcement services to make our community safer. We can build a better future for the country.

A small number of policymaking participants proposed that spending data should include not just the spending figures but also the effectiveness of their spending on prison healthcare and the outcomes of prison health. Participant 42, a chief economist of a national think tank organisation, demonstrated this point:

> Suppose the government is interested in improving its effectiveness. In that case, part of that is encouraging the government to think more carefully about how it translates the money that goes into services into outputs and outcomes for people. The government was focusing too much on the spending going into the service without much thought about the outcomes at the end of the process. It is about trying to make this a bit more visible. The electorate ultimately cares about the output of services, not just the money.

Better data collection and dissemination would facilitate the governance and delivery of prison health in England. These efforts would ensure augmented, transparent reporting of the true costs of imprisonment and violent incidents and illuminate the burgeoning prison population's latent needs—including their complex health needs (NAO, 2017).

Moreover, several policymaking participants called for better modelling of data on the poor health provisions in prisons. After all, they believed that ultimately the health of English prisoners could affect the health of the public. In fact, a few participants quoted a tuberculosis epidemic in Russia between 1997 and 1999 to illustrate this point. As one said, "An example of how poor treatment in prison affects the community is certainly Russia, where multi-drug-resistant tuberculosis caused 20,000 deaths" (Participant 24, a member of a European anti-torture committee).

As further substantiated by Participant 23, an advisor to a European intergovernmental human rights organisation and an international drug and crime organisation, "Prison healthcare is not only for the sake of prisoners; it is for the sake of the whole community". Such an argument could be used to convince taxpayers of the logic of directing funds towards improving prison conditions: they would create a safer society.

Moreover, conducting a thorough impact assessment to forecast the fiscal impact on prisons (and other public sector services) before imposing future funding cuts should become mandatory. Participants suggested that these analyses should be publicised to allow for media and public scrutiny. Drawing on and advancing previous research (Stuckler and Basu, 2013), when citizens can access and engage with the data, politicians can then be truly held accountable for their budget decisions and the effects of those decisions on lives and deaths in prisons. Transparency would expose the systemic government manipulations of data and political misconduct that constitute breaches in public office duties.

As part of ensuring transparency, several policymaker participants urged enhanced accountability of politicians' spending on governmental programmes, which has yet to happen. These participants consistently commented on misspending by former Secretary of State for Transport Chris Grayling (2017–2019), the erstwhile justice minister who also executed the Benchmarking Exercise contributing to the existing prison instability. This misspending, they said, led to further financial drains. For example, as Participant 55, a magistrate and prison health lead of a national health organisation, stated:

> I think that the wider impact of those austerity measures on society needs to be better thought through. Especially when you see massive amounts of waste, like the awful Brexit things that Chris Grayling did, where the ferry contracts signed to ensure critical imports could reach the UK in the event of a no-deal Brexit were cancelled. The government had to pay £33 million to Eurotunnel. It had to cancel all the contracts with P&O Ferries, which cost £50 million. This money would have paid for a significant number of police officers or nurses. Not thinking things through and not thinking about the impact of things means that some areas are left without resources, and, in other areas, resources are wasted.

Connecting the chain of responsibility back to the relevant ministers would also provide a continual thread of evidence that politicians are responsible for directing governmental policies (Boin, 2001; Terry, 1995). As prisons are a hidden department compared to other public services, opening them up for increased accountability and transparency is the way forward.

Finally, in reinforcing better penal policy transparency, there was consensus among policymaking participants that the media must do more to highlight the current prison instability. As Participant 41, a regional prison director of a justice ministry, asserted:

> Prisons appear less safe and more violent, which has come out a lot stronger in the media. The media has got to hit home that perhaps we have got a problem in prisons, and perhaps the amount of staffing that is gone out of prisons impacts it. Then we have seen the political desire to bring back the stability to prisons and take up more prison officers, and that got quite a lot of profiles, as we started to have a bit more investment backing. So, I think it needs to be out there and quite visible.

Several participants believed that the adverse media reporting would have attracted a vociferous response if similar adverse effects were imposed on another setting. Participant 4, an advisor to a European intergovernmental human rights organisation, stated, "If it happened in the community, there would be a lot of disquiet and a lot of uproar in the media. Because it happens in prisons, there is not that same level of concern about it".

Advocacy and monitoring by external organisations

Fifth, like austerity, imprisonment is a political choice. To enable effective responses to existing prison instability, participants called for advocates and researchers to scrutinise the current government's leadership and hold decision makers accountable for their actions or inaction.

Most participants, particularly those operating at the international and national policy levels, advocated using international concordats as minimum standards to protect prisoners' right to health. As the UK government has numerous legal principles enshrining prisoners' right to health, participants argued that these principles should insulate prisoners from arbitrary and unjustified restrictions on their enjoyment of this right. Participant 21, a regional lead of an international health organisation, observed:

> [The international obligations on health] are not a nice-to-do. They are a must-do. Certainly, the courts uphold with rigour any apparent breach of human rights, whether at the European Court of Justice level or English court system. I have been an expert witness in some court cases where

> prisoners have brought challenges to their detention circumstances. The fact that that happens is testimony to the right that prisoners have to safe and decent care that the obligation is on the state to ensure their well-being.

Some participants believed that non-governmental and European oversight organisations could help set the prison reform agenda by holding the English government responsible for its austerity measures' effect on prisoner health. As Participant 18, an academic and an advisor to a European administration organisation, explained:

> It is very important that you have civil society organisations like Amnesty International and the CPT involved . . . in seeing what is happening in prison, writing reports, and telling the rest of the public what is actually happening within them.

Building on existing work (Scott, 2018; Green and Ward, 2004), non-governmental organisations—such as Amnesty International and the Association for the Prevention of Torture, as well as those in the UK, such as the Howard League for Penal Reform, the Prison Reform Trust, and INQUEST—should consistently articulate the impact of austerity on prisoners, remind the state not to breach health standards, monitor compliance, and, as a last resort, name and shame human rights violators.

Participants went further by recommending the establishment of an independent oversight authority to ensure the proper implementation of recommendations resulting from prison monitoring and inspections. Holding the government to account through legal power could also close the crisis-reform-crisis-reform loop.

Legal action

Sixth, participants suggested that prisoners and concerned parties should be encouraged to initiate legal action against government austerity measures. They could do this via the right to life and violation of the prohibition of torture under Articles 2 and 3 of the European Convention on Human Rights. This view was based on the previous successes of prisoners invoking the Convention to improve their health and well-being (van Zyl Smit and Snacken, 2009).

Participant 26, a legal advisor of a supranational court institution, argued that a lack of financial resources should not obstruct prisoners' access to healthcare provisions. The participant explained:

> According to legal standards, lack of financial resources cannot be justified for the reduction of austerity on the level of care for prisoners. There is a legal obligation of the government to try alternative means before attempting to reduce the level of health care in prisons.

Finally, recognising the limitations of the soft enforcement of human rights principles, a small number of participants from both international and national levels suggested encouraging prisoners and concerned parties to initiate legal action against the government's austerity measures that interfered with their rights during imprisonment. In particular, Participant 5, a member of a European anti-torture committee, noted:

> [T]here are very few prisoners in the United Kingdom who would make a challenge before the European Court of Human Rights. In Northern Ireland, there are far more petitions from judicial review by prisoners than there are in Great Britain. . . . [T]here are so few challenges by prisoners in England regarding the conditions of detention that they are required to maintain. This is the complete opposite when we look at deaths in custody and the investigations made by the UK Prisons & Probation Ombudsman.

Courts could then assist in addressing political policies, laws, and regulations that are unresponsive to legitimate demands for healthcare resources (Syrett, 2007). Inspection reports by the HMIP and CPT could be used as supporting evidence to strengthen prisoners' cases.

Some participants also suggested prisoners take legal action via section 1(2) of the Corporate Manslaughter and Corporate Homicide Act of 2007. That section avers that the impediment of access to healthcare, as well as worsening living conditions and increasing violence in prisons, could constitute corporate manslaughter. If so, a gross breach of a duty of care would be occurring owing to serious management failures. Participant 52, the head of policy of a national penal reform organisation, argued for criminal prosecution against the government to reinforce its accountability towards violent incidents that affected prisoners in England:

> We need to push for accountability for institutional failings by looking at how prosecutions could be made through the Corporate Manslaughter and Corporate Homicide Act for self-inflicted deaths, self-harm, and violent episodes in prisons that imperil prisoners.

As one participant noted, a test case is needed to ensure that legal obligations are cemented and enforced through the law, as the 2007 Act has thus far garnered minimal successful prosecution and sanction (Tombs, 2018). Participant 29, an academic and consultant for an international health organisation, explained further, "We need something in case law that this was definitely being contravened and taken, and then it becomes case law". In the absence of these legal challenges, the policymaking participants argued that such inertia highlighted a tacit acceptance towards austerity measures on prisons.

Finally, prisoners' exposure to torture, cruel treatment, or punishment is a human rights transgression amounting to state-sponsored crime (Green and

Ward, 2004). Irrespective of active violations of human rights or passive failures to protect individuals against violations of their rights, academics and advocacy organisations must demonstrate how prisoners' micro-experiences connect to the neoliberal state's reorganisation of markets via macroeconomic austerity and the dismantling of social security systems. The state crime caused by austerity—imposed on one of the marginalised groups within today's society—is a fertile field for health and criminological inquiry and vital for highlighting how austerity has dismantled the safety net of marginalised English citizens.

Conclusion

This chapter reported on participants' practical solutions to reverse the impacts of austerity and improve the stability of English prisons. These solutions fall outside the boundaries of prisons.

First, every participant proposed reducing the size of the prison population to reflect declining prison resources. They believed that abolishing short sentences, considering alternative community sentences instead of imprisonment, and encouraging increased use of suspended sentences would reduce the size of the prison population.

Second, all participants commented that the government needs to make recurrent investment in public services, covering both prisons and community services. Participants also suggested that the government should tackle tax avoidance. Apart from ensuring that these provisions would be adequately funded across all settings, they further proposed that improved funding should ameliorate the built environment of prisons and investment in the prison workforce.

Third, to ensure augmented transparency in penal policies, several participants suggested publicising prison spending data and including projected returns on investments and funding impact assessments in public discussions. Similarly, linking politicians more explicitly with their political activities would ensure greater political accountability to prevent financial waste.

Many participants also proposed that international concordats could be used as minimum standards to protect prisoners' right to health and prevent arbitrary damage to their rehabilitation experience. Finally, participants suggested encouraging prisoners and their network, as well as organisations that have legal standing, to initiate legal actions against the government over austerity's impact on prisons. Citing the potential litigation routes under the European Convention on Human Rights, the Corporate Manslaughter and Corporate Homicide Act of 2007, and the state crime framework, austerity measures can constitute a violation of the right to life and the prevention of torture. They can also constitute corporate manslaughter and cruel treatment, which is considered a human rights transgression amounting to state-sponsored crime.

References

Boin, A. (2001) *Public Institutions: Leadership in Two Prison Systems*. Boulder: Lynne Rienner Publishers.

Bradley, K. (2009) *Lord Bradley's Review of People with Mental Health Problems or Learning Disabilities in the Criminal Justice System*. London: Department of Health.

Chang, H. (2010) *23 Things They Don't Tell You About Capitalism*. London: Penguin.

Corston, J. (2007) *The Corston Report: A Report by Baroness Jean Corston of a Review of Women with Particular Vulnerabilities in the Criminal Justice System*. London: Home Office.

Financial Times (2017) *Multinationals Avoid up to £5.8bn in UK Tax, HMRC Finds* [Online], available from: www.ft.com/content/00de4f00-b754-11e7-8c12-5661783e5589 (Accessed: 10th August 2018).

Green, P. and Ward, T. (2004) *State Crime: Governments, Violence and Corruption*. London: Pluto.

Ismail, N. and Forrester, A. (2020b) The State of English Prisons and the Urgent Need for Reform. *The Lancet Public Health*. 5(7), pp. e368–e369. https://doi.org/10.1016/S2468-2667(20)30142-0.

Keynes, J. M. (1936) *The General Theory of Interest, Employment and Money*. London: MacMillan.

Mills, A. and Kendall, K. (2018) Introduction. In: Mills, A. and Kendall, K., eds. *Mental Health in Prisons: Critical Perspectives on Treatment and Confinement*. Basingstoke: Palgrave Macmillan, pp. 1–22.

Ministry of Justice (2017) *Costs Per Place and Costs Per Prisoner by Individual Prison* [Online], available from: https://assets.publishing.service.gov.uk/government/uploads/system/uploads/attachment_data/file/653972/costs-per-place-per-prisoner-2016-2017-summary.pdf (Accessed: 19th February 2019).

National Audit Office (2017) *Mental Health in Prisons* [Online], available from: www.nao.org.uk/wp-content/uploads/2017/06/Mental-health-in-prisons.pdf (Accessed: 11th January 2018).

National Centre for Social Research (2018) *Support for More Tax & Spend at Fifteen-Year High* [Online], available from: https://natcen.ac.uk/news-media/press-releases/2018/september/support-for-more-tax-spend-at-fifteen-year-high/ (Accessed: 25th January 2021).

Ruckert, A. and Labonté, R. (2017) Health Inequities In the Age of Austerity: The Need for Social Protection Policies. *Social Science & Medicine*. 187, pp. 306–311.

Scott, D. (2018) *Against Imprisonment: An Anthology of Abolitionist Essays*. Hampshire: Waterside Press.

Stuckler, D. and Basu, S. (2013) *The Body Economic: Why Austerity Kills*. London: Allan Lane.

Syrett, K. (2007) *Law, Legitimacy and the Rationing of Health Care: A Contextual and Comparative Perspective*. Cambridge: Cambridge University Press.

Terry, L. D. (1995) *Leadership in Public Bureaucracies*. Thousand Oaks, CA: SAGE.

Tombs, S. (2018) The UK's Corporate Killing Law: Un/Fit for Purpose? *Criminology & Criminal Justice*. 18(4), pp. 488–507.

United Nations General Assembly (2019) *Visit to the United Kingdom of Great Britain and Northern Ireland: Report of the Special Rapporteur on Extreme Poverty and Human Rights* [Online], available from: https://undocs.org/A/HRC/41/39/Add.1 (Accessed: 25th January 2021).

van Zyl Smit, D. and Snacken, S. (2009) *Principles of European Prison Law and Policy: Penology and Human Rights*. Oxford: Oxford University Press.

Chapter 11

Conclusion

Introduction

In 1964, then British Prime Minister Harold Wilson reportedly said that "a week is a long time in politics". Indeed, things can change incredibly quickly. Yet despite all the evidence of its failings, austerity has remained in place in the UK since 2010 and counting.

A primary research question guided my investigation: "How does austerity impact prison health governance and healthcare delivery in England?" Drawing from the perspectives of 87 prison health experts, I argue that austerity is a political experiment that exposes six political fallacies that have shaped and constrained prison healthcare in England since 2010. These paradoxes are: i) the need for austerity and cost-saving measures; ii) the operation of prison health within a punishment structure; iii) the stability of a structured, top-down control of prison services; iv) the political rhetoric of 'tough on crime' and 'we are all in this together'; v) the government's neoliberal responses to prison instability; and vi) continual prison scrutiny of governance and services.

Overall, the findings demonstrate that austerity has failed to reduce the burgeoning national debt, control the governance and delivery of effective and efficient healthcare services, and improve the utility of health among prisoners in England. Although the proposed solutions will not remedy all of austerity's impacts over the last decade, they may facilitate fundamental reform on prison and prison health in England if implemented correctly and robustly.

Why this matters

This book's novel analytical narrative supports arguments that austerity is a political choice and, after a decade, is clearly a failed political ideology. As participants affirmed, politicians claimed that austerity was imperative to reduce the state debt and recover from the global recession emanating from the US and European countries (Gamble, 2014). However, the UK debt-to-GDP ratio reached an apogee in 2019 versus the pre-austerity era in 2010, following the

DOI: 10.4324/9781003182337-11

bank bailout programme of the government (Office for National Statistics, 2021). Austerity has failed to fulfil its objectives in reducing deficits.

The narrative also illustrates British exceptionalism in volunteering for deflation despite not being a member of the Eurozone and lacking an economic imperative (Gamble, 2014). The government's fiscal adjustment programme was comparable to that which the Troika imposed on Greece, Ireland, and Portugal as part of their bailout conditions (ibid.). If recession provided the pretext, startlingly, growth did not provide a reason for relief. The United Kingdom's economy, the fifth largest in the world, is continually growing, exceeding 2% between 2013 and 2018 (OECD, 2018).

This book highlights one of austerity's central political, as opposed to economic, characteristics: upholding it required discrediting evidence and downplaying state adaptability. That it has so clearly failed is further evidence it was economically unsound.

This study also underscores how imprisonment during austerity becomes a double punishment, building on Sykes's (1958) theory of deprivation. This study reports how austerity obstructs access to healthcare and purposeful activities for prisoners, creates precarious living conditions and increases levels of violence that subject prisoners to excessive distress or hardship. That prisons continue to hold these citizens not only belies the notion of healthcare equivalence in prisons but constitutes a human rights abuse.

These findings contest previous studies—in the UK, Europe, and the US—showing imprisonment is an opportunity to improve prisoners' health (Crewe, 2005; Spycher et al., 2021). Current resources and conditions make such improvement difficult. The findings also reveal the deterioration of formal prison governance. Such deterioration indirectly fuelled the rise of prison gangs and organised crime within English prisons and materialised the crisis of legitimacy (Habermas, 1973), which undermines leadership and coordinated action for health delivery.

This study builds on existing scholarly and governmental work arguing that austerity deteriorates safety nets for the communities and primes vulnerable individuals from these communities for prison. Approximately 14 million people in the UK live in poverty, experiencing record levels of hunger and homelessness (UN General Assembly, 2019), evidencing the population's health deterioration. Further, the study supports the conclusions that prisoners' poor health is partly a by-product of their experiences before incarceration (Marmot, 2005; Spencer, 2001; WHO, 2014). Eventually, these individuals arrive at penal institutions with extraordinarily complex health and social needs that have gone unmet due to diminished community services under austerity. This study also builds on the evidence of a 49% real-term reduction in government funding from 2010 to 2018 alongside a rise in demand for key social services (House of Commons Committee of Public Accounts, 2018), which have further reinforced inequalities, especially in deprived communities.

In previous generations, several areas across England depended on employment in mines, steelworks, and shipbuilding. But the deindustrialisation of the 1980s, fitting the neoliberal agenda of reducing state intervention in the economy, left the working class vulnerable (Milne, 2014; Pacione, 1997). This present study not only builds on the assertion that the poor bear the brunt of austerity (Harvey, 2010), but it also underscores the double regulation of the poor (Wacquant, 2000). Participants witnessed a close meshing between the rolling back of the welfare state and rolling out of penal institutions. Their observations also reinforce the recognition of a strengthening of the coercive arm of the state (ibid.).

Various US literature has examined the connection between austerity and deindustrialisation. It finds those living in poverty suffer a reduced lifespan and an increase in the seriousness of criminality that leads to imprisonment (Linkon and Russo, 2002; Nosrati et al., 2018). Social inequality matters for crime and punishment, but crime and punishment are also key in reinforcing social inequality. This study offers a foundation for future quantitative studies that might explore the association between the government's decisions to withdraw funding from a welfare-based approach and the increase in criminality in areas that experienced deindustrialisation during the austere era in the UK.

In addition, this study builds on privatisation lessons from other countries, particularly Australia and the United States. It does so by evidencing how private prison providers escape or lack oversight and quality control monitoring, supporting arguments against the privatisation of prisons and prison healthcare services in the UK. Rather than reducing inefficiency and improving cost-saving and competition, this study illustrates that privatisation achieved the opposite with immense consequences.

Participants' observations exposed how privatisation increases monitoring costs for the government, contradicting the cost-saving agenda. Meanwhile, participants showed that using profit as a moral compass could limit the efficacy of health utility on prisoners. Furthermore, the transfer of HMP Birmingham from G4S to a public sector prison, the bankruptcy of Carillion, and the poor performance of private contractors who delivered the Transforming Rehabilitation programme post-imprisonment exemplify the arguments against privatisation (Ministry of Justice, 2019a; House of Commons Justice Committee, 2019). They provide an early warning that privatisation might cost more in the long run as the government continues to subsidise their failure.

Despite their poor track record across the English criminal justice system, private contractors are forecast to occupy an increasingly significant role in the penal landscape following an outsourcing plan for at least two new prisons, HMPs Glen Parva and Wellingborough (House of Commons Library, 2018; Ministry of Justice, 2019b). Several participants signalled the move's political irrationality. This anomaly is ripe for an academic investigation into the actual costs of privatisation in prisons and the broader criminal justice system. These future studies should expose the contradiction of continuing to trust these private contractors when they persistently fail to deliver on costs, service efficiency, quality, and the broader moral obligation for the state to administer punishment rather than private contractors.

Finally, this book illustrates the impotence of prison oversight mechanisms, which enable the continued infliction of austerity on prisoners and the prison workforce. This study thereby addresses the lacuna that Nicola Padfield (2018) identified. This study finds that civil servants, from policymakers to prison officers, had to maintain impartiality by aligning themselves to justice ministers' visions.

Concurrently, this study provides the first evidence needed to assess parliamentary committees' effectiveness in monitoring prison and prison health and establishes a foundation on which future studies should build. Negative publicity from damning parliamentary inquiries has yet to translate into substantive reforms. Indeed, half of the HMIP recommendations for improvement have not been achieved in 2019/2020 (HMIP, 2020). All monitoring bodies have expressed serious concerns about prison staff's failure to implement improvements following their reports (House of Commons Library, 2019).

Participants also criticised the unwillingness of HMIP, PPO, and IMBs to challenge austerity's degrading of the prison regime and prison healthcare services. Ironically, they impose liability on civil servants who had no choice but to execute political mandates. These findings contradict earlier studies of these boards, which present a more favourable view of their role in highlighting and preventing institutional abuse and upholding accountability (Bennett, 2016; Ramsbotham, 2003).

This study also articulates a new phenomenon. The Lobbying Act of 2014 increasingly prevented third sector organisations from opposing austerity due to contractual clauses and statutory requirements. This trend is generalisable across charitable sector operations across the UK, whereby the work of members of charitable organisations must reflect their funders' views. This consequently mutes, conceals, and obscures these voluntary organisations' voices. Silence and lack of meaningful actions helped create the space and conditions for the deep-seated crisis that austerity continually inflicts on prisoners and the prison workforce.

Why this matters for interdisciplinary prison health research

This study provides theoretical clarity in analysing the complexity of austerity's impact on public sector services. It argues austerity exposes six political paradoxes that have shaped and constrained prison health in England since 2010. This framework reflects the impact of neoliberalism: mutable and tentative 'rolling back' and 'rolling out' policies, hegemonic programmes, and governmentality (Ward and England, 2007). Overall, austerity has failed not only to reduce the burgeoning national debt. It has also failed to control the governance and delivery of healthcare services effectively and efficiently. And it has failed to improve the utility of health among prisoners in England. While maintaining a sensitivity to the uniqueness of other contexts, this framework could potentially be adapted to other public service sectors to examine austerity's impact on different health settings.

Furthermore, this book advances our understanding of civil servants' limited autonomy and independence. Participants found civil servants unable to challenge austerity's impact on prisons and prison health effectively. Irrespective of the organisational strata, all avoided using the word 'austerity' in their daily discussions within their departments and with stakeholders. This avoidance demonstrates their passive and pervasive acquiescence as civil servants. This finding is important given social policy theorists such as Tom Gash et al. (2010) have assumed that public bodies exist to depoliticise decision-making processes and that civil servants are independent decision makers. This book suggests this conclusion is problematic and overstated, at least within the prison service context. Instead, the top-down control mimics the critical realist theory of governance (Marsh, 2011). It reflects how the government maintains a firm grip on hierarchical coordination, inherited from the Westminster model of strong ministerial steering.

The tradition of ministerial involvement in prison services continues to this day. This study does not align neatly with the theory of representational dimension (Sparks and Bottoms, 1996), which argues officials' behaviour is a homogenous reflection of the whole system. Tensions exist within the narrative of prison workers, where they opposed ministerial involvement in the prison service. Nevertheless, overall, this study demonstrates how civil servants have drifted to the margins of decision making, doing their best to execute the ideas the central government had foisted on them. Inevitably, study participants from all organisational levels aligned with politicians' objectives and their ideological hegemony (Gramsci, 1971). This has depoliticised austerity through economic logic, disguised austerity as a political apparatus, and disconnected political accountability to emasculate criticisms.

Additionally, this study highlights the constriction of prison health governance within the prison service's top-down control structure. This is a new form of governance that academics have yet to theorise. It seeks to mesh a government without governance representation of the prison health system and structure with the empirical manifestation of adaptation towards a top-down structure. The concepts of government without governance were fashionable in the 1990s, providing an alternative to the traditional top-down, command-and-control approach of hierarchical steering by the central government (Bevir and Rhodes, 2003; Fidler, 2007; Rhodes, 1996). Yet they tend to leave limited space for the domination of one government agency over another. This new form of governance highlights the zero-sum collision between a top-down and dispersed system, prioritising short-term security and control in the criminal justice system. This governance is riddled with ideological and political interests and thwarts social pursuits, such as rehabilitation. Underlying the structure of prison health governance and delivery is the state's choice to align prison health governance and delivery with the prevailing political ideology (Peck and Tickell, 1994).

This book provides further impetus for the emerging scholarly turn towards informal governance within prisons. This informal governance has flourished because of weak formal governance. Advancing previous research (Gooch and Treadwell, 2020; Maitra, 2010; Skarbek, 2011), this study demonstrates how the microeconomic structure of organised crime thrived in the prison system under austerity. Previous studies (ibid.) were based on ethnographic accounts from 2014 and before, leading to a disparity with current developments. Updating existing scholarship and moving beyond Jürgen Habermas's (1973) crisis of legitimacy theory, this study has shown the lack of detection and enforcement resulting from fewer prison custodians and a broader legitimacy crisis in prison governance. This crisis has resulted in a loss of control of the prison institution, an undermining of leadership, and uncoordinated action for health delivery.

The book also builds on the theory of agnotology, which remains under-theorised in social sciences (Proctor and Schiebinger, 2008). A minority of civil service participants denied the relationship between austerity and prison instability, claiming inadequate hard evidence of causation. Most participants rejected such logic, finding clear causation in austerity for the violent catastrophe following the Benchmarking Programme 2012. These denials nevertheless resemble a process of manufacturing doubt and promoting ignorance and indifference via continual gaslighting (ibid.). Those in power manipulate the public by fragmenting the reality of austerity. Blaming prison instability on the increasing presence of psychoactive substances is agnotology, enabling theorisation of denialism. We cannot fully appreciate the politics of austerity without examining the political response framing the prison crisis.

This book highlights the consistent degradation of the prison rehabilitation construct over the last few decades. A mismatch between policy that recognises rehabilitation as a penal agenda and resource constraints reinforces the conflict between 'policy-in-form' and 'policy-in-use' enacted on the 'front-stage' of policy formulation and 'backstage' of implementation. Furthermore, the stability of the governance and delivery of prison health depends highly on, and therefore suffers from, the ministerial view that rehabilitation initiatives are soft on crime. This dependency is compounded by a vague purpose of imprisonment under Rule 3 of the Prison Rules 1999. It is written to encourage and assist prisoners in leading a good and useful life, yet reinforces punishment over rehabilitation. The pro-punishment sentimentality subverts the complex meaning of prison rehabilitation in prison discourse. This self-contradictory discourse amplifies the theory of bureaucracy (Weber, 1930): the prison service continues to be ill-equipped to translate vague and conflicting goals into integrated actions. Such inability creates ripple effects throughout prison management and the delivery of healthcare equivalence, and eventually impedes prisoners' access to health services. The concept of English prisons as potentially rehabilitative merely cloaks the dominant reality that these are institutions of punishment.

Finally, this book paves the way for international research to determine how the exposure of prisoners to torture, cruel treatment, or punishment via austerity could amount to state crimes. Implicit in the human rights-based definition of state crime is not only active violations of human rights but also passive failures to protect individuals against violations by other individuals or corporations (Green and Ward, 2004). Recent ministerial admissions, including those of Boris Johnson, have conceded that austerity programmes were more wide-ranging, severe, and damaging than initially intended (Al-Jazeera, 2019). The UN's special rapporteur investigation found the UK government had breached its human rights obligations in a 'systematic' and 'tragic' way (UN General Assembly, 2019). Demonstrating austerity as a framework for state crime within the prison system, imposed on society's most marginalised members, is a fertile field for health and criminological inquiry.

Why it matters for policy

Finally, this study highlights urgent policy responses that could strengthen political accountability for the imposition of austerity on prison and prison health. Several participants recommended monitoring per capita spending on prisons and prison healthcare services. International organisations such as the WHO and the CPT could facilitate this given austerity is a global phenomenon. Similarly, participants highlighted a need to quantify the actual costs of imprisonment and ill-health within this austerity setting to form the basis of political, policy, and social discussions, especially on the extent of prison effectiveness. Rather than focusing on austerity's impacts within the prison setting only, connecting the postponement or cancellation of health appointments and longer treatment waiting times to the broader NHS England performance, for instance, would provide a bird's-eye view of the issue.

National research should track the implementation of recommendations from the prison oversight bodies to improve prison health and regime in England. Participants were inconsistent on how much austerity impacts different prison establishments and prisoners. To address the inconsistency, this book suggests closer monitoring of the impacts across prison establishments and prisoner groups in England. Independent external organisations will be best placed to monitor this development within their scrutiny framework. Similarly, tracking mechanisms that connect ministers to their reform agenda—irrespective of success or failure—would reveal their political power in directing civil servants to execute their political vision and raise accountability. Such research could potentially highlight the lack of ownership and compliance. It could also highlight how the broader political climate around Brexit, responses towards the COVID-19 pandemic, and the discussions on withdrawal from human rights commitments often tamper with the implementation of those recommendations. Overall, these research projects could deliver actionable evidence that springboards policy responses.

This book also presents an opportunity to reflect on other domains where austerity policies could compromise health. Future international research could focus on determining how much macroeconomic conditions and political economy frameworks are commensurable with the government's commitment to providing sufficient financial resources for prison health. The research could link these commitments to existing obligations, such as the principle of equivalence of healthcare in prisons under the Mandela Rules, as well as the Sustainable Development Goals 2030 estimated to be between US$3.3 and US$4.5 trillion a year (Ismail et al., 2021; Tangcharoensathien et al., 2015). As politicians face competing fiscal demands, addressing the under-resourcing of health and welfare services in the criminal justice system is important, as is understanding the political archetype that could either nurture or thwart the prison health commitment.

Clarifications on the strengths and limitations of the study

This research contextualises austerity's impact on prison health governance and the delivery of prison healthcare services in England within a comprehensive framework of prison agent narratives. Its findings are significant for countries beyond England, particularly those where austerity shaped prison policy following the 2008 global economic recession. These countries include Portugal, Italy, Ireland, Greece, and Spain. This book presents an opportunity to reflect on the impact of austerity measures in other domains—such as welfare and social care—where policy choices could compromise health. Such explorations would likely indicate that austerity cannot be justified empirically or ethically, given its harmful effects on health governance, the workforce, and the health and safety of the end-users.

As with all research, however, this study has limitations. First is that it can only speak qualitatively. It cannot quantitatively evidence that austerity is responsible for worsening prison health governance and the delivery of healthcare in English prisons. Some policy measures demonstrated austerity's effects over the last decade, particularly the post-2012 Benchmarking Exercise that saw a reduction in prison workforce: it precipitated the increasing violence in prison. Indeed, no plausible alternative explanation exists for the current prison instability. Furthermore, an overwhelming majority of participants explicitly rejected the claim that more proof is necessary. Thereby, they clearly indicated austerity as inflicting harm on prison health governance and healthcare delivery in England.

Considering the study is qualitative, we cannot definitively attribute solely to austerity the findings of instability in the prison health system and the broader regime of prisons. There are longstanding prison issues connected to government policy decisions, and these are broader than austerity. Notably, these include inadequate funding and delivery of prison healthcare services, poor health of prisoners, and statutory commitment on sentencing—which have been discussed within this book. Although quantitative analysis is beyond this study's remit, others might use its interviews more conventionally as a precursor to quantitative research on how austerity impacts the prison health and prison regime. Experimental studies could identify potentially counter-intuitive and important findings regarding fiscal relations, redistribution, and the normative order within prisons. These studies would also help ensure that more conventional quantitative statistical generalisations redress the potential pitfalls of qualitative analysis generally.

Another limitation of this study is its discounting of prisoners' perspectives. While this study attempts to understand austerity's impacts on prison health from 87 prison health experts' perspectives, no interviews occurred with end-users. Future studies should fill this gap to understand experts' possible micro-assumptions, particularly on how the distribution of resources impinges individual prisoners. As such, future research should address how austerity specifically impacts the diverse prison populations, as well as the unequal distribution of spending cuts along gender, age, ethnicity, and nationality, alongside intersectionality among them. As 90% of prisoners will eventually leave prison (House of Commons Library, 2019), future studies could also assess austerity's impacts on prisoners after they return to their communities.

Moreover, the data also focused solely on adult prisons in England and may not reflect conditions in other places of confinement, such as youth offender institutions and immigration removal centres. That said, thinking this study's insights are entirely inapplicable to these environments would be remiss.

Final thoughts

Over a decade has passed since the political rhetoric of austerity emerged in England. Austerity and imprisonment have failed to deliver their objectives: to rapidly reduce the burgeoning national debt and the rate of reoffending. However, after over a decade of failures, the state continues to experiment with austerity, reproducing the same failures, and political reluctance to dispense with them seems as strong as ever. Austerity is an expensive political choice, and the nonfinancial cost of imprisonment during austere times is the egregious violation of human rights. This research offers a starting point, providing a narrative calling for fundamental reform to create a more positive and inclusive system, in line with England's international and domestic commitments to the humane treatment of all people, including those whose behaviour warrants censure.

References

Al Jazeera (2019) *Britain at the Crossroads* [Online], available from: www.aljazeera.com/indepth/opinion/britain-crossroads-191108083530322.html (Accessed: 25th January 2021).

Bennett, J. (2016) *The Working Lives of Prison Managers: Global Change, Local Culture and Individual Agency in the Late Modern Prison*. London: Palgrave Macmillan.

Bevir, M. and Rhodes, R. A. W. (2003) *Interpreting British Governance*. London: Routledge.

Crewe, B. (2005) *The Prisoner Society: Power, Adaptation, and Social Life in an English Prison.* Oxford: Oxford University Press.

Fidler, D. P. (2007) Architecture Amidst Anarchy: Global Health's Quest for Governance. *Global Health Governance.* 1.

Gamble, A. (2014) Austerity as Statecraft. *Parliamentary Affairs.* 68, pp. 42–57.

Gash, T., Magee, I., Rutter, J. and Smith, N. (2010) *Read Before Burning: Arm's Length Government for a New Administration.* London: Institute for Government.

Gooch, K. and Treadwell, J. (2020) Prisoner Society in an Era of Psychoactive Substances, Organized Crime, New Drug Markets and Austerity. *The British Journal of Criminology.* 60(5), pp. 1260–1281.

Gramsci, A. (1971) *Selections From the Prison Notebooks of Antonio Gramsci.* London: Lawrence & Wishart.

Green, P. and Ward, T. (2004) *State Crime: Governments, Violence and Corruption.* London: Pluto.

Habermas, J. (1973) *Legitimation Crisis.* London: Heinemann Educational Books.

Harvey, D. (2010) *The Enigma of Capital and the Crises of Capitalism.* London: Profile Books.

HM Inspectorate of Prisons (2020) *HM Chief Inspector of Prisons for England and Wales: Annual Report 2019–20* [Online], available from: https://assets.publishing.service.gov.uk/government/uploads/system/uploads/attachment_data/file/927361/hmi-prisons-annual-report-accounts-201920.pdf (Accessed: 25th January 2021).

House of Commons Committee of Public Accounts (2018) *Financial Sustainability of Local Authorities: Fiftieth Report of Session 2017–19* [Online], available from: https://publications.parliament.uk/pa/cm201719/cmselect/cmpubacc/970/970.pdf (Accessed: 20th April 2019).

House of Commons Justice Committee (2019) *Prison Governance* [Online], available from: https://publications.parliament.uk/pa/cm201919/cmselect/cmjust/191/191.pdf (Accessed: 21st January 2020).

House of Commons Library (2018) *The Prison Estate. Briefing Paper Number 05646, 12 December 2018* [Online], available from: http://researchbriefings.files.parliament.uk/documents/SN05646/SN05646.pdf (Accessed: 19th February 2019).

House of Commons Library (2019) *Briefing paper Number CBP-04334, 23 July 2019: UK Prison Population Statistics* [Online], available from: http://researchbriefings.files.parliament.uk/documents/SN04334/SN04334.pdf (Accessed: 27th May 2020).

Ismail, N., Lazaris, A., O'Moore, E., Plugge, E. and Stürup-Toft, S. (2021) Leaving No One Behind in Prison: Improving the Health of People in Prison as a Key Contributor to Meeting the Sustainable Development Goals 2030. *BMJ Global Health.* 6, p. e004252. https://doi.org/10.1136/bmjgh-2020-004252.

Linkon, S. L. and Russo, J. (2002) *Steeltown U.S.A.: Work and Memory in Youngstown.* Lawrence: University Press of Kansas.

Maitra, D. M. (2010) An Exploratory Study of Prison Gangs in Contemporary Society. In: Harding, S. and Palasinski, M., eds. *Psychological Perspectives on Youth Gang Behaviour.* Hershey, PA: APMHBS Book Series, pp. 1–28.

Marmot, M. (2005) Social Determinants of Health Inequalities. *Lancet.* 365, pp. 1099–1104.

Marsh, D. (2011) The New Orthodoxy: The Differentiated Polity Model. *Public Administration.* 89(1), pp. 32–48.

Milne, S. (2014) *The Enemy Within: The Secret War Against the Miners.* London: Verso Books.

Ministry of Justice (2019a) *Birmingham Prison Contract Ended* [Online], available from: www.gov.uk/government/news/birmingham-prison-contract-ended (Accessed: 21st February 2020).

Ministry of Justice (2019b) *10,000 Extra Prison Places to Keep the Public Safe* [Online], available from: www.gov.uk/government/news/10-000-extra-prison-places-to-keep-the-public-safe (Accessed: 21st February 2020).

Nosrati, E., Ash, M., Marmot, M., McKee, M. and King, L. P. (2018) The Association Between Income and Life Expectancy Revisited: Deindustrialization, Incarceration and the Widening Health Gap. *International Journal of Epidemiology*. 47(3), pp. 720–730.

Office for National Statistics (2021) *UK Government Debt and Deficit: September 2020* [Online], available from: www.ons.gov.uk/economy/governmentpublicsectorandtaxes/publicspending/bulletins/ukgovernmentdebtanddeficitforeurostatmaast/september2020 (Accessed: 25th January 2021).

Organisation for Economic Co-operation and Development (2018) *Quarterly GDP* [Online], available from: https://data.oecd.org/gdp/quarterly-gdp.htm (Accessed: 25th January 2021).

Pacione, M., ed. (1997) *Britain's Cities: Geographies of Division in Urban Britain*. London: Routledge.

Padfield, N. (2018) Monitoring Prisons in England and Wales: Who Ensures the Fair Treatment of Prisoners? *Crime, Law and Social Change*. 70, pp. 57–76.

Peck, J. and Tickell, A. (1994) Jungle Law Breaks Out: Neoliberalism and Global-Local Disorder. *Area*. 26(4), pp. 317–326.

Proctor, R. N. and Schiebinger, L. (2008) *Agnotology: The Making and Unmaking of Ignorance*. Stanford: Stanford University Press.

Ramsbotham, D. (2003) *Prisongate: The Shocking State of Britain's Prisons and the Need for Visionary Change*. London: The Free Press.

Rhodes, R. A. W. (1996) The New Governance: Governing Without Government. *Political Studies*. 44(4), pp. 652–667.

Skarbek, D. (2011) Governance and Prison Gangs. *American Political Science Review*. 105(4), pp. 702–716.

Sparks, R. and Bottoms, A. E. (1996) Legitimacy and Order in Prisons. *The British Journal of Sociology*. 46(1), pp. 45–62.

Spencer, A. (2001) *Removing Bars to Good Treatment*. London: NHS.

Spycher, J., Dusheiko, M., Beaupère, P., Gravier, B. and Moschetti, K. (2021) Healthcare in A Pure Gatekeeping System: Utilization of Primary, Mental and Emergency Care in the Prison Population Over Time. *Health Justice*. 9(11).

Sykes, G. (1958) *The Society of Captives: A Study of a Maximum Security Prison*. Princeton, NJ: Princeton University Press.

Tangcharoensathien, V., Mills, A. and Palu, T. (2015) Accelerating Health Equity: The Key Role of Universal Health Coverage in The Sustainable Development Goals. *BMC Medicine*. 13, p. 101. https://doi.org/10.1186/s12916-015-0342-3.

United Nations General Assembly (2019) *Visit to the United Kingdom of Great Britain and Northern Ireland: Report of the Special Rapporteur on Extreme Poverty and Human Rights* [Online], available from: https://undocs.org/A/HRC/41/39/Add.1 (Accessed: 25th January 2021).

Wacquant, L. (2000) The New "Peculiar Institution": On the Prison as Surrogate Ghetto. *Theoretical Criminology*. 4(3), pp. 377–389.

Ward, K. and England, K. (2007) Introduction: Reading Neoliberalization. In: England, K. and Ward, K., eds. *Neoliberalization*. Hoboken, NJ: Blackwell, pp. 1–22.

Weber, M. (1930) *The Protestant Ethic and the Spirit of Capitalism*. Oxford: Basil Blackwell.

World Health Organization (2014) *Prisons and Health* [Online], available from: www.euro.who.int/__data/assets/pdf_file/0005/249188/Prisons-and-Health.pdf (Accessed: 12th April 2018).

Chapter 12

Methodological appendix

Introduction

This research is the first in-depth, large-scale qualitative study exploring the impact of macroeconomic austerity on prison health governance and delivery. This chapter demonstrates the rigour and transparency of this research. It presents the rationale and philosophical underpinning of the research, for which constructivist grounded theory provides the core approach. Subsequently, it explains the process for accessing and recruiting participants and the procedures for data collection and analysis. These expert interviews highlight issues pertaining to 'studying up' with elite participants and the challenges in undertaking health research in a highly regimented environment with 'street-level bureaucrats' (Lipsky, 1980). Finally, given the study is qualitative, measures were undertaken to establish the trustworthiness of the research project, including the principles of credibility, ethical conduct, and sincerity.

How I orientated the research

I chose a constructivist approach to grounded theory (Charmaz, 2006) for this study. This is a suitable methodology for a new, emerging phenomenon and therefore this study. The choice was made fully consciously from an epistemological, ontological, and subjective viewpoint, underscored by the project's research imperatives and practicalities.

Epistemologically, constructivism asserts that knowledge and meaning about the world are constructed by participants (Appleton and King, 2002). A constructivist stance encourages me to 'study with the participants'. This involved providing them with a safe space to engage with the topic, humanising the research interactions and avoiding a mechanistic process of engagement. This approach also recognises the relativism of multiple social realities. The informants' experiences, and the contexts of these experiences, helped theorise austerity's impact on prison health governance and delivery.

Simultaneously, rather than suggesting truth is discoverable only in a posteriori knowledge, the ontological perspective of constructivist grounded theory

DOI: 10.4324/9781003182337-12

acknowledges the existence of multiple realities. Realities, as constructed by the research participants, are shaped by the intersections of political, cultural, and social norms, leading to a theory that "is situated in time, place, culture and situation" (Charmaz, 2006, p. 131).

From a subjectivity viewpoint, an approach based in constructivist grounded theory acknowledges overtly the subjective role of the researcher in the process of both generating and analysing data (Charmaz, 2014). My background as a former community and prison commissioner in the public health sector for nearly a decade has helped ensure I am conversant with the prison health governance and the delivery of prison healthcare services in England and ensured that I have not examined the phenomenon superficially, since I can draw on my first-hand experiences witnessing it across prison institutions.

In embracing practicality, constructivist grounded theory encourages me to be acquainted with the existing literature to augment my knowledge before entering the field. Classical grounded theorists objected to engagement with the existing literature before beginning data collection (Glaser and Holton, 2004). However, researchers like myself do not exist in a vacuum. Thus, the context around individual perceptions and their conceptual frameworks cannot be side-lined. Having background knowledge reinforces my credibility and, in turn, contributes to the authority of the ensuing arguments (Ismail, 2020a).

How I recruited the research participants

A 13-month period of research fieldwork was undertaken intermittently between January 2018 and September 2019, with 87 prison health professionals who operate within the international, national, and local governance structures. Given the interdisciplinarity and scale of the investigation into the governance strata of prison health in England, the sample size was inevitably large. Figure 12.1 demonstrates the number of participants who were contacted and subsequently participated

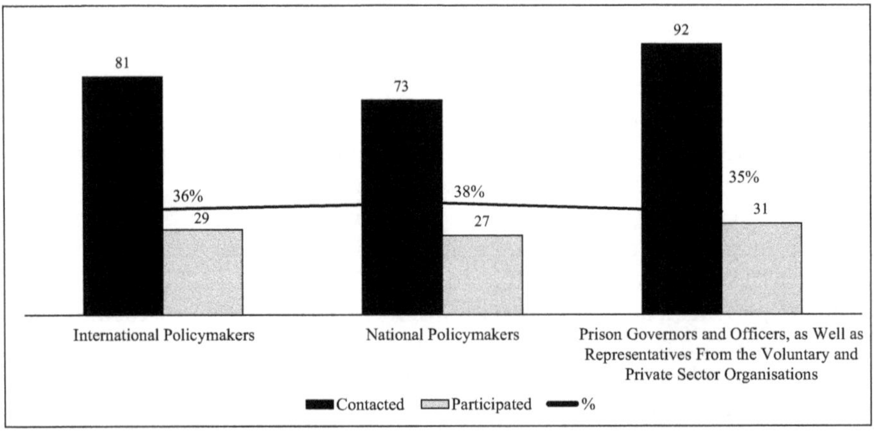

Figure 12.1 Number of participants who were contacted and participated in the research

during the three research phases. Of 246 potential participants who were approached, 87 (35%) agreed to take part. Drawing on a large group of potential participants helped to minimise the uncertainty around non-participation.

At the first fieldwork stage, 29 policymakers from key organisations relevant to international prison work, such as the UN, the WHO, and the Council of Europe, were invited to provide accounts on the research topic, together with those from other non-governmental organisations, such as Amnesty International and the Association for the Prevention of Torture. This was followed by the second wave of fieldwork, where 27 national policymakers participated, from governmental (e.g., HMPPS, NHS England, and PHE) and non-governmental organisations, reflecting the broad composition of the prison health terrain in England.

To reflect ground-level experiences, 22 prison governors and officers across 17 prison sites—ranging from high-, medium-, and low-security prisons, as well as resettlement prisons, and with a mixture of public and private sector institutions—took part in the final stage of the research. Additionally, nine representatives from the voluntary and private sector organisations who were commissioned to deliver the prison health agenda across English prisons took part in this research.

Despite the varied sample, all stakeholders were guided to address the same aim, namely to highlight austerity's impact on prisons, regardless of the stratum that they occupied. As Kathy Charmaz (2006) indicates, "the studied experience is embedded in larger and, often, hidden positions, networks, situations and relationships. Subsequently, differences and distinctions between people become visible" (pp. 130–131). As such, I was alert to similarities and differences between participants to ensure all perspectives were considered sufficiently.

Recruitment of elite participants

This study further redresses the paucity of 'studying up' research in the prison health field. Building on previous methodological studies on elite participants (Lilleker, 2003; Littig, 2009), the methodological contribution is demonstrated via interviews with 56 international and national experts. These experts occupied authoritative positions and engaged with policymaking activities in the prison health field, and they could influence political outcomes on prison health. The sparsity of research with political and policy elites is not unique to the prison health field, considering their position in an asymmetrical distribution of knowledge and their insularity from the public, which can be attributed to their power (Hunter, 1995; Ostrander, 1995).

I carefully planned and executed invitation strategies. These strategies included examining official documents on international and European prison health, where the names of the authors and consultees were recorded, to identify potential research participants.

Purposive sampling was first used by "seeking out individuals where the processes being studied are most likely to occur" (Denzin and Lincoln, 1994, p. 202). I selected participants based on four inclusion criteria: a) perspectives that reflect the diverse disciplines covered by this research; b) the richness of experiences that reflect participants' seniority in the field; and c) participants' decision-making capacity, based on their position in the organisational hierarchy.

Subsequently, I implemented theoretical sampling when some data categories became saturated and participants introduced new concepts, following preliminary data analysis (Milliken and Northcott, 2003). For instance, there was the emerging issue of privatisation, given that this had increasingly become a policy option in prison health since 2010 to reduce operational costs and promote the efficient operation of prisons. I contacted new participants who might have perspectives that could either further support or challenge these provisional findings. As theoretical constructs evolved, I sought further information from these participants to refine the emerging ideas.

Finally, I used snowball sampling where, at the end of each interview, I speculatively asked the participants, "Who else should I talk to about this research?" This strategy proved to be useful. On many occasions, I was given the contact details of potential interviewees and, after interviewing them, I asked the same question, which allowed me to use their authority to access colleagues operating in a similar or deeper way within the same field.

Recruitment of the 'street-level bureaucrats'

According to Michael Lipsky (1980), the term 'street-level bureaucrats' denotes frontline staff who use power and discretion in delivering public services. Prison governors and their officers, as well as the workforce of the private and voluntary sector organisations who deliver healthcare and healthy living provisions in English prisons, fall into this category.

From the outset, 34 prison institutions were purposively sampled to take part in the research. I sent invitations to prison governors by email, with the intention that prison officers from those sites also be invited to take part. In total, 17 prisons agreed to participate, representing 50% of the contacted establishments, with 22 prison governors and officers providing accounts on the topic. I selected the range of prison establishments to reflect the following different characteristics: public and private prisons, male and female prisons, and prisons with an older prisoners' wing.

The sample also included the different categories of prisons: high security, local or training, resettlement, or open prisons. I also considered other key factors. Institutions requiring pressing improvement, based on the urgent notification triggered by the Chief Inspector of Prisons to the Secretary of State for Justice (HM Inspectorate of Prisons, 2019), were selected, as were the ten most challenging prisons affected by high levels of violence and drugs (Ministry of Justice, 2018). Finally, I also approached stakeholders who were part of the management structure of the Prison Governors' Association and the Prison Officers' Association for this research project.

Like the process with elite participants, I adopted theoretical sampling to explore the emerging issue of how austerity is perceived to impact closed, medium-sized prisons more heavily than high-security or open prisons. Pursuing these emerging avenues required me to work simultaneously on data analysis and participant recruitment to support or challenge the emerging account.

As part of snowball sampling, academic collaborators from Public Health England and an academic institution served as a conduit by introducing me to five prison governors. Four immediately accepted the research invitation. Using known contacts and affiliates, I established a connection with the interviewees and avoided cold canvassing (Ismail, 2020b). Notably, the snowball sampling was used least in the street-level bureaucrat interviews, especially where access to institutions would need to be carefully justified and permission from the Ministry of Justice sought first (ibid.).

Consent and confidentiality

All participants were informed verbally during the interview about its aim, the procedures that would be followed, the length of the interview, and the questions that would be asked. They were given the opportunity to ask questions before giving their consent for participation. Written informed consent was obtained from all participants. I assured participants that their consent was ongoing and that they could withdraw from the study at any time. They were also guaranteed confidentiality at both individual and organisational levels to promote candour, considering that austerity is a politically contentious topic.

How I collected the data

Data were collected via face-to-face, telephone, and online interviews. In keeping with constructivist grounded theory, a semi-structured interview format was used. Through directed, but open-ended, exchanges with participants, interviews aimed to elicit the participants' accounts of their experiences and perspectives on how they governed and delivered the prison health agenda during austere times, which are usually absent from official documents on prison health.

Face-to-face interviews

Considering the politically sensitive nature of the research topic, I prioritised face-to-face interviews. A total of 61 face-to-face interviews were conducted. The average duration of each interview in this mode was 53 minutes. The interview length helped to establish rapport and trust with the participants to elicit more in-depth responses (Lincoln and Guba, 2000).

I interviewed most of the elite participants at their respective office locations. Most participants were based in central areas in their respective countries

(England: London, Leeds, Reading, Oxford) or in major European cities, such as Vienna, Geneva, Amsterdam, Strasbourg, and Dublin. Most interviews happened at their offices. Similarly, most face-to-face interviews with prison governors and their staff, as well as with representatives from the private and voluntary sector organisations, took place at their establishments.

Telephone interviews

I conducted telephone interviews (n=16, average: 48 minutes) as a substitute for in-person interviews when the participants had time constraints that prevented an in-person meeting. However, they were only offered if suggested by informants. Disclosure on what is considered a politically sensitive topic is easier in person (Sturges and Hanrahan, 2004), particularly as I was unknown to some participants before the research engagement.

Establishing trust over the telephone was more difficult than in person (Healey and Rawlinson, 1993), and the participants provided less detailed responses. They might have felt uncomfortable sharing stories over the phone, particularly in the absence of visual cues (Sturges and Hanrahan, 2004).

Online interviews

There were nine online interviews conducted via Skype. Each interview lasted an average duration of 49 minutes. The literature considers online interviews an alternative to the gold standard of face-to-face interviews (McCoyd and Kerson, 2006).

Using Skype minimised the number of opportunities that would have otherwise been lost because of access and distance. However, visual and interpersonal aspects of the interactions remained key barriers. Drop-outs were relatively common and to be expected, where the conversation had to be stopped or repeated, because the screen had frozen and the participant was unable to hear my questions or I their response.

Additionally, it was impossible to conduct online interviews with local participants as the lack of IT facilities and the risk-averse culture in prisons that prioritises safety and security prevented this technology from being used in that context. Since the fieldwork was undertaken, however, the COVID-19 pandemic took place, which might have improved the technological advancement and receptivity towards its use as a means of communication.

Interview guide

Before data collection, I devised an initial interview guide. It began with an open question (i.e., "In what ways did this study appeal to you?"), followed by a list of broad, provisional topics that would help to guide the interview process loosely while also allowing my approach to remain informal and flexible. The questions moved from the non-intrusive to the more intrusive (Lilleker, 2003). Loaded questions, closed questions (i.e., yes or no), and poorly structured questions were avoided.

The participants were encouraged to talk freely. Where appropriate, I provided latitude for the participants to deviate from the initial question and then returned to the questions using the interview guide or prompts.

Probes

Deep and rich responses are vital to the trustworthiness of qualitative research. Therefore, it was important for the interviews to go beyond mere soundbites. To elicit this depth, I drew on one or more of Patton's (2002) and Lilleker's (2003) techniques for probing participants:

- Detail-oriented probes helped to obtain more information about the phenomenon described by the participant;
- Elaboration probes required the participants to expand their initial response;
- Clarification probes were used by rephrasing the participants' answers;
- Contrast probes provided participants with something to push off against;
- Criticism probes included introducing criticism from the previous interview to the next participant to help understand what his or her position was and to obtain a new perspective, as part of data triangulation.

The use of the probes signifies active listening, a non-judgmental approach, and a willingness to reciprocate between parties (Kvale, 1996). Fluid and dynamic exchanges occurred between the research participants and me because I established rapport with the participants.

Transcribing

All interviews were audiotaped and transcribed verbatim. Overall, the transcripts generated over 1,474 pages and 689,664 narrative texts for analysis. Interviews were transcribed within one week of the interview to help ensure the data collection and analysis would occur simultaneously.

How I analysed the data

I undertook the analysis stage iteratively, concurrently with the data collection for each interview phase. I analysed the data and used this process to inform future data collection (Pope et al., 2000), which prompted me to modify the interview questions and highlight emerging avenues of further inquiry.

The process commenced by reading the transcripts four times before the coding. This helped me to immerse myself in the data and be empathically introspective. I imported all transcripts into NVivo 12 software (QSR International, Australia) to organise data created by multiple interviews, manage complex data, identify emerging ideas and patterns, and link meanings to different parts of the analysis.

The coding process started with the labelling of each line of text by focusing on specific words or phrases. Subsequently, the coding process became more focused, as the differences in codes were reconciled and as the categories were matched to other categories as part of the analysis (Dey, 1993). The process continued with axial coding, a process which reassembles the data to give coherence to the developing theory (Charmaz, 2006).

Additionally, I used a constant comparative method. This entailed going back and forth during data analysis so that the data were inspected thoroughly at each stage and the relationships between the emerging categories identified. I wrote memos to situate my analysis into the broader analytical process, while the categorising process helped me connect all major categories.

Condensing the data from 87 interviews and devising cross-cutting theories across all interviews proved challenging. To further refine the emerging theories from the analysis, I devised an additional stage called 'The Fourth Order' to consolidate the axial codes to form a central research thesis (Ismail, 2020a). Here, all the axial categories from the different interview phases underwent a further deductive and synthesis process to form a central research thesis that austerity exposes six political paradoxes that have shaped and constrained prison health in England since 2010. The central thesis was realised when these categories covered all the major themes from the interviews.

Finally, I analysed the transcripts until data saturation was achieved. Data saturation was reflected by the absence of any new themes appearing in the interviews. First, I drew on a five-dimension framework (Aldiabat and Le Navenec, 2018; Bowen, 2008; Morse et al., 2009): 1) examining the investigation's nature and complexity; 2) the interdisciplinary nature of the research established the sample's heterogeneity; 3) theoretical sampling prompted further focus on the emerging theories from the initial interviews; 4) triangulation of the sample selection; and 5) the use of subjectivity and intuition to determine data saturation. Second, this research devised a new variance called 'participant saturation', where key stakeholders recommended as participants were already interviewees (Ismail, 2020a). On achieving this saturation, interviewing additional stakeholders for the research is futile (ibid.). Doing so ensured inspection of every angle, which is the very requirement of data saturation within the grounded theory methodology.

How I ensured the study findings are trustworthy

It is important that qualitative research establishes the trustworthiness of findings, and that these findings demonstrate the credibility and plausibility of the data collection, analysis, and interpretation. This is demonstrated through the specific measures related to credibility, ethical conduct, self-reflexivity, and transparency that contribute to the study's trustworthiness.

Credibility

To establish credibility, I undertook measures to ensure thick descriptions, multivocality, data source triangulation, member checks, and peer debriefing. In ensuring thick descriptions of the investigated phenomenon (Guba and Lincoln, 2005), I provided rich and varied findings from different participants with diverse backgrounds.

I triangulated data sources during the interview phase to look for similarities or dissimilarities between participants' viewpoints and experiences (Shenton, 2004). When similar results emerged from different sites, I concluded that findings had credibility.

After completing the interviews, I undertook member checking, which was a process of "taking findings back to the field and determining whether the participants recognise them as true or accurate" (Lindlof and Taylor, 2002, p. 242). I produced a two-page briefing note that was circulated to the international and national policymakers who participated in the research.

Finally, I presented the tentative findings of the study with the aim of further refining the theory at five conferences across Europe and North America between 2018 and 2019. Doing so helped to inform the research phase and provide alternative interpretation for some data.

Ethical conduct

The participation risks of this research were reviewed through procedural and relational assessments (Tracy, 2010). In terms of procedural ethics, ethical approval was granted by the Faculty Research Ethics Committee at UWE Bristol in December 2017 (reference: HAS.17.11.054). For the research with the national policymakers and the local prison actors, approval from the National Research Committee of the Ministry of Justice was obtained in January 2019 (NRC Reference: 2018–381).

Some participants might have felt unable to refuse their colleagues' invitation to participate, particularly when they were recruited via snowball sampling, which could potentially amount to coercion. To mitigate this risk, I reiterated that participation was voluntary and that the participants were given sufficient time and space to reflect on the invitation before deciding. In addition, these participants hold senior positions within their respective organisations, and, therefore, this potential vulnerability could have been mitigated because they could decline my invitation.

Considering that the health and justice community are closely networked, often, the interviewees were inquisitive about who else I had been or would be interviewing. Here, I was particularly vigilant about not disclosing the names of the participants or the content of discussions to other participants to ensure that all discussions remained confidential.

Checking my positionality

I was cognisant that my self-awareness of my own background and views and my corresponding self-reflexivity could have possibly shaped the research process. While my insider status helped me understand this topic, I was mindful of my own thought processes so that I did not unduly influence the participants' accounts. In addition, I opted for self-disclosure of my background to the participants using my email and letter signature, as well as mentioning my background and how I came to be investigating this area, at the beginning of each interview. This disclosure of insider status was useful in building rapport, balancing the power between the participants and researcher, and gaining their respect (Bosworth et al., 2005).

Self-reflexivity also raised the question of intersectionality and the power dynamic between the participants and me. For instance, elites were portrayed in the literature to be male, older, and of a higher social class compared to the researcher (Winkler, 1987). Similar observations were also made for prison governors and staff, although the class portrayal of this group was absent in the academic literature. Nearly three-quarters of the participants were men. In all cases, there was an age gap between me and the interviewees. Nevertheless, I felt like I was treated as an equal. This was partly because of my insider status.

Conclusion

In this chapter, I have explained and critically examined the research process that I used to study the impact of economic austerity on access to health services in English prisons, including interviewing 87 actors involved in prison health governance and delivery. The knowledge, meaning, and experiences of the impact of austerity was couched in the language of the participants, while I acknowledged my subjective role as an insider in the prison setting. The approach of grounded theory involved managing the data collection and analysis simultaneously.

Grounded theory is a fluid methodology. However, in a world driven by credibility, rigour, and transparency, the principles of constant comparison, as well as two methodological innovations on the newly devised "fourth data order" and "participant saturation" frameworks, were valuable research compasses.

Finally, I have elucidated the notion of trustworthiness from the perspectives of credibility, ethical conduct, and sincerity. In particular, I have emphasised self-awareness of the way my background shaped the research and the way it cannot be divorced from it. I hope transparency about my own strengths and weaknesses has been demonstrated through the discussion of the power dynamic and intersectionality between myself and the research participants, while prompting future replicability of the process in prison research, as well as projects in the broader social sciences field.

References

Aldiabat, K. M. and Le Navenec, C. (2018) Data Saturation: The Mysterious Step in Grounded Theory Method. *The Qualitative Report*. 23(1), pp. 245–261.

Appleton, J. V. and King, L. (2002) Journeying from the Philosophical Contemplation of Constructivism to the Methodological Pragmatics of Health Services Research. *Journal of Advanced Nursing*. 40, pp. 641–648.

Bosworth, M., Campbell, D., Demby, B., Ferranti, S. M. and Santos, M. (2005) Doing Prison Research: Views From Inside. *Qualitative Inquiry*. 11(2), pp. 249–264.

Bowen, G. A. (2008) Naturalistic Inquiry and the Saturation Concept: A Research Note. *Qualitative Research*. 8(1), pp. 137–152.

Charmaz, K. (2006) *Constructing Grounded Theory: A Practical Guide Through Qualitative Analysis*. London: SAGE.

Charmaz, K. (2014) *Constructing Grounded Theory*. 2nd ed. London: SAGE.

Denzin, N. K. and Lincoln, Y. S. (1994) *Handbook of Qualitative Research*. London: SAGE.

Dey, I. (1993) *Qualitative Data Analysis: A User-Friendly Guide for Social Scientists*. London: Routledge.

Glaser, B. and Holton, J. (2004) *Remodelling Grounded Theory. Forum Qualitative Sozialforschung/Forum: Qualitative Social Research* [Online], available from: www.qualitative-research.net/index.php/fqs/article/view/607 (Accessed: 1st December 2019).

Guba, E. G. and Lincoln, Y. S. (2005) Paradigmatic Controversies, Contradictions, and Emerging Confluences. In: Denzin, N. K. and Lincoln, Y. S., eds. *The SAGE Handbook of Qualitative Research*. 3rd ed. Thousand Oaks, CA: SAGE, pp. 191–216

Healey, M. and Rawlinson, M. (1993) Interviewing Business Owners and Managers: A Review of Methods and Techniques. *Geoforum*. 24, pp. 339–355.

HM Inspectorate of Prisons (2019) *HM Chief Inspector of Prisons for England and Wales: Annual Report 2018–19* [Online], available from: www.justiceinspectorates.gov.uk/hmi-prisons/wp-content/uploads/sites/4/2019/07/6.5563_HMI-Prisons-AR_2018-19_WEB_FINAL_040719.pdf (Accessed: 25th January 2021).

Hunter, A. (1995) Local Knowledge and Local Power: Notes on the Ethnography of Local Community Elites. In: Hertz, R. and Imber, J. B., eds. *Studying Elites Using Qualitative Methods*. Thousand Oaks, CA: SAGE, pp. 151–170.

Ismail, N. (2020a) Challenges and Practicalities in Adopting Grounded Theory Methodology When Conducting Prison Research. In: Maycock, M., Meek, R. and Woodall, J., eds. *Issues and Innovations in Prison Health Research: Methods, Issues and Innovations*. London: Palgrave Macmillan, pp. 69–89.

Ismail, N. (2020b) Challenges in Conducting Interviews Regarding Prison Health with Prison Governors and Prison Officers in England. *SAGE Research Methods Cases: Medicine and Health*. https://doi.org/10.4135/9781529735208.

Kvale, S. (1996) *InterViews-An Introduction to Qualitative Research Interviewing*. Thousand Oaks, CA: SAGE.

Lilleker, D. G. (2003) Interviewing the Political Elite: Navigating a Potential Minefield. *Politics*. 23(3), pp. 207–214.

Lincoln, Y. S. and Guba, E. G. (2000) Paradigmatic Controversies, Contradictions and Emerging Confluences. In: Denzin, N. K. and Lincoln, Y. S., eds. *Handbook of Qualitative Research*. Thousand Oaks, CA: SAGE, pp. 191–215.

Lindlof, T. R. and Taylor, B. C. (2002) *Qualitative Communication Research Methods*. 2nd ed. Thousand Oaks, CA: SAGE.

Lipsky, M. (1980) *Street Level Bureaucracy: Dilemmas of the Individual in Public Services*. New York: Russell Sage Foundation.

Littig, B. (2009) Interviewing the Elite—Interviewing Experts: Is There a Difference? In: Bogner, A., Littig, B. and Menz, W., eds. *Interviewing Experts*. Hampshire: Palgrave Macmillan, pp. 98–116.

McCoyd, J. L. M. and Kerson, T. S. (2006) Conducting Intensive Interviews Using Email: A Serendipitous Comparative Opportunity. *Qualitative Social Work*. 5(3), pp. 389–406.

Milliken, P. J. and Northcott, H. C. (2003) Redefining Parental Identity: Caregiving and Schizophrenia. *Qualitative Health Research*. 13(1), pp. 100–113.

Ministry of Justice (2018) *Minister Announces' 10 Prisons Project' to Develop New Model of Excellence* [Online], available from: www.gov.uk/government/news/minister-announces-10-prisons-project-to-develop-new-model-of-excellence (Accessed: 21st February 2020).

Morse, J. M., Stern, P. N., Corbin, J., Bowers, B., Clarke, A. E. and Charmaz, K. (2009) *Developing Grounded Theory: The Second Generation*. Walnut Creek, CA: Left Coast Press.

Ostrander, S. (1995) "Surely You're Not in This Just to be Helpful": Access, Rapport, and Interviews in Three Studies of Elites. In: Hertz, R. and Imber, J. B., eds. *Studying Elites Using Qualitative Methods*. Thousand Oaks, CA: SAGE, pp. 133–150.

Patton, M. Q. (2002) *Qualitative Research and Evaluation Methods*. 3rd ed. Thousand Oaks, CA: SAGE.

Pope, C., Ziebland, S. and Mays, N. (2000) Qualitative Research in Health Care: Analysing Qualitative Data. *BMJ*. 320(7227), pp. 114–116.

Shenton, A. K. (2004) Strategies for Ensuring Trustworthiness in Qualitative Research Projects. *Education for Information*. 22, pp. 63–75.

Sturges, J. E. and Hanrahan, K. J. (2004) Comparing Telephone and Face-to-Face Qualitative Interviewing: A Research Note. *Qualitative Research*. 4(1), pp. 107–118.

Tracy, S. J. (2010) Qualitative Quality: Eight "Big-Tent" Criteria for Excellent Qualitative Research. *Qualitative Inquiry*. 16(10), pp. 837–851.

Winkler, J. T. (1987) The Fly on the Wall of the Inner Sanctum: Observing Company Directors at Work. In: Moyser, G. and Wagstaffe, M., eds. *Research Methods for Elite Studies*. London: Allen & Unwin, pp. 129–146.

Index

Note: Page numbers in *italics* indicate figures, and references following "n" refer notes.

For Product Safety Concerns and Information please contact our EU
representative GPSR@taylorandfrancis.com
Taylor & Francis Verlag GmbH, Kaufingerstraße 24, 80331 München, Germany

www.ingramcontent.com/pod-product-compliance
Ingram Content Group UK Ltd.
Pitfield, Milton Keynes, MK11 3LW, UK
UKHW020316270926
475702UK00050B/839

* 9 7 8 1 0 3 2 0 2 1 9 5 9 *